Washington Architecture 1791-1861
Problems in Development

Daniel D. Reiff

U.S. Commission of Fine Arts • Washington, D.C. 1971

Daniel Drake Reiff (B.A., M.A., Ph. D., Harvard University),
headed and edited the summer architectural surveys of the
Commission of Fine Arts from 1967 through 1970; he was also
coauthor of two of the surveys. During 1969 and 1970 he was
the Acting Assistant Secretary of the Commission, during which
time this study was undertaken.

For sale by the Superintendent of Documents, U.S. Government Printing Office
Washington, D.C. 20402 - Price $3.50
Stock Number 1000–0004

Preface

The development of architecture in Washington is one of the strangest phases in American history. Instead of being an important center for the diffusion of new architectural styles or developments, as one would expect from a nation's capital, Washington reached architectural maturity with painful slowness, in spite of the fact that many of the nation's leading architects built in the city during its formative years, from 1791 when it was first planned, until the outbreak of the Civil War in 1861.

The contrast between hopes and reality was striking from the beginning. Although the city was conceived and laid out by Maj. Pierre Charles L'Enfant, a talented Frenchman with considerable imagination, in order to rival the grand capitals of Europe, Washington in fact was for years an underdeveloped town with muddy, ungraded streets, tracts of barren or swampy ground throughout the sparsely settled site, and only a half dozen government buildings of any real architectural distinction. In addition to these structures, only two significant semipublic buildings had been erected by the beginning of the Civil War—the Smithsonian Institution (begun in 1847) and the Corcoran Art Galley (begun 1859).

To complete this inauspicious picture, the private houses of Washington and contiguous Georgetown showed a very conservative and unadventurous nature, with the few mansions of real architectural merit finding no imitators. Surprisingly, even the numerous impressive Greek Revival government buildings of the 1830's inspired no houses to follow their lead with peristyle or portico.

What were the reasons for this strange lack of vigor? It would seem natural that a new and growing capital, of all places, would also be an architectural center of influence. Following the Greek Revival period, even James Renwick, Jr. and Andrew Jackson Downing, two of the most famous and influential architects of the mid-Nineteenth century, had only a very slight local influence, although both erected several buildings, and Downing even laid out the Mall to be the first large public garden in the United States. With such a hopeful beginning in 1791—the city planned by L'Enfant under the active concern of Thomas Jefferson and George Washington—its failure to fulfill the early promise is at first baffling.

These are intriguing problems, and the aim of this study is to examine some of the possible answers, including the actual nature of the L'Enfant plan, the context of public and private building in Washington, and the reasons for the lack of influence of major architects, both Greek Revival and Picturesque. It was not really until after the Civil War, in the 1870's, that Washington began to catch up with the mainstream of American architecture.

L'Enfant's plans for laying out and developing the capital will be examined first, for here, ironically, we can find the roots of many of the basic problems that were to plague Washington for over 70 years. The attitude of Congress toward the city and its development is also vital during this period up to the Civil War and reveals additional reasons for the Capital's fitful growth. In discussing the actual buildings erected, however, only two types will be examined: the governmental and semipublic structures, and the domestic architecture. Other building types will be largely left to one side. Churches generally follow quite closely the predominant style elsewhere in the middle Atlantic States—from late Georgian through Greek, Gothic, and Romanesque Revivals—and are thus not the best indications of the local architectural climate. Stores and commercial buildings are similarly not particularly helpful, for until the 1850's they were generally very close in style to, and often converted from, residential structures. And the Washington schools, which became models of superb design efficiency in the later Nineteenth century, did not reach this distinctive level until after the Civil War. Thus, these types will be brought in only peripherally while considering primarily the public and domestic buildings, and what they can tell us about the development of Washington architecture.

While the plan for the embellishment and planting of the Mall which Downing drew up and set in motion is not "architecture," it nevertheless was very closely linked with it in theory, and further helps to confirm the general lack of influence of works from major architects.

It was not until the 1870's that the architectural climate of Washington finally began to change, 80 years after the original grand conception. At long last, after overcoming innumerable difficulties, the Capital began to assume the appearance of a major American city.

Acknowledgements

This study could not have been undertaken without the interest and helpful suggestions of Charles H. Atherton, Secretary of the Commission of Fine Arts. I am particularly indebted to Professors John Coolidge and Eric Carlson of Harvard University who read the work in manuscript and offered valuable criticisms and suggestions.

Research on this study would have been far more difficult but for the generous cooperation of many, especially Miss Virginia Daiker, Division of Prints and Photographs, Library of Congress; Mrs. Elden Billings, Librarian, Columbia Historical Society; Mr. George Pettengill, Librarian, American Institute of Architects; and the staffs of the Department of Interior Library, the Washington Public Library, and the National Archives. Individuals who assisted me on specific points are gratefully acknowledged in the footnotes.

I am also indebted to Donald B. Myer, Assistant Secretary of the Commission of Fine Arts, for his editorial efforts and to Miss Marylyn Shaw of the Commission of Fine Arts for typing the final manuscript.

D.D.R.

Contents

List of Illustrations

CHAPTER I

L'Enfant and the Development of Washington

MOST of the problems that were to hamper the development of architecture and the growth of Washington until the 1870's had their roots in the very origins of the city. The painfully slow growth of the capital was due in large part to not following Maj. Pierre Charles L'Enfant's ambitious scheme for the rapid initial improvement and development of the plan he had so carefully conceived and laid out. For such a huge area of undeveloped land to become a city, some compelling method of settlement was certainly necessary, and the nature of his plan and his scheme of development were mutually dependent. With this understandable failure to implement his huge project was linked the slowness in deciding on and building necessary public structures. This apparent lack of government interest in the new city did not further the swift settlement of the Capital. Also important was the District Commissioners' lack of "grand vision." L'Enfant was an artist, and they were men of affairs. Furthermore, they were unable to spend the large sums that L'Enfant required for fulfilling his plan. These factors assured the slow, laborious, and fitful growth of the city. Had the Commissioners' more practical nature, and the paucity of government funds been taken into full account by L'Enfant, his plan and mode of development might well have been different.

When we examine the origins of his plan, what the theory behind it was, and the results he hoped for, we can begin to see why he failed, how so many of the later problems began, and how essential and persistent they would be.

The uncomfortable and cumbersome peregrinations of the Continental Congress made it clear to all that a permanent seat of government was needed. Between 1774 and 1789 they had met in eight different cities. In addition, the threat of armed violence that was presented in Philadelphia in 1783, when about 300 unpaid soldiers surrounded Independence Hall, assured the Congress—especially after the state legislature refused to call the militia for protection —that a permanent capital city completely under their own jurisdiction was advisable.[1]

The debate for the location of the new city, which everyone felt would be a great economic and political boon to the state in which it was located, began in 1783. At once there was regional animosity, since many representatives wanted the Capital in the north, the economic and population center of the country, and others in the south, near the geographic center. It was not until 1790 that agreement was finally reached. The Capital would remain in Philadelphia for 10 years, and then would move to a new site on the Potomac River where a federal district "not exceeding ten miles square" was to be established. In order to reach this agreement, northern members of Congress voted for the southern location, in return for southern support of the Federal assumption of the states' war debts (heaviest in the northern states). This agreement was engineered by Thomas Jefferson. George Washington was gratified

---

[1] These early developments are discussed in greater detail in H. Paul Caemmerer, *A Manual on the Origin and Development of Washington* (Washington: U.S. Government Printing Office, 1939), pp. 1–8. See also John W. Reps, *Monumental Washington* (Princeton: Princeton University Press, 1967), pp. 1–2. The texts of many of the early documents are presented in Allen C. Clark, "Origin of the Federal City," Columbia Historical Society *Records*, XXXV-XXXVI (1935), pp. 1–18.

with the location on the Potomac, not only because it was in an area he knew well (about 15 miles north of Mt. Vernon) but also because of his interest in the Patowmack Canal, a project to aid and improve commerce from the interior, down the Potomac River. Washington had been active in this venture since 1785 when he had become the founder of the new company.[2]

The "Act for establishing the temporary and permanent seat of the Government of the United States" became law on July 16, 1790, and specified two important items. The act appointed three Commissioners to survey the area and noted that "the said commissioners, . . . shall have power to purchase or accept such quantity of land on the eastern side of the said river, within the said district, as the President shall deem proper for the use of the United States, and according to such plans as the President shall appprove, the said commissioners . . . shall, prior to the first Monday in December, in the year one thousand eight hundred, provide suitable buildings for the accommodation of Congress, and of the President, and for the public offices of the government of the United States." [3] Both the plan and the necessary government buildings are mentioned, but all that is stated about how this was to be financed was that "for defraying the expense of such purchases and buildings, the President of the United States be authorized and requested to accept grants of money." This, clearly, was a moneysaving but short-sighted device, which relied on the good will or calculation of the states desiring the capital. When offering land within their boundaries in 1789, Maryland had pledged $72,000 and Virginia $120,000 toward construction in the new city.[4] These funds were now the only money at the disposal of the President and the Commissioners.

Pierre Charles L'Enfant was chosen by Washington to study the site, and lay out the plan of the city —and, though never begun, to design the public buildings as well—because he was probably the most well qualified person Washington knew. Writing in November, 1791, to Dr. David Stuart, one of the Commissioners, Washington stated:

> For such employment as [L'Enfant] is now engaged in, for projecting public works, and carrying them into e[ff]ect, he was better qualified than any one, who had come within my knowledge in this country, or indeed in any other. . . .[5]

When L'Enfant came to the United States in 1777 he was only 22 years old, but his early training as an artist in Paris at the Academie Royale de Peinture et de Sculpture (from 1771) was of importance. Although there is no direct evidence that he ever studied architecture, he was artistically talented, his general ability was considerable, and he was certainly influenced by residing in Paris, and probably also in Versailles (where he had lived as a child).[6]

His artistic talents were soon recognized in America, and for about 6 months during 1778–79, while living in Philadelphia, the Frenchman assisted Baron von Steuben in preparing his manual *Regulations, Order and Discipline for the Army of the United States* (1779) by providing diagrams and plans. Soon, "whenever something in any way connected with art was wanted during the War or for years after the War, he was appealed to." [7] L'Enfant, as we know, drew Washington's portrait at Valley Forge in 1777, as well as that of other officers; [8] in 1782 he (presumably) designed the original Badge of Military Merit (later, the "Purple Heart") , and in 1783 the badge for the newly founded Order of the Cincinnati. In 1783, he took the designs to France in order to supervise striking of the medals, and establish the society in that country.[9] As late as 1791, Alexander Hamilton asked him to design a coin for the government, but by that time L'Enfant was too busy on the plan of the Capital to give it any attention.[10]

L'Enfant was also called upon, in 1782, to design an open classical pavilion in Philadelphia for a celebration in honor of the Dauphin; and, in 1788, he designed the domed baldachino that sheltered George Washington in the Federalist pageant in New York City, in support of ratification of the new

[2] See Historic American Buildings Survey No. DC-147, p. 2; published in [Daniel D. Reiff and William R. Gwin], *Georgetown Architecture—The Waterfront* (Washington: Commission of Fine Arts and the Historic American Buildings Survey, 1968) , pp. 107–124.

[3] The full text is given in Caemmerer, *Manual*, pp. 7–8. The three Commissioners chosen by Washington—Thomas Johnson, Daniel Carroll, and Dr. David Stuart—were all public figures, well known in the area, who lived in Maryland or Virginia, generally near the ultimately chosen site. See W. B. Bryan, *A History of the National Capital* (New York: The Macmillan Company, 1914–16) , I, 120–122.

[4] Ibid., p. 6.

[5] H. Paul Caemmerer, *The Life of Pierre Charles L'Enfant* (Washington: National Republic Publishing Co., 1950) , p. 175.

[6] The early life of L'Enfant is discussed at length in Caemmerer, *Life*, pp. 5–24. See also Reps, *Monumental Washington*, pp. 5–8.

[7] Caemmerer, *Life*, pp. 66–67.

[8] Ibid., p. 46.

[9] Ibid., pp. 77–80.

[10] Reference to the "devices for the coin" is in Hamilton's letter of May 24, 1791, to L'Enfant, quoted in Caemmerer, *Life*, pp. 123–125.

Constitution. L'Enfant's architectural work in that city appears to have been considerable; in addition to designs for decorations (and possibly the portico) of St. Paul's Chapel in 1786–88, he also designed or remodeled over a dozen mansions in and about New York. His plans for the remodeling of Federal Hall in 1788 (figs. 1–2), and his supervision of the work, certainly made him one of the best known local architects of the day.[11] At a later date he even claimed that when he left New York to lay out the Federal City he had "proposals already . . . placed under my immediate agency [for] the erecting of Houses to the amount of *$1,000,000*," and that the plan called for this amount to be doubled.[12] Even if this is somewhat exaggerated, it is clear that L'Enfant was indeed active in architecture up until he left for the Federal City. And since the *Gazette of the United States* at that time called his remodeled Federal Hall "on the whole superior to any building in America,"[13] he was clearly recognized as a man of talent. He also had imagination and vision—as well as personal charm—which appealed to Washington.

L'Enfant had written to the President in 1789, even before the site of the new city had been fixed, in order to offer his own services in founding the Capital. Although one of his reasons for so doing was that it provided a great "occasion of acquiring reputation, to whoever may be appointed to conduct the execution of the business," he also wished to become a useful citizen and "share in the undertaking." But more important was the vision he saw in the possibility of designing a totally new Capital:

> No nation perhaps had ever before the opportunity offered them of deliberately deciding on the spot where their Capital city should be fixed, or of combining every necessary consideration in the choice of situation—and altho' the means now within the power of the country are not such as to pursue the design to any great extant it will be obvious that the plan should be drawn on such a scale as to leave room for that aggrandisement & embellishment which the increase of the

FIGURE 1. Federal Hall, New York City, by L'Enfant, 1788. (From *The Massachusetts Magazine,* June 1789.)

wealth of the Nation will permit it to pursue at any period however remote.[14]

It is therefore not surprising that when Washington began to study the proposed site, L'Enfant was among those chosen to perform the work.

Preliminary work on siting the capital began in the spring of 1791.[15] Although the original act of July 16, 1790, had specified a site on the Potomac anywhere from the Eastern Branch upstream 80 miles, Washington preferred the location between Georgetown and the Eastern Branch, and at the end of January 1791, he had a preliminary survey made in this area for the Federal District. Then, in a letter

[11] The architecture of L'Enfant is briefly discussed in Caemmerer, *Life,* pp. 103–118. It is surprising that more work has not been done on L'Enfant as an architect. In 1944, Talbot Hamlin pointed out that he may have been a very important influence for architecture in the new republic. See Talbot Hamlin, *Greek Revival Architecture in America* (New York: Dover Publications, 1964), p. 122, note 3.

[12] Memorial submitted to the Commissioners of the City of Washington, August 30, 1800, in "L'Enfant's Memorials," C.H.S. *Records,* II (1899), p. 84.

[13] Caemmerer, *Life,* p. 117. No date or reference is given. Two engravings of the remodeled building are reproduced, pp. 111 and 112.

[14] Letter by L'Enfant to Washington, Sept. 11, 1789, in Caemmerer, *Life,* pp. 128–129. L'Enfant's spelling, as can be seen, left something to be desired.

[15] A fuller account of the preliminary work is found in Caemmerer, *Life,* pp. 127–150, and in Elizabeth S. Kite, *L'Enfant and Washington 1791–1792* (Baltimore: The Johns Hopkins Press, 1929), pp. 31–52. See also Reps, pp. 9–15.

FIGURE 2. "View of the Old City Hall, Wall St., In the Year 1789," drawn by Diedrich Knickerbocker Jr., engraved by Hatch & Smilie. From *The New-York Mirror*, November 19, 1831 (based on a late Eighteenth century engraving).

of February 3, 1791, he wrote to two friends in Georgetown, asking them to buy, as quietly as possible, for the ultimate use of the government, land both adjacent to Georgetown and to the Eastern Branch.[16] The following day he sent Andrew Ellicott, "Geographer-general to the Government," to the site in order to map out the entire 10 mile square "Federal Territory" (fig. 3) and ascertain the shorelines and the general topography.[17] Then, on March 3, Washington had the original act amended to specify an area at this location, which would also include Alexandria, located on the south shore of the river.[18] Finally, in early March 1791, L'Enfant was sent to make a more detailed map of the topography of the specific site of the city. The letter from Thomas Jefferson (then Secretary of State) of early March sets out his duties:

> The special object of asking your aid is to have a drawing of the particular grounds most likely to be approved for the site of the Federal town and buildings. You will therefore be pleased to begin on the Eastern branch and proceed from thence upwards, laying down the hills, valleys, morasses and waters between that and the Potomac, the Tyber, and the road leading from Georgetown to the Eastern branch and connecting the whole with certain fixed points on the map Mr.

Ellicott is preparing. Some idea of the height of the lands above the base on which they stand would be desirable.[19]

As yet, no actual plan was proposed. Although Washington apparently thought quite early that the entire area might be ·used for the city, Jefferson's preliminary sketches (1790 and early 1791) [20] assumed the location would be between Rock Creek (adjacent to Georgetown) and Tiber (or Tyber) Creek (fig. 4). An alternate site was between Tiber Creek and the Eastern Branch, stated also in a letter from Jefferson to L'Enfant on March 17, 1791.[21] This idea of two locations was fostered by Washington—with L'Enfant's survey beginning at the Eastern Branch—in order to reduce the price of land adjacent to Georgetown. It was only at the time of his visit to Georgetown on March 28–30 that Washington informed the proprietors of the contemplated land that he felt that the entire site should be laid out as one city,[22] not just one of the two proposed locations. By playing off the interests of Georgetown against those of the hamlet of Carrollsburg on the Eastern Branch, he persuaded them to agree to reasonable terms for the entire area.

It was also at this time, on March 30, that Washington gave L'Enfant oral instructions to lay out the plan of the enlarged city. His mission completed successfully, Washington wrote Jefferson on March 31 that he had been "fortunate as to reconcile the contending interests . . . and to unite them in such an agreement as permits the public purposes to be carried into effect on an extensive and proper scale. . . ." [23]

The preliminary examinations of the site by L'Enfant prior to the arrival of Washington at the end of March not only laid out the topography, but also pointed out a number of basic features that any plan should take advantage of.[24]

The flat and gently rising ground, especially in the eastern section, was perfect for laying out streets. However, because there was also hilly ground toward Georgetown and Jenkins Hill (present site of the

16 Kite, p. 32.

17 Ibid.

18 Caemmerer, *Manual*, p. 8.

19 Caemmerer, *Life*, p. 135.

20 See Reps, figs. 4 and 7.

21 Op. cit., p. 137. "There are certainly considerable advantages on the Eastern branch; but there are very strong reasons also in favor of the position between Rock Creek and Tyber. . . ."

22 See Kite, p. 43, and Caemmerer, *Life*, pp. 141–142.

23 Caemmerer, *Life*, p. 145.

24 See his letter to Jefferson of Mar. 11, 1791 (Caemmerer, *Life*, pp. 136–37), and also the "Note relative to the ground lying on the eastern branch . . ." probably given to George Washington on Mar. 28, 1791, in Kite, pp. 43–48.

Capitol building), these features should be taken into consideration. A simple grid pattern, which might look fine on paper, would not be successful on both high and low-ground. The hills also provided superb sites for important public buildings (especially Jenkins Hill) which would thus be visible at a great distance. High ground near Georgetown, north of the Tiber, was also admirable for private estates, which would overlook the city and the river. The hills toward Georgetown were the perfect location for military defenses as well.

The depth of the Eastern Branch, and the irregularity of the shore on the Potomac side of that point of land at the mouth, provided good sites for wharfs and docks. A bridge, however, was needed across the Eastern Branch, with another above Georgetown at the "two sisters" (now three sisters) island.

Any plan, L'Enfant felt, should be conceived on a large scale, but so arranged that it would be convenient for early settlers and also could be extended as years went by. This had to be kept in mind when the plan was made.

Thus, while his first duties were only to set down the topography, L'Enfant also analyzed it with an eye to how a city could be adapted to it, and what advantages the natural features provided. Although in his March 11 letter to Jefferson, L'Enfant had conceived of the city as being situated below Tiber Creek (the land above it being too hilly), after he had completed the survey as Jefferson had directed, he felt that the city could indeed spread all the way to Georgetown, facilitated by a paved road from Georgetown to the Eastern Branch Bridge. He therefore came to the same conclusion as had Washington, that the city should encompass all the land from the Eastern Branch to Georgetown. In a letter to L'Enfant on April 4, 1791, shortly after their meeting, Washington outlined the area that he had in mind, which included all this area, as well as all of Jenkins Hill. He urged L'Enfant to include as much ground as there seemed any possibility of getting from the proprietors.

When L'Enfant began actual work on laying out a plan for the Federal City, his preliminary survey of the topography was of immense value. In his notes supplied to Washington on March 28, he had implied that any plan should take advantage of the specific topography. But now, for inspiration, he wanted to examine plans of other major European cities and so wrote to Jefferson on April 4 to request

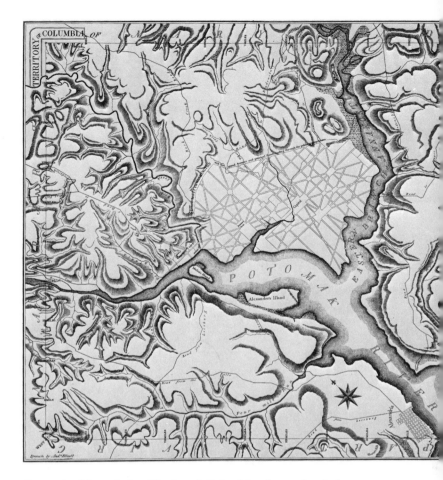

FIGURE 3. Plan of the District of Columbia, drawn by Andrew Ellicott, 1791. (Reproduction by the U.S. Coast and Geodetic Survey, 1898.)

any that he might have. L'Enfant assured him that he "would reprobate the Idea of Imitating," and that rather "it is my wish and shall be my endeavor to delinate on a new and original way the plan the contrivance of which the President has left to me without any restriction soever." [26] He also requested specific information on what public buildings or other features he should plan for. Jefferson sent him a dozen maps: Frankfurt, Karlsruhe, Amsterdam, Strassburg, Paris, Orléans, Bordeaux, Lyons, Montpelier, Marseilles, Turin and Milan, but none of London which L'Enfant had also originally asked for.[27]

[23] Caemmerer, *Life*, pp. 144–145.

[26] Ibid., p. 146.

[27] Ibid., p. 147. In this discussion of L'Enfant's planning of Washington, no attempt has been made to investigate possible sources of the plan in those of other cities. This is a complicated problem and has been examined in some detail by a number of scholars. See particularly, Paul D. Spreiregen (ed.), *On the Art of Designing Cities: Selected Essays of Elbert Peets* (Cambridge: The M.I.T. Press, 1968).

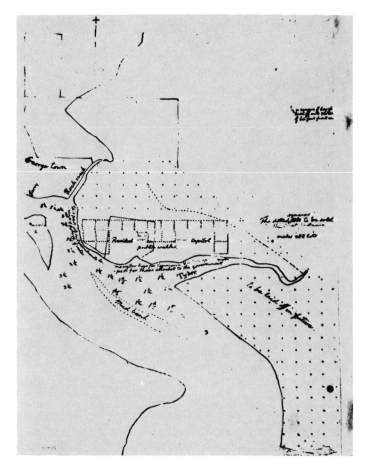

FIGURE 4. Sketch plan for the Federal City, by Thomas Jefferson, 1791.

After nearly 3 months of work, L'Enfant visited George Washington at Mt. Vernon and took him a "progress map" together with a long report dated June 22, 1791.[28] In this significant document, he expands and explains the basic points of his preliminary survey. Two months later he took his completed map (fig. 5) to Philadelphia (late August 1791) to arrange for an engraving of it as Washington had requested. Around the borders of this map he had inscribed a full description of the layout of the city.[29] This text is the most succinct description of his intent. At the same time he brought a Memoir to accompany the map, which explained the mode of development to be followed, but also had a few fur-

ther specifications on the arrangement of the city.[30] From these three sources the plan for the Federal City as of August 1791, can be summarized.

The relation of the street plan to the topography is clearly brought out. The two major heights of ground gave the basic focal points—the ridge north of Tiber Creek chosen for the President's House, facing south, and Jenkins Hill, to the east, selected for the Congress House. As L'Enfant stated, "having first determined some principal points to which I wished to make the rest subordinate I next made the distribution regular with streets at right angles *north-south* and *east west* but afterwards I opened others on various directions as avenues to and from every principal place." [31] The grid of streets thus formed the basic division, amenable to efficient use and sale. The avenues he notes serve many purposes: they connect major points directly, link existing roads, join the various squares both physically and visually, contrast with the grid regularity, and provide a greater variety of good lots with fine views.

This brings up an important point about his basic plan. As seen in his preliminary "Map of Dotted Lines," (fig. 6), from the two major points chosen as foci, he has drawn dotted lines extending outward in several directions. These are sight lines to other natural features, and also proposed avenue lines which lead to major points (such as the ferry crossing at the Eastern Branch, or the ford into Georgetown, or the new road to Bladensburg [New York Avenue] which was to follow a natural valley). Combined with this is the street grid, with the closest spaced lines following the most level and open ground, or running up valleys. At a number of places where the two systems cross, squares are established. What is significant is that these squares generally fall on the 50-foot contour line, so that the avenues which then are drawn to connect them run mainly on high level ground.[32] This obviously gives the lots on the avenues and the squares the advantage of a more level siting, and for those facing south, a view down hill. This gives particular meaning to L'Enfant's pointing out the "advantageous ground over . . . which the avenues are mostly directed." [33] In his plan this is emphasized (section III) by stating that the avenues and streets meet at "predetermined points" i.e., the

[28] C.H.S. *Records*, II, pp. 32–37. See also the copy by Roberdeau in Kite, pp. 52–56.

[29] Reproduced in Kite, pp. 62–66. These notes were subsequently published in the *Gazette of the United States*, Philadelphia, Jan. 4, 1792 (Caemmerer, *Life*, p. 163). The text is also reproduced around the border of the map made in 1887 by the Coast and Geodetic Survey as an exact copy of the original, which by then was badly faded and worn.

[30] C.H.S. *Records*, II, pp. 38–48.

[31] Ibid., p. 33.

[32] This was observed by Charles H. Atherton, Secretary, Commission of Fine Arts, in a study made in 1961.

[33] C.H.S. *Records*, II, p. 33.

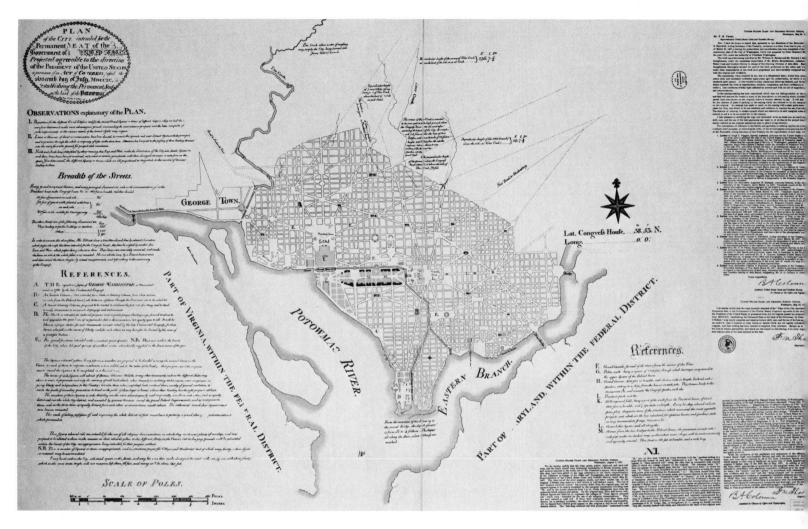

FIGURE 5. L'Enfant's map of the Federal City, 1791. (Reproduction by U.S. Coast and Geodetic Survey, 1887.)

flat land uniformly at the 50-foot level wherever it coincided best with level ground for right-angle streets. Thus, the street plan was created not as a grand abstract pattern, but for very functional ends; and it was, largely determined by the topography of land sloping up from the river to the surrounding hills, but interrupted at several points by more prominent outcroppings.

The location of public buildings and major residences is also gone into in considerable detail, and is of particular interest for showing where L'Enfant wanted buildings to be located. Although this placement was in part, as we shall see later, determined by his scheme for the settlement and development of the huge plan, the major factors were again the topography. The positions of the President's House and the Congress House, early decided upon, were also deciding factors.

As mentioned above, the Congress House was placed on Jenkins Hill, "which stand[s] as a pedestal waiting for a monument," [34] and the President's House on the rise of ground north of Tiber Creek, with a majestic view down the Potomac for about 10 miles. This was a site that Washington had himself noticed on his March inspection. These two locations were not only the foci for radiating streets, but also largely determined where other major buildings were to be placed. The greatest majority were to rise between the President's House and Congress House on the avenue which connected them (and which also extended directly to Georgetown's main street to the northwest, and to the proposed Eastern Branch bridge to the southeast). Convenient therefore to both branches of government, the "three grand Departments of State" (presumably State, Treasury, and War) were to be on this avenue. Also along this

[34] Ibid., p. 35.

7

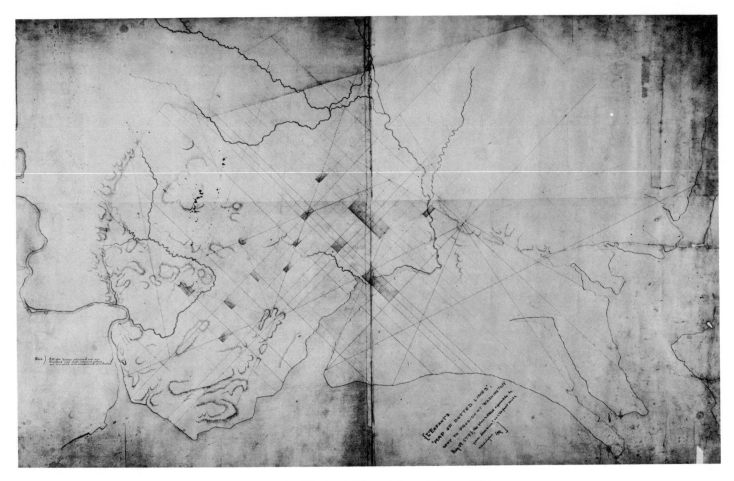

FIGURE 6. L'Enfant's Map of Dotted Lines, 1791.

avenue, near the midpoint, were to be located other important structures: the National Church (D on his final plan; see fig. 7), the square for the Judiciary Court (exact site not specified), the national bank, a playhouse, and the market and exchange. Thus, clustered around and on squares just north of the avenue would be religious, judicial, and commercial interests. On the south side of this avenue where there are numerous cross streets, were to be located shops, the printing and stationery offices, etc., and many of the first houses.

The second major link between the President's House and the Congress House—or more accurately their respective gardens—was the carriage drive and gardens (H; see fig. 7), with the equestrian statue of George Washington (voted by the Continental Congress in 1783) at A forming the pivot south of the President's House and west of the Congress House. These pleasant grounds would be bordered with embassies, as well as with places of "public resort" such as theatres, assembly rooms, and academies.

This rather strange combination does not appear to have been fully worked out in L'Enfant's own mind. Other official residences would apparently be built on the eastern side of the south extension of the President's Park (south of the equestrian statue), with a view of the river.

The third location for major buildings was facing onto the various "grand squares" which he had created. These squares are numbered on his map and tinted yellow. The locations would be developed by the states, which would erect "statues, columns, obelisks" and the like in these squares, and construct buildings around them, in part to give each state its own specific area of the city, but also to aid in settlement since the squares were arranged almost equidistant around the central area. Other squares not assigned to states could be devoted to colleges, academies, or other societies. Two squares north of what became Pennsylvania Avenue, toward the Capitol, are reserved for churches.

Two lesser locations for buildings are dealt with

8

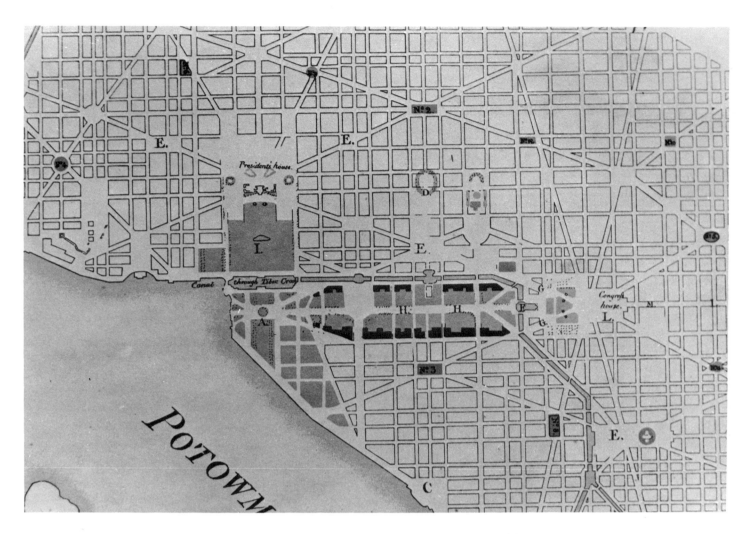

FIGURE 7. Detail, L'Enfant's map of the Federal City, 1791.

briefly. The canal from in front of the Congress House south to the Eastern Branch would spur commerce and along it (as on the Eastern Branch) warehouses would rise. The long street from the Congress House east to a second East Branch crossing was, on the map, set aside for shops and arcades.

Thus, while L'Enfant suggests areas for a number of buildings, no rigid system or compact grouping was really implied. The sites for major buildings, besides the President's House and the Capitol, were all near the center of the city, and fronted on squares (or gardens), or a major avenue, or were located at the center of a square.

The hills toward Georgetown which he had previously suggested as good locations for fortifications are no longer considered in this light. They become part of the street pattern, with their proximity to Georgetown making them even more likely as fine country seats.

The harbors and wharfs early envisioned on the Eastern Branch are expanded on the final map to line both the Potomac side of the point and extending up the Eastern Branch beyond the first bridge. By turning the Tiber Creek into a canal and continuing it south in front of Jenkins Hill, this Eastern Branch port, where the water was deep enough, could also receive vessels coming down the river from Georgetown without venturing out into the Potomac, which is much wider below the mouth of Tiber Creek, and has numerous mud flats at that point. This new canal was also necessary for early transportation of building material into the very center of the city. This area, however, was not discussed in any great detail. Similarly, the bridges proposed earlier are now only mentioned in passing. His final map indicates the one above Georgetown, and at the ultimate west end of Pennsylvania Avenue, which crosses over Rock Creek into Georgetown. At the far southeast end of this same avenue a draw-bridge would cross the Eastern Branch, and further upstream would be a second bridge on the extension of East Capitol Street.

The large scale of the city—necessary to provide for future expansion, make it worthy of a great new republic, take full advantage of all the natural features, and provide enough land to ultimately raise money—gave rise to many problems. The major one was how to settle such a vast area. The plan, with emphasis on diagonal streets and the ring of states' squares around the center, was in part adapted to this end, as will be seen below. L'Enfant's main intent in the size, however, was to assure the Federal City of ample space for growth into one of the great world capitals.

The public grounds are not mentioned in the first report of L'Enfant, but these last three documents have ample reference to them. The President's House, of course, has a "park" which extends south to the Tiber (and Potomac); the Congress House has a "garden" which covers the west slope of the hill. These two areas are linked by a mile-long "public walk" which has the Tiber Canal at the north edge, and at the west end, directly below the President's park (to which the public walks are joined by two bridges) is the equestrian statue of Washington, as a focal point or pivot. To the south of it, extending the President's park (and the view) is another park with its east side at an angle so that the view from the President's House would be unobstructed by buildings. So that the equestrian statue also would not obstruct the view (the site being marked by a rise of ground), L'Enfant planned to lower this hill and use the earth to fill in the overly wide mouth of Tiber Creek.

The central public walk (the present Mall) was to have a carriage drive or "grand avenue" 400 feet wide down the center, gardens at each side, and flanked also (though he is not completely consistent at this point) by embassies, and public buildings for entertainment. Thus the "grand walk" formed a tree and garden lined link, using the equestrian statue as a pivot, between the President's House and the Congress House, and provided good views for both. The carriage drive, though ostensibly merely a pleasure route going to the river overlook west of the equestrian monument, also could be used as a pleasant approach to the President's House.

These points summarize the major features of the new city. It should be noted, however, that some of his features were not completely his own invention. As mentioned above, the great size of the city was also contemplated by Washington.[35] The use of the "highest summit of lands" for the Congress House and a similar prominence further to the west, toward Georgetown, for the President's House, was a relationship already decided upon by Jefferson, as noted in his memorandum to Washington of March 11, 1791,[36] before any word from L'Enfant had even been received. The scale, however, was far smaller, with the Capitol no further east than about Twelfth Street. His sketch plan of the area (fig. 4), probably accompanying this memorandum, shows this relationship of President's House and Capitol, with the Potomac and Tiber Creek to the south. It also shows that Jefferson conceived of the two buildings as linked by a public walk bordering the Potomac and Tiber Creek. Furthermore, when sending maps to L'Enfant on April 10, 1791, before L'Enfant's planning had really begun, Jefferson emphasized that he felt that "very liberal reservations should be made" for public grounds, and that the area around the Tiber (which was too shallow for navigation) would be a good place. He also noted that "those connected with the government will prefer fixing themselves near the public grounds in the center." He mentions also that the Eastern Branch would probably be the best location for commercial development because of the deep water.[37]

It is obvious, then, that while L'Enfant closely analyzed the site and fitted the needs of the city to it on a monumental scale, some of the basic ideas in the broadest sense were already conceived of by Jefferson and Washington. These helped L'Enfant to come to the final arrangement of his plan.

The problem of actually establishing and making grow a city of this extent was not faced by either Jefferson or Washington. And the size of L'Enfant's city was gigantic. After Washington's meeting with the Georgetown proprietors he wrote to Jefferson on March 31, 1791, of his success and mentioned that the area he had obtained was "from three to five

---

[35] See also his letter to Jefferson of Mar. 31, 1791, in which he mentions his agreement with the proprietors to take all the land "from Rock Creek along the river to the Eastern Branch, and so upward to, or above the Ferry, including a breadth of a mile and a half. . . ." This was to be ceded to the Government on the condition that the whole "shall be surveyed and laid off as a city (which Major L'Enfant is now directed to do)." Caemmerer, *Life*, p. 145.

[36] Caemmerer, *Life*, p. 139.

[37] Ibid., p. 147.

thousand acres." [38] The actual city which L'Enfant laid out, according to his map of August 1791, contains close to 5,700 acres. Virtually all of it was undeveloped, with the land—some hilly, some more level—thickly covered with trees, crossed by several streams, and at places bordered by marshes. As a comparison, neighboring Georgetown comprised about 300 acres at that time, extending little further north than O Street, thus containing only about 5 per cent of the area of Washington. And Georgetown had been growing slowly since 1751 when it was incorporated and laid out.

Furthermore, the Federal City had no *raison d'être* other than to serve the legislature and provide for the government which, when in session, had only 26 senators and 64 representatives in 1790, and a small number of clerks. Both Alexandria and Georgetown, flourishing towns of several thousand each, were active trade centers. In Georgetown the street pattern had directly grown out of its position as a port and trade center. West Landing and The Keys ran along the shore; the next major street up the slope to the north ran almost parallel to the shore and connected Chain Bridge at Little Falls to the west with the ford of Rock Creek to the east. Almost perpendicular to these two streets, at the center of the town, was High Street which began at the waterfront (called Water Street at this point) and climbed the hills almost due north, bending to best ascend the eminences above the town. The compact community had grown around these major streets and the waterfront with a few major estates and farms on the hills above.

For the Federal City, L'Enfant realized that if such a gigantic tract of land were to be laid out and developed successfully, modes of settlement that would assure growth, and means of providing a viable existence in addition to the support of Congress, would have to be provided. His plan of the city was made with problems of settlement in mind, as well as the other factors. We can briefly summarize the obvious requirements:

1. A central area for concentrated early development.
2. All major streets and squares cleared and graded, and streets paved in order to facilitate communication over the long distances and encourage building on them.
3. Adequate water supply.

4. A commercial potential established.
5. All major government buildings begun at once so as to form obvious focal points and spur private building near them.
6. For future development, squares and focal points to be developed by the states, to encourage settlement around them.
7. All improvements, clearly, to be effected by the Federal Government, which had full jurisdiction.

L'Enfant's discussion of these points is found in his report to Washington of June 22, 1791, the long Memoir to Washington dated August 19, 1791, and on the map he took to Philadelphia at the end of August of that year. These have all been mentioned above. In addition, there is the important report "for renewing the work at the Federal City" to George Washington of January 17, 1792,[39] which was accompanied by a long schedule of "Operations Intended for the ensuing Season" and a financial estimate for this work.[40] Other details are given in various contemporary letters, and in the appendix to his letter to the District Commissioners of May 30, 1800.[41]

A primary concern of L'Enfant's was to begin in the city in the area between the President's House and the Capitol, not only because this was where the government buildings were to be, but also so that a compact village could be well started. He envisioned shops, government related business (such as printing and stationery), row houses, boardinghouses, hotels for foreign ministers, and even the homes of the District Commissioners. Clearly, service facilities would soon grow up in this area. This early settlement, he felt, should be encouraged by grants of lots to those who would immediately erect buildings on them. The public walks adjacent would be an added amenity, and if playhouses and other amusements were erected, people would readily settle in this area.

A second major consideration was preparing the city so that such development could easily begin. Among the priorities in the 1792 agenda were leveling and grading some of the principal streets to the quality of good turnpike roads, grading certain other important streets, and bridging Rock Creek. Before any major building was to be done, the streets were to be "completely paved and ready for hous[es]" for

38 Ibid., p. 145.

39 Kite, pp. 110–116.
40 Ibid., pp. 116–132.
41 Caemmerer, *Life*, pp. 395–410.

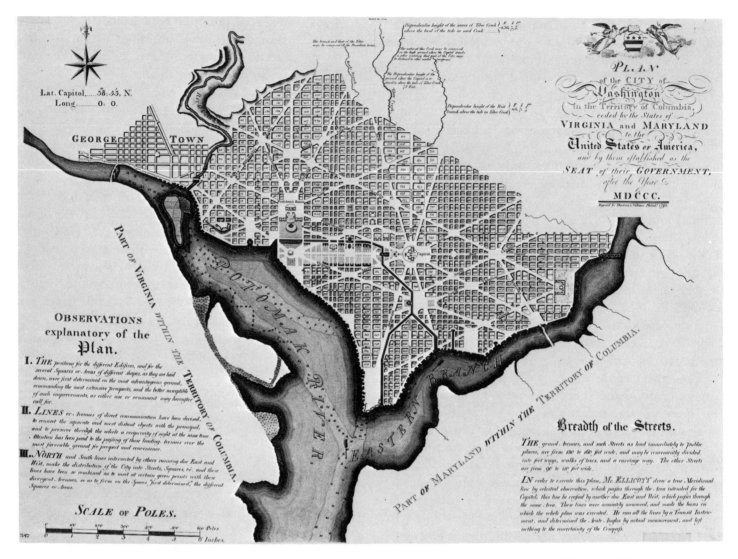

FIGURE 8. Engraved plan of the Federal City, by Andrew Ellicott, based on the drawings of L'Enfant, 1792.

until this was done, and the streets given their proper level, it would be impossible to tell how high or low the resulting building frontage would be.[42] The avenue to Georgetown was also to be completely paved. On his map he specifies that all major streets would be 160 feet wide, which included an 80-foot-wide carriageway in the center, 30-foot-wide gravel walks with trees on each side of it, and finally a 10-foot-wide pavement on each side. With these improvements, communication would be easy and builders attracted to the completed streets.

Another factor was the water supply. Although there were many streams and springs, one of the first items of business during 1792 was to be a more permanent supply. "Aqueducts already begun must be

continued in various places to convey . . . water . . . in such quantity as will be of general use to the city." [43] This also had to be completed before other improvements were begun.

Tiber Creek also had to be made into a canal and continued down to the Eastern Branch. This was necessary from the beginning to transport building material. Related to this, mills for plaster and cement, lumber mills, brickyards, blacksmith shops, scows for transporting stone from the Aquia Creek quarries—these also had to be established. After the initial years the canal would also contribute to the city's commercial possibilities.

After this groundwork had been well started, all the major buildings should be begun also. This was

---

[42] Ibid., pp. 401–402.

[43] Kite, pp. 118–119.

important for several reasons. The hotels and rent houses that he hoped to have built in the center of the city would not, he felt, be constructed "unless *some shining progress is made in the grand work* which the publick has to effect—*the continuance of that progress evidently provided for,* and the whole machine put in such motion *as will convince the friends as well as enemies to its success* that it will *be accomplished in all parts. . . .*"[44] It would then give assurance to those thinking of building in the new city. Furthermore, with work begun at once, there would be at least six public buildings completed by 1800 and, because various stages of each could be coordinated, efficiency and savings would ultimately result.

L'Enfant also had plans for the continuing growth of the city. By assigning the squares around the center of the city to various states, outer nodes of development would arise, all reasonably close to the center, and connected to that center (and each other) by paved avenues. On his map he notes that the states would improve them within a limited time. Since they were also visible from each other, rapid growth along the connecting streets would result. This was one of the reasons for the plan of diagonal streets in the first place.

L'Enfant believed that the Federal Government would finance all of this from the beginning since, of course, there was no population or trade to tax, and the city was being created by fiat by the government in the first place. Even George Washington, when discussing with the original proprietors of the land on March 29, 1791, had assured them that a "Town house or exchange" would be built for them at the center of the city.[45] Since L'Enfant was familiar with the great public works in Europe, his assumption of generous government control was probably present from the beginning.

Leaving nothing to chance, L'Enfant also had exact ideas as to how this should be financed. Until the land was improved, all the lots owned by the government for sale as a source of revenue (10,136 lots, half of the total) would obviously have a minimal value compared to their price when they faced graded and paved streets with completed government buildings nearby, a reliable water supply, and the prospect of some commercial success for the city. Until this could be effected—in about 6 years—a large loan should be taken by the government, with the salable lots providing convenient collateral.

His estimate for the first year's work was $300,000, and this amount would be continued for 4 years (through 1795) so that the initial total would be $1,200,000. By 1797 he felt that the sale of lots could begin.[46] After 1800, when Congress was to move to the city, the legislature would provide more capital themselves to help free the land to be sold from a mortgage held by a foreign bank.

It is clear that the $300,000 per year, even if extended through 1797 ($1,800,000) and taking the grants by Maryland and Virginia (almost $200,000) into account, was a low estimate. Though his 1792 estimate includes payment for 1,070 men and 74 teams of oxen or horses, it omits completely the salary for the Director General (presumably himself), his three assistants, the Surveyor of the City, his assistant, a head carpenter and head mason, and payment for the three District Commissioners—all of which would have to be honorable and munificent. This might add as much as $140,000 more for the 6 years.[47] Since L'Enfant was not noted for his thrift,[48] and since inflation would decrease the value of the dollar by about 45 per cent by 1800, one can see that the initial expense would have been closer to $3 million.

The scheme for development as outlined above was indeed genius; it was the proper complement to a most skillful plan. L'Enfant solved a problem that had never before been faced in America with originality and considerable insight. Had he actually been an architect or planner, trained in Europe, he might have been tempted to impose a "grand plan" on the site which could have been more dramatic, though probably less well fitted to the site. And had L'Enfant's ingenious plan for development been followed, the Federal City might well have started on quite a different level. It was not to be effected, however. The impediments were too large and numerous; L'Enfant himself, after many difficulties, was

44 Letter to Washington, Jan. 17, 1792. Caemmerer, *Life,* p. 195.
45 Ibid., p. 155.

46 Kite, pp. 124–129.
47 This rough estimate is arrived at by giving L'Enfant a salary of $4,000 each year—in 1802 he claimed $8,000 for 1 year's work, and inflation had been about 45 per cent since 1790—and the 10 others $2,000 each year, certainly a generous sum. In 1792 Jefferson wrote the Commissioners that Washington thought that $2,500 to $3,000 might be sufficient payment for L'Enfant. See Caemmerer, *Life,* p. 227.
48 In his commissioning the Order of the Cincinnati medals in Paris in 1783, L'Enfant spent much more than intended, both for the medals and for his own expenses. See Caemmerer, *Life,* pp. 82–84.

dismissed from his post by Jefferson on February 27, 1792.[49]

The reasons why L'Enfant's plan for development was not carried out—and why many subsequent problems rose with each year—fall into several broad categories. There were the conflicts between the strong-willed L'Enfant and the three Commissioners, which led to his dismissal; the Commissioners' lack of grand vision and their desire for rapid results to be visible; Congress' distrust of central government power; the total absense of adequate government financing; other far more pressing priorities for government attention and spending; and, land speculation in the new city.

A primary problem was the insoluble conflict that grew up between the Commissioners—David Stuart, Daniel Carroll, and William Johnson—whom Washington had appointed to supervise the planning and development of the Federal City, and L'Enfant. One initial point of friction that increased as months went by was that L'Enfant considered the planning of the city completely his own project, not subject to any other modification. He understood his appointment by Washington as giving him total freedom in *all* ways, not just in what sort of plan he arrived at.[50] Confident of his own ability and originality, and completely caught up in the *grandeur* of the project, he insisted—with some reason—that the plan had to be expanded and developed completely his way, or it would be a disaster. Since, by law, L'Enfant was under the Commissioners' direction, a conflict in authority was inevitable.

L'Enfant approached his work as a creative artist in the service of a Noble Patron—in this case, Washington. He assumed that his payment would ultimately be a munificent honorarium—he did not consider himself "employed" to perform a specific task. Thus his feeling that he was responsible only to Washington, who gave him freedom to design as he saw fit, distorted his relationship with the Commissioners from the start.[51]

Another point of friction with them was that L'Enfant assumed, again from not understanding the nature of his employment, that the map he was working on was his own personal property,[52] and that he would eventually reap a small fortune when it was published and sold. Thus the desire of Washington and Jefferson and others to have an engraving made, their sending of drawn copies to foreign heads of state, and the other "unauthorized" copies made for various reasons, were actually quite justified, but gave the high spirited L'Enfant the impression that everyone was trying to steal his work and rob him of his just due.

In proceeding with the scheme of development in 1792, there was also considerable conflict with the Commissioners. L'Enfant began to take over the direction of the actual work—opening the quarry, grading and leveling, brick making, laying foundations. The Commissioners had other suggestions as to what should be started first (such as making bricks rather than cutting stone) but L'Enfant utterly refused to follow their directions.[53] He also proceeded in having the house of Daniel Carroll of Duddington pulled down, since it was being built in one of the grand squares (southeast of the Capitol) which he had mapped out. L'Enfant, assuming that all steps of his plan would proceed at once, required that the house be removed to leave the square open, and had the house demolished by his own men. This did not ingratiate him with the Commissioners, whose duty it also was to deal with the often difficult proprietors of the land. L'Enfant's refusal to follow any of their directions or suggestions made joint effort impossible.

There also seems to have been some gossip and slander, supposedly spread by L'Enfant, disparaging the ability of the Commissioners, which exacerbated the relationship; the mysterious removal of survey stakes by some unknown party did not strengthen mutual trust.[54]

---

[49] Caemmerer, *Life*, pp. 212–213. Letters and other material dealing with his dismissal are reproduced in this same volume, pp. 169–215. See also the memorials subsequently submitted, C.H.S. *Records*, II, pp. 72–110. This material is also fully discussed in Kite.

[50] Writing to Jefferson on Apr. 4, 1791, L'Enfant requests maps of various cities to look at, but assures him that his plan will be "new and original. . . ." "The President has left me without any restriction soever." Caemmerer, *Life*, p. 146.

[51] In one of his last letters to L'Enfant before he was dismissed, Jefferson tried to set down the relationship in unequivocal terms: The Commissioners "will of course receive your propositions, decide on the plans to be pursued from time to time, & submit them

to the President to be approved or disapproved, & when returned with his approbation, the Commissioners will put into your hands the execution of such parts as shall be arranged with you, & will doubtless see from time to time that these objects, & no others, are pursued." Letter of Feb. 22, 1792. Caemmerer, *Life*, p. 209.

[52] This is mentioned as early as August 1791. In a letter from Jefferson of Aug. 18, he talks of the engraving of the map and either Ellicott or L'Enfant to proceed with this matter. L'Enfant has written in the margin of his letter: "What right could this man [Ellicott] have thereto?" Caemmerer, *Life*, p. 156. In his Memorials, L'Enfant complained that the taking over of his map deprived him of his rights in the sale of copies. *Life*, p. 388.

[53] Caemmerer, *Life*, pp. 199–202.

[54] Ibid., p. 202. Also, Kite, pp. 135–137.

It was, clearly, utterly impossible for L'Enfant and the Commissioners to work together. Washington himself realized how difficult a person L'Enfant was.[55] On December 2, 1791, he wrote one of several warnings, trying to set the relationship right:

> I wished you to be employed in the arrangements of the Federal City. I still wish it: but only on condition that you can conduct yourself in subordination to the authority of the Commissioners, to whom by law the business is entrusted, and who stand between you and the President. . . .
> Having the beauty and regularity of your plan only in view, you pursue it as if every person & thing were *obliged* to yield to it. Whereas the Commissioners have many circumstances to attend to, some of which, perhaps, may be unknown to you; which evinces in a strong point of view the propriety, the necessity, and the safety of your acting by their directions.[56]

All was to no avail, and as mentioned, L'Enfant was dismissed on February 27, 1792, since he "absolutely decline[d] acting under the authority of the present Commissioners." [57]

A second major factor in the failure of the plan was the different views of the plan held by L'Enfant and the Commissioners. L'Enfant presumed that his plan would be rapidly put into effect, with Washington overriding any problems. He did not take into consideration all the conflicts and personal and legal problems that the Commissioners had to deal with. L'Enfant also assumed that money would be raised without further issue, since the city was the will of Congress. The Commissioners, however, were more realistic, and knew the problems in effecting an undertaking of this size. They could not envision the undertaking ever brought to completion and were rather intent on a small, modest beginning to show that progress was being made—sale of lots on good terms, erection of at least a few houses, beginning the two major buildings. They undoubtedly understood the somewhat hostile mood of Congress, the lack of funds, the need for showing progress. Coming to Georgetown once a month for their meetings, they surely had that thriving town as a model of what could be erected, and knew of its practical problems.

The capital probably seemed a fanciful city of preposterous distances.

Another major reason for failure was, of course, the attitude of the Congress. Although they had indeed voted to set up a capital under their own control, the sentiment as to where such a capital should be was not unanimous and for decades there was agitation to move it to some other location, even after work was begun on the Potomac site. Thus, requests for huge sums of money—or slow progress —could possibly jeopardize the whole project. There was also lengthy and heated debate over how strong the central Federal Government should be, and many states, with vivid memories of British domination and the despotism of powerful royal governors, did not relish a strong central government. While both Washington and Hamilton realized that a powerful government was obligatory, they had to use their utmost skill in assuring a strong Federal constitution. Its slow ratification by the various states, after much debate, is an index of this hesitancy. Thus, a grand, highly expensive, and seemingly ostentatious city, far larger than any established state capital, would be the last project that jealous states would be willing to support.

But even if Congress had been perfectly willing to give full support to a new Capital, it is doubtful if they would have been willing to take out a loan—as L'Enfant wanted—for over $2 million in a period when the country was already in financial difficulties. The selection of the original site, as mentioned, had been part of the bargain in Hamilton's funding bill, in which the debts of the Continental Congress were to be taken over and paid in full. It also included assuming the debts of the various states in waging the Revolutionary War, since this had been in common cause. The Federal Government was to exchange full value government bonds for the devalued state bonds. In exchange for the southern Capital site, southern states voted for this assumption, though it benefitted the north most. This assumption was most important in keeping the tenuous union together, and in helping to establish a firm national currency. The states' debt, however, was $20 million. For years, Congress tried valiantly to pay off this huge sum, so that new borrowing was out of the question. And assuredly, individual states would hardly be willing to be taxed for a project which would seem to them a dangerous precedent for government power, a gigantic city giving them no apparent benefit.

---

[55] In a letter to David Stuart on Nov. 20, 1791, he observes: "It is much to be regretted—however common the case is—that men who possess talents which fit them for peculiar purposes should almost unvariably be under the influence of untoward dispositions or are sottish, idle,—or possessed of some disqualification by which they plague all those with whom they are concerned. . . ." Caemmerer, *Life*, p. 175.

[56] Ibid., p. 182. For a discussion of the many duties that the Commissioners had to attend to, see William Tindall, *Standard History of the City of Washington* (Knoxville: H. W. Crew & Co., 1914), esp. pp. 119–122.

[57] Kite, p. 151.

The Federal Government income was also not large to begin with. In 1792 the Treasury receipts amounted to close to $3,370,000, primarily from customs duties. In addition, necessary loans totaled over $5 million.[58] The expenses for that year were estimated in 1792 at about the same figure ($3,688,000). This included $368,653.56 "for support of the civil establishments," a similar sum for the Navy, $87,463.60 for pensions, and about $2,850,000 for payment of the interest on the total public debt, foreign and domestic.[59] Any surplus was used to reduce the debt, which, as of January 1, 1792, stood at $77,227,924.66.[60] In a country this much in debt, anxious to pay it off, the borrowing of more to build a grandiose national Capital would have seemed to many utter folly. It is worth pointing out that L'Enfant's estimated annual expense for the Federal City was $300,000 (plus supervisory expenses), a sum very close to the entire amount spent in 1792 for the civil government, "including 40,000 dollars for foreign offices."[61] Although L'Enfant claimed in 1800 that Hamilton, then Secretary of the Treasury, had said he would supply all the money wanted and more, this seems improbable.[62]

A further reason for the failure of the plan was that there were far more important things that had to be done. Before the Revolution, the colonies had been protected by British troops and ships; now the Navy had to be greatly strengthened and regular troops paid to protect the western frontiers. Internal improvements—mainly canals and roads—were vital for the growth of commerce, to help give the country a needed sense of unity, and to aid in their mutual defense. Industry needed rapid assistance now that European goods were being heavily taxed (for national revenue); the fishing and shipping industries also needed encouragement. The civil wars in Europe, beginning in 1793, made it all the more important that the United States become as inde-

pendent as possible. These and many other problems affecting the very existence of the new country had to be solved. In this context, a grandiose Capital would be an impossible expense, especially at a time when the very nature of government financing was being debated. If the new city were to grow, it would have to be by its own efforts.

A final factor that prevented the growth of the city was land speculation. L'Enfant had foreseen that unless public lands available to be sold were held until the city was more than a wilderness, people would buy them at a low price and hold them, for an eventual profit, rather than build on them. This is in fact what happened. In his Memorial of August 30, 1800, L'Enfant deplored this speculation, which he felt ruined the development of Washington. The general value of the lots was low for this and other reasons. "From the Sale of House Lots and the intermissive Supply [of funds] obtained it has not in seven years lapse enabled the Completion of even one half of the main Edifices."[63] For a small town of a few hundred acres, with public buildings of brick, the sale of lots might well have adequately financed a neat community—but certainly not a city of nearly 6,000 acres with large stone edifices. Even George Washington, probably realizing that an appeal for funds to Congress would be foolish and probably dangerous, promoted the early sale of lots in the fall of 1791, in part also to show Congress that progress was indeed being made.

Thus, for many reasons the scheme of development by L'Enfant failed at the time. In fact, it seems remarkable that it got as far as it did, considering the other demands on the Congress, factionalism, and the state of Federal finances. The struggling city that emerged in 1800 had its later problems already well rooted in the unfulfilled original plan of the city.

When the Capital was moved from Philadelphia to Washington in 1800, the new city already had several major flaws which would persist for three-quarters of a century.

None of the basic improvements—one might almost say "capital improvements"—that L'Enfant envisioned had been made. The streets and squares were not graded or paved, only cleared of trees (with the stumps remaining). A water supply was not established; planting along major streets had not been undertaken. Furthermore, a means of commer-

---

[58] "Statement of the annual receipts into the Treasury, 1789–1809," *American State Papers*, Documents, Legislative and Executive of the Congress of the United States, 1st–13th Congresses, Vol. VI (Washington: Gales & Seaton, 1832), Serial 10, p. 424.

[59] "Estimates for Annual Expenditure, 1792," *American State Papers*, Documents, Legislative and Executive of the Congress of the United States, 1st–13th Congresses, Vol. V (Washington: Gales & Seaton, 1832), Serial 9, p. 146.

[60] Op. cit. p. 425.

[61] Op. cit., p. 146.

[62] In his Memorial of Aug. 30, 1800, he asserts that it was "the Secretary's intention to have provided me at once with as many Pounds Sterling as I had at the time computed of Dollars wanted." Caemmerer, *Life*, p. 377.

[63] Ibid., p. 233.

cial development was not yet established. There also was an obvious lack of government interest in the city since no special appropriations had been made. Two major government buildings had been begun, and two lesser ones, but there was no firm commitment to future funding of growth. In addition, the precedent of the architect being responsible to a government committee of laymen, not otherwise qualified to interpret his work, and with their own ideas, was established.

Private development, by lack of basic improvements or incentives, was also not encouraged, and was even discouraged by speculation. The city was totally dependent on Congress for support and money, yet it had no representatives—and it was the House of Representatives that was responsible for raising funds. Because of the vast distances of the plan, settlement without these improvements was even more difficult.

These are problems that would be persistent in the ensuing years, and gave a most unpropitious background to the new city. It forms a basis for understanding much of the success and failure in the subsequent architecture.

CHAPTER II

Congress and Building in Washington, 1800-1861

FROM an examination of the manner in which L'Enfant laid out the Federal City, and the apparent intent of Congress and George Washington, a number of basic premises are established for the development of the city and its architecture. The city was to be completely under the control of Congress in all ways. The government had authorized the city, selected the site, and planned it; they also owned all the avenues and streets, half of the building lots, and about 540 acres of land reserved for major public buildings and open spaces. Their control and extent of ownership was thus undisputed.

The city also was to exist primarily for the benefit of Congress, and since they had complete control, and owned most of the land, it would appear obvious that it was their duty to support, develop, and improve the city themselves. This would include grading, roadways, paving, water supply, and so on.

Implicit in the above, all the public buildings that were needed by the Federal Government, as well as most of those by the residents—clerks, functionaries, tradespeople, mechanics, farmers, and other local residents—would have to be provided by Congress.

Furthermore, since the city had no representatives in Congress and no way of making its wishes known other than by petition, the Congress would have to be awake to both the Federal Government's needs, and to those of the city which were dependent upon them. And since the city was dependent on Congress for its existence, the government was bound to provide some means of continuing livelihood for the city during the many months of the summer when the legislature was not in session. Development of port facilities similar to Georgetown and Alexandria (also within the Federal District), seemed the best mode.

Finally, in addition to the actual need of the various improvements outlined above, the fact that Washington was the Capital of the country and would be visited by foreign representatives and diplomats, travelers, and traders, suggested the desirability of rendering the city both attractive and convenient to foreigners who would return home with reports of what America and its Capital were like.

When we look, however, at what official structures were actually built in Washington and what general improvements were made by the Federal Government, we will see that the actual state of affairs was far different from what it should have been. The attitude of Congress toward the city, and what the local inhabitants had to do, will go far in showing why the first 60 years of Washington's growth were unfruitful ground indeed for the active development of important architecture.

Before December 1800, when Congress moved to Washington from its 10-year stay in Philadelphia, only a limited amount of work had been accomplished. The management of the city at that time was under the direction of three Commissioners, with the advice of President Washington and his Secretary of State Thomas Jefferson.

In the original plans for the Federal City, it was contemplated that L'Enfant would also design the needed buildings, and it was to him that Jefferson wrote some suggestions. In a letter of April 10, 1791, he states:

> Whenever it is proposed to prepare plans for the Capitol I should prefer the adoption of some one of the models of antiquity which have had the approbation of thousands of years; and for the President's house I should prefer the celebrated fronts of modern buildings which have already received the approbation of all good judges. Such are the Galerie du Louvre, the Gardes meubles; and two fronts of the Hotel de Salm.[1]

The "model of antiquity" proposed for the Capitol was probably the Roman temple form which Jefferson had himself chosen for the Richmond capitol 6 years earlier. For the President's House, the more delicate Eighteenth century French classicism which he had been able to admire when in Paris from 1784–89 was more appropriate. It is clear from this that Jefferson was not simply interested in the latest handsome Federal-style structure, such as Charles Bulfinch was building in Boston, but a new and more severe classicism that would be a clear break from the Georgian and British past. At the time, L'Enfant's most famous building, the new Federal Hall in New York City (1788–89) was still Federal in style in many ways, though his strong interest in a more monumental treatment, with a projecting portico, is clear.[2] The building was, however, firmly linked with the Eighteenth century tradition, especially in its cupola and flat brickwork (figs. 1–2). This mixture of older and newer forms may have been in part determined by the former Federal Hall which L'Enfant had to incorporate; he kept the two side wings when filling in the central portion with his columned portico, though changing them somewhat to conform to the new proportions. Thus, Jefferson's suggestion of looking to an even more classical style does not seem out of place.

Actually, however, though there is apparently no visual corroboration, L'Enfant might well have con-structed buildings of far greater blocky classicism than even Jefferson envisioned. In the appendix to his Letter to the Commissioners of May 30, 1800, he criticized the design of the Capitol as being more like a palace than "a basilick consecrated to the august representation of the people," which, rather than being "pretty," should be of a "massy Sullen [and at] the same time grand aspect."[3] He further stated that "the whole composition is of too Slander a Module . . . for having not sufficient masses nor boldness of profile and being too laboured never can be of good aspect;"[4] he also thought that the building was too small for the site. We see then, that L'Enfant's concepts were closer to those of the important Greek Revival architects Benjamin H. Latrobe and Robert Mills years later, than to the structures actually built by 1800.

Since L'Enfant was soon relieved of his position, the Commissioners established a competition for the Capitol and the President's House. An advertisement announcing such a competition, and giving specifications, was inserted in newspapers throughout the country in March 1792.[5]

The design for the President's House by James Hoban was selected by the Commissioners and George Washington in July 1792, and work was shortly begun.[6] As Jefferson had desired, the building was unlike anything in the United States at the time and had the overtones of European grandeur (fig. 9). The design was strongly Palladian, as adapted in Britain in the Eighteenth century. As has often been pointed out, it resembles closely a design from James Gibbs's *Book of Architecture* of 1728 (fig. 10) as well as Leinster House in Dublin (1745–47).[7] For a new national architecture, attempting to discard the Georgian and Federal styles, this building combined European associations and a classical basis, with permanent ashlar construction into a design both handsome and beautifully proportioned. Work on this structure was slow, however, and by December 1800, when President John Adams moved into it, the interior was far from complete.

---

[1] H. Paul Caemmerer, *The Life of Pierre Charles L'Enfant* (Washington: National Republic Publishing Co., 1950), p. 149.

[2] L'Enfant's work on the New Federal Hall is discussed in Talbot Hamlin, *Greek Revival Architecture in America* (New York: Dover Publications, 1964), p. 8. More recently it has been thoroughly examined, and the floor plans reconstructed, by Louis Torres in "Federal Hall Revisited," *Journal of the Society of Architectural Historians*, XXIX, 4 (December 1970), pp. 327–338.

[3] Caemmerer, p. 402.

[4] Ibid., p. 403.

[5] W. B. Bryan, *A History of the National Capital* (New York: The Macmillan Company, 1914–16), I, 187.

[6] Ibid., p. 195. Hoban's prize was an award of $500 and a gold medal; he was also employed at 300 guineas a year to superintend the work.

[7] Both are illustrated in *The White House: An Historical Guide* (Washington, D.C.: White House Historical Association, 1964), p. 13.

The second major building was the Capitol. The development of this structure is far more complicated. It too was subject to a competition, advertised in March 1792, in which the necessary rooms were specified, but little else was required. None of the submissions was considered satisfactory, but the drawings of Stephen Hallet were thought the best and he was requested to continue work on them. Then, Dr. William Thornton requested permission to submit plans late, was so permitted, and his drawings of February 1793 were at once seen to be the most successful (fig. 11). Washington and Jefferson were both enthusiastic and the design was approved. Unfortunately, in order to compensate Hallet for the now rejected work he had been doing, the Commissioners employed him to study the Thornton plans and provide cost estimates. This was obviously an error in judgement and ethics, since Hallet was determined to effect various changes of his own contrary to Thornton's design, of which he was highly critical. To make matters worse, although James Hoban was to be the Supervising Architect, Hallet was also appointed to be the assistant supervisor and the draftsman.[8] Since Hoban was fully occupied with the work on the President's House, Hallet had an overly large degree of freedom and, as Hoban said, had "the boldness or foolishness" to change Thornton's plans and even the construction. When informed of these deviations, Washington "expressed his disapproval in a style of such warmth as his dignity seldom permitted,"[9] according to Thornton. Hallet was dismissed on November 15, 1794. Thornton, who had become one of the District Commissioners in September 1794, was now also made Commissioner of Federal Buildings and so had more direct control over his design. But since Hoban was still overworked, George Hadfield became the next Supervising Architect, only to resign (but soon return) when Washington would not permit him to make changes. Even the Commissioners had their say, eliminating ventilating flues in the Senate, and changing materials to be used elsewhere. Thornton's objection to this, and the use of some poorly carved ornament, was overruled in 1797 and 1798. "Thorn-

FIGURE 9. The President's House, by James Hoban. (From Charles W. Janson, *The Stranger in America*, 1807.)

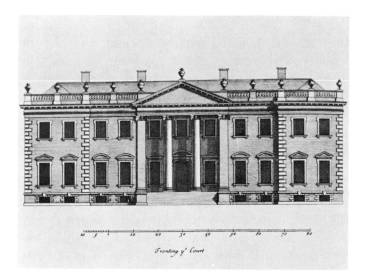

FIGURE 10. Design for a house to have been built in Greenwich, England, 1720. Plate 47 from James Gibbs, *A Book of Architecture, Containing Designs of Buildings and Ornaments* (1728).

ton was always the advocate of good construction and material, but his confreres did not always uphold him when his plans caused an increase in the first cost."[10] Hadfield, who made certain errors, quit in May 1798, and Hoban once again came in charge.

These problems with the Capitol are here outlined to show the difficulties the Commissioners had in pursuing the building, and why, by 1800, only the north wing was completed. Not only the many con-

---

[8] Glenn Brown, *History of the United States Capitol* (Washington: U.S. Government Printing Office, 1900), I, 5–17. This two volume work is a thorough account of the intricate problems involved in building the Capitol in all its various stages. See also *Documentary History of the Construction and Development of the United States Capitol Building and Grounds*, H. Rept. 646, 58th Cong., 2d sess, Ser. 4585.

[9] Brown, p. 18.

[10] Ibid., p. 23.

FIGURE 11. The Capitol, east elevation, first design (revised), by Dr. William Thornton, 1800.

flicting wills, but the shortness of funds delayed the building.

The full design by Thornton, not to be completed until almost 30 years after it was begun, was, like the President's House, unlike anything else in the United States. His design, in cut stone (in spite of the original requirement that the structure be of brick), discarded all sense of small scale Federal-style buildings. He produced a design of considerable originality, both large in its essential volumes, yet refined in its details.

The building as Thornton designed it had a massive central portion based on the Roman Pantheon (fig. 12), with a deep octastyle porch which caught shadow dramatically, and behind which was a low capping dome.[11] This section was placed on a rusticated basement story. Flanking this central rotunda where two wings, each five bays across and each connected to the domed central portion by a wide single bay, somewhat recessed. In contrast with the central element, these wings had flat pilasters articulating the surface, both at the sides and (in his revised ver-

FIGURE 12. The Pantheon, Rome, 125 A.D.

sion) at the ends. These pilasters, and other Palladian details, gave it a more delicate surface treatment; these blocklike wings would therefore contrast with the more massive sculptural central unit. Thornton's design, by combining the massiveness of a Roman model with the more delicate, yet still classical, wings, united the two styles Jefferson had found most appropriate.

Both the President's House and the Capitol were clear statements of a new classicism, a clean break with older Federal Style brick architecture. The new style had the enthusiastic support of both Washing-

---

[11] The similarity with the Pantheon is not only due to the general relationship of a pedimented portico with a low dome somewhat behind it, but also to closer details. Both poricos are ocastyle and of the Corinthian order. The dome on the Pantheon has six low stepped rings around the base (above one larger low band); Thornton's drawing also shows six rings. His revised drawings show also indications of an oculus in the same manner as in the Pantheon. The size of the central portion of the capitol is smaller, however, the portico of the revised plan (see Brown, I, plate 28) being ca. 85 feet wide, and that of the Pantheon ca. 115 feet.

22

FIGURE 13. F Street at Fifteenth Street, N.W., looking northwest, 1817. Watercolor by Baroness Hyde de Neuville.

ton and Jefferson; this was one hopeful indication of future national encouragement of imaginative architecture.

Only two other government buildings were erected by the end of 1800. President Washington had wanted the executive buildings close to the President's House and approved the site to the east and west of it. Even when the new president, John Adams, wanted to have them built near the Capitol, Washington's will prevailed.[12] In 1797, George Hadfield designed a structure for the Treasury Department, which was to be located east of the President's House, about parallel to its south facade. This same design was duplicated and used by the Commissioners for the Executive and War Department building which was to be built on a corresponding spot to the west of the President's House. No views of these two structures before 1814 have been found. After their destruction, however, they were rebuilt using the

original walls, and probably followed the original design. As rebuilt in 1817, each was a 2½ story brick structure with a low stone basement and a stone string course below the second floor windows. The entrances to the Treasury building were from the east end (on Fifteenth Street, N.W.) and probably at the opposite end as well as the north and south sides. These long sides were broken by a wide three-bay gabled pavilion at the center which projected slightly. To either side of this central feature were six bays of windows. The hip roof apparently had three dormers at the east and west ends, and four on each side. The only prominent classical motif seems to have been a Palladian window at each end of the second floor. A portion of this building appears in a watercolor of 1817 (fig. 13). The original building, begun in 1798 and finished in 1800, measured 147 feet by 56 feet 6 inches.[13]

[12] [Donald J. Lehman], *Executive Office Building* ("General Services Administration Historical Study" No. 3; Washington: U.S. Government Printing Office, 1964), p. 5.

[13] Lehman, pp. 6–7. Figure 13c shows the rebuilt State and War building (in the 1860's used by the Navy) with the two additional stories; the lower portion, however, is probably little changed. Only in the northern pair of buildings, constructed in 1818–20,

FIGURE 14. Hollis Hall, Harvard University, Cambridge, Mass.

FIGURE 16. Wheat Row, 1313-1321 Fourth Street, S.W., 1793

FIGURE 15. Old North, Georgetown University, begun 1792-93.

Thus, the Hadfield buildings are a continuation of simple brick Georgian and Federal structures, lacking any porticos or extensive classical detailing. In general appearance they followed a common type of rectangular, utilitarian building with a central pedimented pavilion common in the Eighteenth century, such as Hollis Hall (Harvard University) of 1762–63 (fig. 14). Such types were also built with a decorative cupola on the roof, as in Nassau Hall (Princeton University) of 1754–56, and elsewhere. In Washington, both Old North at Georgetown University, begun in 1792–93 (fig. 15), and the group of houses called Wheat Row, of about 1793, (fig. 16), are similar in form. This plain and somewhat backward style

was undoubtedly a result of a desire to economize, so that what funds were available could be used on the Capitol.

These four structure were the only government buildings more or less ready by December 1800. The only other piece of major construction was a causeway and a three-arch stone bridge across Rock Creek built in 1792.[14] This connected Georgetown and the post road which ran through Washington; the bridge, however, soon collapsed.[15] In 1800, a second bridge was built at M Street, north of this. But other improvements were negligible. Some streets had been cleared of trees (though stumps were left) but none was paved; springs still supplied the only water; Pennsylvania Avenue was still bisected toward the Capitol by a stream and a marsh; Tiber Creek was unimproved; streets and parts of the Mall were used by individuals for growing crops; and other enclosed parts of public reservations were put to use as pasturage. By 1800 only 109 brick houses had been built, although there were 263 frame structures permitted after the original building code, which specified only brick or stone houses,[16] was modified to encourage building. And the population by 1800 was only 3,210 (including slaves), only a few hundred more than Georgetown.[17] Since the buildings that had been erected were widely scattered over the city, the sylvan character was largely unbroken, except for the most populous areas along Penn-

[14] Bryan, I, 314.

[15] Ibid., pp. 189–190.

[16] William Tindall, *Standard History of the City of Washington* (Knoxville, H. W. Crew & Co., 1914), pp. 122–123.

[17] Constance McLaughlin Green, *Washington, Village and Capital, 1800–1878* (Princeton: Princeton University Press, 1962), p. 21.

was the original form embellished with an Ionic portico on their north sides, with the central pavilion expanded from three to five bays.

FIGURE 17. Washington in 1800. Drawn by Parkyns, engraved by Heath; published in 1804.

sylvania Avenue above and below the President's House, around the Capitol, at Greenleaf's Point (near the junction of the Potomac and Eastern Branch), and lesser structures around the Navy Yard.[18] The city was truly a bleak vision to the Congress which arrived in the winter of 1800 (fig. 17). The capital as it appeared then has been described thus:

> Two unfinished stark white citadels towered above the terrain from hilltops on opposite shores of a dismal swamp, more like ruins amid the fallen fragments of their own stone than new and rising edifices. Where monuments had been planned, brush piles moldered and rubbish heaps accumulated. Where majestic avenues were to sweep, swaths of tree stumps stood, rough quarried stones marking the intersections. Where houses were to be, barren hillocks, stripped of vegetation, rose like desert islands amid a sea of bogs and marshes.[19]

There are many reasons for this dismal state in 1800, when the government took up residence. They are worth enumeratiing, for they indicate problems that the city would continue to have.

There was a lack of adequate money to pursue work on the Capitol, President's House, and other improvements (dredging, grading, filling, paving, fencing, etc.) due to the poor sale of lots, inability of securing adequate credit locally or abroad, and a reluctance to ask for it from Congress. Thus, the apparent official progress was very slow, discouraging private investment and settlement.

Doubts also existed as to whether the government would really move to the new Federal City. An Englishman, by the name of Weld, visited the District of Columbia in 1796 and claimed that there were people in Philadelphia "doing all in their power to check the progress of the building in the city, and to prevent the Congress from meeting there at the appointed time." [20] And many Congressmen did not

---

[18] James Sterling Young, *The Washington Community 1800–1828* (New York: Columbia University Press, 1966), p. 67, fig. 2. This study of early Washington gives a lively picture of the Capital from the 1790's through the 1820's. See especially pp. 19–26.

[19] Young, p. 42.

[20] Theodore W. Noyes, "Some of Washington's Grievances," No. 1, *Washington Star,* Feb. 18, 1888, p. 2.

wish to move to a city without any of the civilized amenities that Philadelphia could offer.

Confidence in the Federal City to thrive and grow was also low because of the poor sale of lots, slow or defaulted payments, land speculation, disastrous and poorly run lotteries to raise money, bankruptcy of many landholders, and slow construction of public buildings. These factors discouraged large and small investors equally.[21]

The very concept of a great national capital was anathema to some, and not in the least interesting to many. Both Washington and Hamilton, who did the most to assure the site on the Potomac was chosen, were convinced that a strong central government was essential, not only to preserve the new freedom, but also to keep the new country unified and promote its growth. But probably a majority of people, including Congressmen, were afraid of a strong national government. All their previous experience had been with state governments, which still affected them far more in daily life than any central government primarily devoted to foreign affairs, the Army and Navy, etc. Thus, it has been suggested: "Fundamentally, it would appear that the government itself was an institution of too little significance to attract population and wealth to its residence."[22]

Furthermore, from the very beginning, Congress showed virtually no interest in the Capital City, and (as in all other cities), simply assumed that the municipality would provide for grading and paving, street lighting, markets, schools, poor relief, and other such burdens. This was a basic fault in conception, that Congress failed to see themselves as generous benefactors of a capital they had willed into being, and paid no attention to the basic necessities the city needed, but which its meager population could not supply adequately.

In the actual building of the first structures there was a scarcity of workmen, and the Commissioners even contemplated importing them from Europe. Minor labor disputes did not assist these difficult beginnings.[23]

Most foreboding of all as concerned the future of government architecture, there was a basic conflict between the government authorities (the Commissioners) and the architects. As we have seen, Thornton's plans for the Capitol were foolishly given to Hallet, a competing and rival architect, for cost esti-

mates. He was also put largely in charge of the work. Changes made by him, his successors, and the Commissioners themselves, would seem to violate the architectural conception of Thornton's original plan. This tinkering with the original conception could not but alter and probably debase the archietect's intent. In a similar spirit, Hadfield's plans for the Treasury building were duplicated without his permission, and without further compensation. The sense of architecture as a profession, rather than a mere trade, just then beginning to come into focus, was bound to create problems between a board used to builders and pattern books rather than a creative architect who dealt in overall concepts, not changeable parts.

When money was available, as for the President's House and the Capitol, and the architect given free rein, buildings of the latest and most viable style were produced, appropriate to the new purposes. But when the emphasis was on economical construction (as the Treasury, and State and War buildings), structures that were common and ordinary were the result. If, as slowly came to be accepted, the government should be housed in the best possible buildings, too penurious an attitude would clearly result in disappointing architecture.

Finally, a sense of leadership was essential. Under Washington (with the aid of Jefferson) the desire for a grand city with first-rate architecture was uppermost. Intelligent appreciation and understanding assured what successes came. But when Adams became president in 1797, it was clear that his interests lay elsewhere, and only when Jefferson became president in 1801 did the official interest in architecture revive again. Similar ups and downs would continue.

These problems help to indicate why the architectural climate of Washington was not very encouraging, even before Congress took up official residence in the Capital City.

The first 35 years of government residence in Washington set the tone of development. When we examine what Congress spent for its own convenience, and what for the city, and also see what Washington City itself spent, we can understand the nature of early difficulties. Several reports, of 1820, 1830, and especially 1835, set forth clearly the conflict of duty and the grievances of Washington, and help point to the reasons that Congress took virtually no interest in the development of the new city.

---

[21] Early land dealings are discussed fully in Bryan, I, 214–240.
[22] Young, p. 27.
[23] Bryan, I, 322.

FIGURE 18. The Capitol, about 1828, as completed by Charles Bulfinch. Drawn by W. H. Bartlett, engraved by R. Brandard.

In these first decades, what did Congress do for the improvement of their new Capital? Their work falls into two areas, work that benefitted themselves only (or in major part) and those that were primarily for the benefit of the city and its citizens (which naturally included Congressmen as well as government workers).

Work on the Capitol, of course, continued.[24] In 1803 Jefferson appointed Benjamin H. Latrobe as Surveyor of Public Buildings to continue work on the building. Latrobe modified Thornton's plan slightly and proposed ways to complete the central portion. His desire was to simplify the style somewhat, especially on the interior, to conform more to the latest architectural thought which turned increas-

ingly to Greek inspiration rather than to broader Palladian and Roman classical bases. Latrobe managed to complete both the north and south wings by 1811. Congress then made no further appropriations, in part due to continuing controversy over the expense, the method of construction, and other criticism, and in part due to the approaching war with England. After the destruction of Washington by the British in 1814, the structure had to be entirely rebuilt and Latrobe, rising to the occasion, redid the interiors along the former lines but now with a more consistent stylistic unity. By 1817, however, he resigned his position, due to great friction with one of the Commissioners, criticism for his slowness, and other difficulties, and the completion of the central portion was left to Charles Bulfinch. This architect made minor interior changes, altered the east facade somewhat, and redesigned the dome to make it more prominent. By 1827 the Capitol was at last complete (fig. 18). In

---

[24] The full account of the various building campaigns, construction problems, etc., is found in Brown, I, which covers the period up to 1850. See also Talbot Hamlin, *Benjamin Henry Latrobe* (New York: Oxford University Press, 1955).

FIGURE 19. The President's House, by Hoban, with portico of 1829, by Benjamin H. Latrobe.

FIGURE 20. Department of State, about 1830.

spite of many hands, it was one of the handsomest and richest buildings in the United States, rivaling many comparable structures in Europe.

Although the President's House was not complete in 1800, slow progress over 7 more years finally brought the work to an end, and included pavilions and terraces on the east and west sides which had been designed by Latrobe, at Jefferson's request. After the destruction of 1814, it was rebuilt by Latrobe, with the porticos which he had proposed on the north and south sides in plans of 1807. The south portico was completed in 1824, the north in 1829, giving the building the appearance it has today (fig. 19).

The Treasury building and the State and War

building were both reconstructed after the 1814 invasion using the original walls, and probably the original plan. They were completed by the spring of 1816. But in 2 more years, due to severe overcrowding, two more office buildings were erected to the north of each, in 1818–20.[25] Although slightly larger in size, their style was based on the earlier structures (fig. 20). The central pedimented pavilion was now five bays rather than three wide, and each building was ornamented on the north (or Pennsylvania Avenue) side with a portico of six Ionic columns, giving the brick structures considerably greater formality. The ends had rectangular, rather than Palladian, windows at the second floor.

These buildings were the extent of government construction, during the first 35 years, devoted to its own offices and accommodation.

During this same period, only three structures for the city were erected at government expense: a jail (1802–03); a court house (1823–24), which was actually only a wing of the city hall then being built by the city at its own expense; and a penitentiary for the District (1826–33). The last two would have been paid for by the central government, rather than by the municipality, in any location. Thus, Congress built virtually nothing beyond that which was necessary for its own operation.

Other improvements to the city at government expense were almost exclusively on streets and avenues around the Capitol and the President's House, or on Pennsylvania Avenue which connected the two. A pittance was expended on enclosing the public burial ground on the Eastern Branch, with the only sizable expenditure being $150,000 for completing the Tiber Canal through to the Eastern Branch. This was, however, as much an advantage for the Navy Yard and the construction of stone government buildings as for any hoped for commercial benefit to the city. The administration of the canal and further expenses were left to the city.

This very meager improvement, made only for necessary government buildings and the streets actually used by Congress was, with few exceptions, the whole extent of government interest in developing Washington between 1800 and 1835. Actual costs will be outlined below.

During the same period, the city, which grew from 3,210 to about 20,000, had to take over the prime

25 W. C. Bryan, *A History of the National Capital* (New York: The Mamillan Company, 1914–16), II, 67–68.

duty of other necessary improvements. Although the original three Commissioners for the city had been appointed by an act of Congress, the city government after 1802 was wholly local. From 1802 until 1871, this government consisted of a mayor (sometimes elected, sometimes appointed by the President, according to periodic revisions of the city charter by Congress), and two councils. From the beginning, the Common Council was elected by local residents (those qualified consisting of the "free white male taxpayers"), and from 1804 the smaller Council of Aldermen was elected as well. Therefore, the local government was essentially autonomous, with little influence in, or aid from, the Congress.[26]

In part, because of this lack of contact with Congress, the city was regarded by most Congressmen as being similar to any other American municipality, requiring no special considerations. It had to build its own market houses, infirmaries, fire engine houses, its own city hall, and other necessary public structures. But probably the heaviest burden was the need of clearing and attempting to pave the enormously extensive and wide streets and avenues, as well as paying a portion for country roads. The city also had to provide its own wells, pumps, and street lights; support its own police and fire engines; and care for all the poor and indigent who flocked to the capital from neighboring states in hope of government relief or compensation—these in addition to their own poor. Another great burden which arose in the late 1820's was the large debt contracted by the city in investing in Chesapeake and Ohio Canal stock. Although many citizens had not wanted the canal continued through Georgetown to Rock Creek (where, via the shoreline and the Tiber Canal, boats could come into the center of the city), the government had prescribed this extension in 1828, and the city was authorized to buy stock. Thus, the debt from this overextension was in part due to government expectations.[27] All of these problems were made worse because the city received no taxes on the large government land holdings nor any compensation for city improvements which had increased the value of government lots or aided the government as well as the city.

A comparison of actual expenses by both the government and the city during this period will point up the extent of this imbalance: [28]

Expenses of the Government for its own buildings:
Prior to 1814; Capitol, President's House, etc.	$1,214,292.98
Rebuilding same, plus two new buildings	2,014,586.61
Other work, 1831-34, including repairs	113,213.39½
	3,342,093.98½

Expenses of the Government for city buildings:
Jail and penitentiary	210,780.63
Contribution toward City Hall (courthouse)	11,116.00
	221,896.63

Expenses of the Government for paving streets:
Pennsylvania Ave., footways from Capitol to Executive Offices, trees on Pennsylvania Ave., etc. (Items not specified as around Government buildings amount to ca. $11,500)	208,927.67½
Total	3,772,976.29

Outstanding debt of the city:
This is mainly the expense of the C. & O. Canal, but includes also some for salaries in the asylum and public schools, street lighting, pumps, etc.	1,806,442.59

Expenses for city streets:
Paid by the city, to 1835	429,971.00
Paid by private citizens, over	200,000.00
Total	2,436,413.59

It should be observed, however, that unlike the government expenses, these noted above of the city are not complete. Considerably more was raised by taxes and spent without figuring into the city debt and it is not included. The only significant expense by the government for the city was the $150,000 spent on the Tiber Canal which, as noted previously, equally benefited the government.

What distressed the city most was that in view of this imbalance, the government had actually made, or would make, considerable profits from the land they owned. The value of the land sold, and that assessed but unsold, stood at about $2 million by 1835. Considering that government expenses on street paving, the Tiber Canal, the jail, penitentiary and courthouse amounted to less than $600,000, the city felt that there was a reprehensible imbalance in their finances.

These obvious inequalities were recognized by the city, but Congress turned a deaf ear to their entreaties. As early as 1810 a committee of the House of Representatives declared that "the founding and execution of so extensive a city . . . must obviously require the aid of vast resources," and that

[26] For a discussion of the early government of Washington, see Carroll D. Wright, "The Economic Development of the District of Columbia," *Proceedings of the Washington Academy of Sciences*, I (1899), pp. 174–78, and also Henry E. Davis, "The Political development of the District of Columbia," *Ibid.*, pp. 205–212.

[27] *Report of the Committee on the District of Columbia*, Sen. Doc. 97, 23rd Cong., 2d sess. (1835), Ser. 268, p. 7.

[28] Ibid., pp. 16–19.

the city should be assisted.[29] Nothing came of this and similar admonitions. Even very modest legislation was not implemented. In 1820 an act of Congress gave a new charter to the city, and contained the provision that the Commissioner of Public Buildings, or others in charge of government disbursement in the city, were to reimburse the city "in just proportion" for any streets *"thereafter"* opened and improved where they fronted on government squares. But the expense of this was to be defrayed out of sale of city lots, "and from no other fund." [30] This was not only inadequate, since the majority of streets which did not pass by government lots were still to be paid for by the municipality, but it was also ineffectual, for apparently no payments were made.

In the oration delivered by John Law in 1820 at the cornerstone laying of the City Hall, Congress was excoriated for its continued neglect.[31] Law pointed out that the city, though created by Congress, had received very little indeed from the government to date. "No appropriation of public money was applied to the city before the year 1798, and the sum of 100,000 dollars, which was then advanced, was merely loaned to the Commissioners, on interest, to be repaid by instalments." Subsequent major expenses had been made only for the convenience of Congressmen, and by 1814 the sum spent on public buildings was not even equal to the value of the original land given to the government. Not only had the government made no effort to encourage or aid local development, but it had not even tried to improve any of its own lands. The 320 acres of the Mall are cited: "No attempt to improve the latter has been made; not a tree has been planted; not even a common fence encloses it." Furthermore, he complained, national institutions, such as a military academy or a university, which would have given confidence and encouragement to the city, were not established. A number of "positive errors" in addition to the general neglect are listed, and he observes: "the voice of history might have instructed our legislators that human means and judicious encouragement were necessary to erect and people a

city." These and other omissions he felt were just grounds for the city to complain.

The duty of Congress to Washington was spelled out clearly in 1830 in a report from the District Committee regarding the paving of Pennsylvania Avenue. It was shown that to date the city had spent vastly more than its fair or required share in local improvements, and that the additional burden of paving this avenue was not warranted.[32] If it were to be paved, the government should do it, and the report went on to point out the financial inequalities as outlined above.

Financial difficulties for the city continued to mount. In 1834, at a crisis level, Washington citizens petitioned Congress "for relief from the heavy pecuniary responsibilities" that they bore.[33] The major cause here set forth was the city's oversubscription in C. & O. Canal stock, a project that had cost more and progressed slower than any had anticipated. The city could pay neither the interest nor principal of the debt, which would be taken over by foreign banks if Congress did not assume it. The petitioners explained: "If we erred in the magnitude of our obligations to a great national work, we erred in common with the illustrious founder of our city in appreciating its future consequence and opulence."

The second cause for the large debt, the petition explained, was the expense borne by the city for most of the city improvements, including streets. "As the seat of government of a great empire, [Washington] was so laid out as to involve expenses, at the least triple of those incurred in ordinary towns. When to this consideration is added the exemption from taxation for twenty-four years, of property belonging to the nation, at least equal in value to that owned by individuals, the excessive burdens imposed on private property become evident."

In response to this crisis, Senator Samuel Southard and a committee investigated the affairs of the city, and submitted to Congress the most complete report to date on the financial difficulties, and what duties Congress should assume.

At the beginning of his report, Southard made quite clear the enormity of the present problem: "The city is involved in pecuniary obligations from

---

29 Quoted in Green, pp. 33–34.

30 *An act to incorporate the inhabitants of the City of Washington and to repeal all acts heretofore passed for that purpose,* 3 Stat. 583 (1820), 16th Cong., 1st sess., ch. 104.

31 *Ceremonies and Oration at Laying the Cornerstone of the City Hall of the City of Washington,* Aug. 22, 1820 (Washington: Jacob Gideon Jr., 1820). The oration by John Law occupies the body of the pamphlet, pp. 8–15.

32 *Report of the District Committeee on Paving of Pennsylvania Avenue,* H. Rept. 184, 21st Cong., 1st sess. (1830), Ser. 200.

33 *Memorial of the Citizens of Washington, for Relief from the Heavy Pecuniary Responsibilities under which they are laboring,* Sen. Doc. 29, 23d Cong., 2d sess. (1834), Ser. 267. Georgetown submitted a similar petition at the same time.

which it is *utterly impossible* that it can be relieved by any means within its own control, or by any exertions it may make, unaided by Congressional legislation." [34] The total outstanding debt, was the "enormous sum" of $1,806,442.59. Southard emphasized that there was no reason to suspect any irregularities; "the Committee did not find in their conduct anything which should excite in Congress a reluctance to come to their relief." He enumerated a number of reasons for this huge debt:

1. Expenses for opening and paving streets. Because of the size of the city, the scattered settlements, the great width of streets and avenues, and the total lack of any previous improvement, the expenses, borne almost completely by the city with an inadequate population, was enormous. "The expenditure upon the streets . . . has unquestionably been one of the principal causes of the embarrassment of the city; and the committee believe that it is one which ought not to have been thrown on the inhabitants to the extent which it has been." He also listed a number of factors which suggested the injustice of this burden: the city had been planned and the streets made very wide without consulting any inhabitants; the streets in fact belonged to the Federal Government; the government exercised complete control over the streets (and had even sold some for private lots) so the size could not be changed by the city; and over half the land adjacent to them belonged to the government. "If the streets are its property, and . . . under its control, it is not easy to perceive why it should call upon . . . others to keep that property in order." If streets were to be considered a joint convenience, then the expense must be shared.

2. Government land was untaxed, though in other cities such land is taxed and the revenue spent on local improvements. Washington's tax base was therefore half of what it should be. While taxing the government lands was not proposed, taking this situation into consideration in making appropriations was mandatory.

3. The City Hall, for which the city had already spent $80,000, was not complete in 1823 so Congress had contributed $10,000 for circuit court chambers, and gave the city a right to have a fund-raising lottery (which failed miserably, and increased their debt). But since 1824, half of the building had been used by the government as a court. Southard pointed out that expenses for courts in other parts of the United States greatly exceeded the paltry $10,000 spent.

4. The canal debt was indeed enormous. He pointed out that had the canal not been extended through Georgetown, but had ended just above it as originally planned, Washington could still have profited from it with no further expense. But the enlargement "was induced by the government, and prescribed by the law of 1828 authorizing the subscription," and the city bought more than it should have. Thus the government was in part responsible for this debt. As many of the other improvements of the city, it was motivated by a desire to please Congress and help as much as it could to improve the city and keep the legislature from moving to another location.

Senator Southard put this in perspective by pointing out that the 541 acres of public reservations owned by the government had cost it nothing, since the price paid, $36,099 had been derived from the sale of some of the 10,136 city lots it had been given in the original transaction. Now this public land would be worth $1,500,000 if sold as building sites. Furthermore, the money the government had expended on public and government buildings came from three sources: from lots sold, money provided by the states, and from the Treasury. The committee felt, however, that such a means of financing was not appropriate, and that all expenses for public buildings should be from the common treasury, with appropriations (in lieu of taxes on government buildings and lands) and the sale of lots all going to help develop the city. Had the government property been taxed equal to the private lots, about $2 million would by now have been available to the city.

> In the investigation of the subject . . . the committee have been unable to separate the interest of the District from the interests of the United States. They regard it . . . as the creation of the Union for its own purposes. . . . And if this was the design, it is not easy to comprehend either the principle which would prevent the Government from a liberal appropriation of national resources to accomplish the object, or the policy which would confine the city to the means possessed by the inhabitants for its improvement.

The bill which was passed in response to this report provided, however, only for the assumption of the canal debt, and not the interest or other expenses. But the Southard report nevertheless brought the needs of the city forcefully to the notice of Congress, and argued for the justness and desirability of sharing in the expenses.

---

[34] S. Doc. 97, 23d Cong., 2d sess., Ser. 268, p. 1.

What were some of the reasons for this neglect of the city by Congress? A summary of the major points will make this gross neglect more understandable, and provide reasons why it would continue.

There was essentially a profound lack of unity in the Federal Government, and a lack of influence of the President, which hampered joint efforts. Most of the Congressmen were in Washington for only a few years, and when in the city, stayed for only a few months. No sense of unity with other members, or the townspeople, could develop. For example, two-thirds of the Representatives of the 13th Congress served only two terms,[35] and therefore new politicians not understanding the local problems continually arrived. Furthermore, every 4 years the head of state might change, and with him a percentage of the government officials. Flux made unity difficult..

The sense of party unity was also slight. The main groupings, as Mr. Young has shown in his detailed study, were by boardinghouses in which cliques generally from the same region of the country came together, having similar local interests. This strengthened parochial concerns, to the greater isolation both from other parts of the country, and from Washington. These groups also prevented Congressmen from mixing with local residents more.

The Congressmen's strong sense of individualism was also a devisive factor. No Congressman wanted to appear to agree with anyone else too closely, and personal independence and expression were uppermost.[36]

The two political parties or alignments had almost no cohesion or sense of unity. They almost never met as a group, and members often disliked being identified by party, preferring to be considered from one region or another.[37] The President, who in theory could help unify his followers, had far less influence than one would think, except by purely personal skill. Congressmen took pains not to support his ideas for fear of being considered his "lackey."[38]

There was also a distrust of political power itself, which weakened any sense of unity. This grew not just from past experience, or a desire to uphold regional interests, but also because the Constitution itself made these divisions of power, the checks and balances, so very clear. The antagonisms between the various branches were real.

All these factors made unity and common effort impossible. Jefferson complained that Congress was "not yet sufficiently aware of the necessity of accommodation & mutual sacrifice of opinion for conducting a numerous assembly" and that rather, "the object of the members . . . seemed to be merely to thwart, by every means, the wishes of their political antagonists."[39]

It has even been suggested that a reason that Pennsylvania Avenue was paved and repaired so desultorily was the Congress did not need to be linked to the executive branch, and in fact preferred the separation.[40]

A second reason for congressional neglect was the nature of the Congressmen themselves. Not only were they regional in interests, they were also very conservative in outlook and with little imagination for seeing the needs of the city. Their first responsibility was to their home constituents, and they resisted other pressures. As the country grew, more and more Representatives, especially from frontier states with greater needs of their own, put their claims before all else. The District was lost in the shuffle. And the pressure from constituents was real: when Congress tried to vote themselves a pay increase in 1816, about two-thirds failed to be reelected.[41] As one Congressman noted, it was not considered proper that they should use tax money "to live in ease and affluence—to contract habits and tastes above the intelligent part of [our] constituents, and inconsistent with the plain republican manners of [the] country."[42] Many factors contributed to the gradual decline in the caliber of Representatives.

> The new rules of precedence relegated representatives to an inferior social position; and, as John Calhoun had forseen in 1817, the defeat of a bill to raise congressional salaries to a figure equal to or above those of presidential appointees had the effect of lowering the prestige of the House until the most able men in the country were no longer eager to stand for election. Certainly after 1818 the House contained fewer distinguished men than once it had.[43]

A further reason for the neglect was economic. Congressional conservativeness manifested itself also in a desire for general thriftiness, and an effort to reduce the national debt—at least two issues upon which there was general unity. Congress was always ready to economize: military spending was cut just

---

[35] Young, p. 89.
[36] Ibid., p. 94.
[37] Ibid., p. 137.
[38] Ibid., pp. 129–130.

[39] Ibid., p. 96.
[40] Ibid., pp. 75–76.
[41] Ibid., p. 59.
[42] Remarks of Mr. Ross of Pennsylvania, in *Annals of Congress*, XXX (14th Cong., 2d sess.) , p. 515, quoted in Young, p. 59.
[43] Green, p. 107.

before the War of 1812, with disastrous result. In this light, expenses on the city of Washington, which would appear to constituents as self-agrandizement and favoritism to one city, were avoided. As to the national debt, John Quincy Adams stated in his message to Congress of 1825: "It is exceedingly desirable that [the public debt] should be extinguished altogether." [44]

Furthermore, Congress was antipathetic to any government project which had no immediate, tangible, readily forseeable benefit. This was both from a sense of economy and shortsightedness, and a desire to not exceed their constitutional power. Because of this, all efforts for cultural or scientific improvements were of little success. The idea of a national university met total indifference, although George Washington himself had pleaded for one, and had left his stock in the Patowmack Canal Co. as endowment. Attempts to establish a university in 1805–06 met with no success,[45] and even J. Q. Adams' impassioned plea in 1825 fell on deaf ears.[46]

Other scientific efforts, many with genuine usefulness for commerce and navigation, were defeated also. The Coast and Geodetic Survey had a fitful existence from 1807 to 1818, and then was essentially terminated because no quick results were seen, and Congress felt too much money had been spent.[47] It was not revived until 1832. In 1825 Adams had proposed extensive aid to science and the arts; he emphasized that the constitutional authority to "promote the general welfare" was not just limited to agriculture, commerce, and manufactures, but also included "the cultivation and encouragement of the mechanical and of the elegant arts, the advancement of literature, and the progress of the sciences, ornamental and profound." If Congress refused to exercise its powers "for the benefit of the People" in all ways, it would be "to hide in the earth the talent committed to our charge—would be treachery to the most sacred of trusts." [48] Congress made no response, and the government astronomical observatory Adams had requested was not built until 1843.

When it cost nothing, Congress did indeed occasionally give away land for the use of educational institutions. The first such munificent gift was allowing the Columbian Institute to use six acres of the Mall below the Capitol for a botanical garden.[49] Later, lots were given to Georgetown College and Columbian College. This reluctance to support efforts to improve science and the arts helped to prevent any embellishment of Washington.

There was also a specific lack of conern for the problems of Washington City, and an assumption that the city would somehow take care of itself. In general, Congress begrudged any time it had to spend on District affairs. As early as 1803, a Representative declared that as the city grew, it would take more and more of Congress' time and presently would be equal to that spent on the rest of the United States! [50] And in 1830, the chairman of the House District Committee complained of the unpleasantness of his job, because of the ungenerous "temper and spirit with which the most ordinary appropriations for the benefit of this District are received. . . . Some gentlemen seem to regard the District of Columbia as a rat under an exhausted receiver, where political empirics may display the quackery of legislation without any danger of being called to account for their folly or their ignorance." [51] This was in part due to the lack of representation of the city in Congress so that no one had the interests of the city his sole duty. Petitions of citizens were regarded as irritants.

The assumption that the city would somehow take care of itself was common. Care of roads was always the duty of the municipality. So was poor relief and care for the sick. As early as 1802 the city was spending up to 42 per cent of its income on care of the poor, both local and those flocking to the seat of national government in hope of aid.[52] By the 1830's it was shown that in the local hospitals 75 per cent of the patients were nonresidents of the city.[53] The jails were similarly overburdened; but since these services were traditionally locally administered, Congress provided no assistance until the 1840's.[54]

The weakness of the local government coupled with the indifference of Congress made any local development difficult. The mayor and his two

[44] James D. Richardson (comp.), *Compilation of the Messages and Papers of the Presidents 1789-1897* (Washington: U.S. Government Printing Office, 1896–99), II, 305.

[45] Bryan, I, 553–554.

[46] Richardson, p. 311.

[47] A. Hunter Dupree, *Science in the Federal Government* (New York: Harper & Row, 1964), pp. 29–32. This study has a full account of the government's relations to the development of science, and points out the early reluctance of Congress to finance anything without immediate results.

[48] Richardson, p. 316.

[49] Green, p. 69.

[50] Noyes, p. 2.

[51] Bryan, II, 128.

[52] Young, p. 26.

[53] Green, pp. 135–136.

[54] Ibid., p. 90.

boards, one of aldermen and one of councilmen (both elected by the people) were not up to the difficulties. "Their powers and resources were altogether insufficient for purposes other than those pertaining to an inconsequential town."[55] Only under Mayor William W. Seaton (1840–50) did the local government achieve much influence with Congress, but this was primarily due to Seaton's own ability and character, rather than to a change in the city government.

The regional animosity over the slavery question also inhibited growth of the District. Both local residents and Congressmen were divided on the slavery issue and from the 1820's on, agreement between conflicting interests was more and more difficult. The north, furthermore, wanted Washington to be free of slavery entirely, with sale of slaves there prohibited. Southerners, however, saw this as the first wedge of possible future restrictions and saw the status of the Capital City an index of other changes. In such a climate of antagonism, concerted effort was difficult. Local feelings were not improved when the use of slave labor on public buildings during the 1820's often left freemen unemployed.[56]

There was also a general dislike of Washington as a city by Congressmen. This is not hard to understand. They were required to leave family and friends at home until the 1830's and 1840's's because of the lack of adequate housing, and the relative shortness of sessions. Their life was dull and dreary, with none of the amenities or beauties of an established city such as Philadelphia; the climate was disagreeable to many; the roads and transportation frustrating; and the general spirit of the city depressed and depressing. They impatiently waited for the end of Congress, and many spent their time gambling.[57] Many came with high hopes of honors or public service, and when disappointed identified their discontent with the city.[58]

Certainly one of the most pernicious checks to the development of the city was the possibility that Congress might move the capital to another location. This was a threat that existed more or less actively until the 1870's. In 1807, there were pleas to move the capital back to Philadelphia, "the very focus of

foreign and domestic intelligence."[59] After the destruction of Washington in 1814 it was seriously debated whether or not to move the capital. A committee of Congress finally reported that they found it "inexpedient to remove the seat of Government at this time from Washington City." This was voted on with "inexpedient" changed to *expedient* and the resulting tie was broken by the speaker in *favor* of the change. But on the third vote, when the new location of Philadelphia was inserted, the decision to move the capital was defeated narrowly.[60] Thus was the sense of disappointment with the city, and the feeling that the original commitment as to the site of the capital was not inviolable. Petitions for removing the seat of government to other locations were common thereafter, generally to more western states.[61] In 1888, Theodore Noyes lamented the "miserable state of the city for three-quarters of a century, during which Congressional disfavor or indifference checked its growth," and especially condemned "the efforts of capital-movers [which] shut out new settlers, and discouraged its residents from improving lands."[62]

Government architectural development was undoubtedly hindered by the attitude of Congress toward architecture. Their idea of economy in construction was what was cheapest to *build,* not cheapest in the long run, and so the original Treasury building and State and War building were constructed in the common manner with wood interior framing. In less than 3 years each had been badly damaged by fire, with the loss of records in both. In the Capitol, Congress would not believe that Latrobe's south wing, in masonry and brick vaulting, was less expensive by $100,000 than the plaster and wood north wing. It looked more expensive, and thus was! As Latrobe wrote, "to them it was beauty itself that was the *extravagance*—no cost comparisons could contradict that! What could any architect do in the face of such an attitude?"[63] Latrobe had also warned about using inexpensive materials in the

[55] William B. Webb, J. Woolridge, et al., *Centennial History of the City of Washington, D.C.* (Dayton, Ohio: H. W. Crew, 1892), p. 188.

[56] Green, p. 98.

[57] Ibid., pp. 107–108. Reference is to the 1820's.

[58] *National Intelligencer,* July 13, 1822, quoted in Bryan, II, 63.

[59] Noyes, p. 2.

[60] Ibid.

[61] In 1848, for example, there were a number of petitions from Ohio, with the one from Cincinnati recommending that city as "a position more central, and exempt from a traffic in slaves now allowed within the District of Columbia." S. Jour., 30th Cong., 1st sess. (1848), Ser. 502, p. 380. During this same year other petitions came from Baltimore, Md.; Massachusetts; and Maine.

[62] Noyes, "Some of Washington's Grievances," No. 2, *Washington Star,* Feb. 25, 1888, p. 2.

[63] Hamlin, *Latrobe,* p. 291.

Tiber Canal, but to no avail. Wood-lined locks were built, and soon proved utterly worthless.[64]

There was also considerable meddling from the President and Congress in architectural matters which was generally for the worse. Jefferson's faulty idea of how to roof the House of Representatives chamber in 1806 is an example; his skylights leaked, as Latrobe had warned. These interferences made the architect's work more difficult.

Furthermore, working for a group, rather than individuals, made satisfaction more difficult. Criticisms on slowness and costs by people who were ignorant of any architectural matters, or who knew only the builders' tradition, did not help. In a period when the architect as a professional was coming into his own (Latrobe being one of the first major examples), there was bound to be friction between people used to builders whose plans and details could be shuffled around more readily, and the new architect who was now more interested in overall concepts of design and the unity of the whole construction, and also the introduction of new construction techniques (such as brick vaulting, etc.) which often went hand in hand with new architectural forms. Such plans could not be torn apart and recombined on paper by a layman. This was not helped by the long tradition of combining several architectural designs to unite various desired features. Even as late as the 1830's the designs of a number of architects were combined in New York City's Custom House.[65]

Another reason for poor local development was the uncertainty of continued appropriations from a fickle Congress. This made work of all sorts slower. By not being able to apportion work on a building as the architect saw best—but rather as funds permitted—it increased costs as well. Latrobe, as early as 1806, bitterly complained of the uncertainty of appropriations and pleaded for a change in funding, to no avail.[66] This was to be a problem until the end of the century.[67] Working for the government was usually a dubious honor. "Hallet, Hadfield and Latrobe all suffered loss rather than gain by their association with the capitol."[68]

A final reason may have been that the official building in Washington was retarded by the lack of need. When Congress came to the Federal City in 1800, there were 138 Senators and Representatives, and 126 officers and clerks. The increase was rapid in the first few years, so that by 1816 Congress had grown to 218 members, and the clerks, etc., employed in Washington to 535. From this point, increase in members of Congress was slow; by 1831 it was 261, by 1851 it was 295. Employees grew more rapidly, however. In 1831 they reached 666, by 1841 were 1,014, and in 1851 had grown to 1,533 in number.[69] Thus there was no need for large and capacious buildings until the government was large enough to occupy them. The most dramatic surge in government activity, and in employees, did not occur until the Civil War.

These dozen factors, including social, political, and economic elements, are the major reasons that even after the government took up residence in the Capital, almost nothing was done during the first 35 years to nurture this unique Capital, and why the hope for numbers of large, splendid government buildings soon embellishing the city was unfounded.

The late 1830's and the 1840's saw improvement in the interest taken by the Federal Government in Washington affairs. Although there were still many who disapproved of spending national funds for "purely local improvements," others saw the obvious need to assist the city grow. Furthermore, the needs of the government were expanding, at last necessitating a series of new buildings. Many Congressmen also began to realize how primitive the streets, water supply, sewers, and ungraded and unlandscaped open spaces were. Though improvement was slight, it was an advance over past performance and encouraged the city.

The most obvious change was in new government buildings. While these did not affect the city directly, they did affirm the will of Congress to stay in

---

[64] Ibid., p. 351ff.

[65] Town and Davis, William Ross, and John Frazee all had a hand in designing this handsome building. The Commissioners in charge combined the various schemes. See Hamlin, *Greek Revival Architecture*, p. 154.

[66] Brown, I, 38.

[67] R. H. Thayer (comp.), *History, Organization and Function of the Office of the Supervising Architect of the Treasury Department* (Washington: U.S. Government Printing Office, 1886), pp. 33–34. "One of the most fruitful causes [of] expense in the completion of buildings is the system of making partial appropriations, which prolongs the period of construction and adds materially to the contingent expenses. This method also often prevents the making of advantageous contracts, as at no time can a conract be made beyond existing appropriations."

[68] Hamlin, *Greek Revival Architecture*, p. 23.

[69] Statistics are drawn from U.S. Bureau of the Census, U.S. Department of Commerce, *Historical Statistics of the United States, Colonial Times to 1957* (Washington: U.S. Government Printing Office, 1960), pp. 691, 710.

FIGURE 21.   Treasury Building, by Robert Mills, begun 1836. Photograph taken about 1860.

Washington, give hope of an expanded and more active government, and of course provided more local employment. These new buildings can be examined briefly.

The Treasury Department, crowded into the small original building next to the President's House, was forced to move into temporary quarters in 1833 when the old building burned. The new structure, which was to contain space for the executive offices, the Patent Office, and the Post Office Department temporarily, was proposed in 1836. A number of new sites were discussed, including in Lafayette Square, and on the land south of the President's House, or, between F and G Streets at Seventh and Eighth Streets, N.W. Only this latter site conformed with the placement of public buildings as envisioned by L'Enfant (in the area between the President's House and the Capitol); in fact, this site was the eastern half of the lot designated on L'Enfant's map

as D, where the national church was to be located.[70] The other two sites that were proposed had been left as open spaces on the original plan. Clearly, many Congressmen made no attempt to follow the guidelines set down in 1791.

Two designs for the new Treasury Building were submitted, one by William P. Elliot (a draftsman in the Patent Office), and one by Robert Mills, then in private practice in Washington after having been a clerk in the Treasury Department until 1834.[71] The

_____

[70] These street letters and numbers are those presently in use, which also correspond to those on the Ellicott map of 1792. This map, while following the L'Enfant drawing in most ways, does change the location of certain streets. Thus, on the L'Enfant map there is only one block separating the Patent Office site and that of the City Hall to the east; on the Ellicott map, there are two. The geographic relationship of the buildings is, however, unchanged.

[71] Mills was not then employed by the government in any capacity; and although after being appointed Architect of the Treasury he styled himself "Architect of Public Buildings," no such

FIGURE 22. Treasury Building, south wing, by Ammi B. Young, 1855-60.

FIGURE 23. Treasury Building, south wing, by Ammi B. Young, 1855-60.

Mills design, a long building facing east with a short wing (to the west) at the center, was selected.[72] Controversy in Congress over the location, however, at last gave the final selection to President Jackson who decided it should be on the original Treasury site, east of the President's House, and connected to the old Executive Building at the north end. Since the design was unchanged, and the chosen site more restricted than the others, the Mills building was right on the sidewalk line of Fourteenth Street (fig. 21). And although the south end did not then block the vista down Pennsylvania Avenue, it was obvious that when a south wing was added to it, the view would be obstructed. When this was realized in Congress in 1836, work had already begun and considerable debate arose whether to tear down what was erected and begin again or leave it as it stood. Nothing, however, was ever decided, and the work continued.[73]

The Mills wing, almost the whole length screened by a monumental Ionic colonnade or peristyle, was to be a fireproof building and so the plan, brick groin vaulted rooms on either side of a barrel vaulted central corridor, was in part determined by the structural logic of such a building.[74] It was also partly determined by the requirements of providing 114 offices. The exterior was of Aquia sandstone (as were the President's House and the Capitol) above Mills' objection that it would not last well. This, of course, was quite true, the masonry all having to be

FIGURE 24. Treasury Building, west wing, by Isaiah Rogers, 1862-64.

replaced in 1909 by granite. This wing was completed in 1840 and the south wing (figs. 22–23), designed by Ammi B. Young, was built in 1855–60, following the same style as Mills had begun.[75] The west wing (fig. 24), designed by Isaiah Rogers, was begun about 1862 and completed in 1864 (including the northwest corner) and the north wing, by A. B. Mullett, was started after the demolition of the old Executive Building in 1866, and completed in 1869.

The design as set by Mills was appropriate and much admired. The fireproof nature and the economy of brick vaulting made it a permanent and durable structure. The large, simple exterior design was not, of course, a mere copy of a Greek temple but, as the best of the Greek Revival designs, solved new problems within a vocabulary of Greek concepts

position actually existed. I owe these facts to Donald J. Lehman, General Services Administration historian, who has studied Mills and the Treasury Building extensively.

[72] Bryan, II, 244.

[73] Ibid., pp. 245–246.

[74] William H. Pierson, Jr., "Robert Mills' Treasury Building," *JSAH*, XXVIII, 3 (October 1969), pp. 211–12.

[75] The overall design of the south and west wings were provided by two small-scale drawings by Thomas U. Walter. Although these were followed in general, the final design of these wings was clearly due to Young, Rogers, and Mullett. This information is courtesy of Denys Peter Myers, Historic American Buildings Survey, Washington, D.C.

FIGURE 25. Patent Office, south facade, by William P. Elliott. Photograph taken about 1864.

of form with considerable originality. The free use of Greek elements enabled the large office building —a new type never before built in the United States —to be given a sense of unity of concept that, had it been constructed in brick with the older vernacular trim, would have been impossible to achieve.

The second structure was the new Patent Office, which was built on the site originally set aside by L'Enfant for a national church (between F and G Streets between Seventh and Ninth Streets, N.W., one of the locations contemplated earlier for the Treasury. The building was begun in 1836 following the designs of William P. Elliot, although Mills, an architect with considerable experience and knowledge in constructing fireproof buildings, was the supervisor of the construction. This south wing, also of sandstone, was even more monumental and severe than Mills' own Treasury, and consisted of a huge two story Doric portico at the center with wings on either side (fig. 25). These wings were articulated by pilasters supporting a plain Doric entablature, the whole resting on a one-story rusticated basement. The interior of this wing, completed by 1840, was vaulted by Mills (fig. 26). Just as in the Treasury Building,

the interior divisions (halls, offices, and alcoves) were largely the same as the structural divisions of groin and barrel vaults. The pilasters and corner piers which animated the exterior also acted as buttresses for these vaults, thus creating a particularly happy congruency of interior structural units with exterior form. This coincidence of structure with design, of interior space with exterior form, with the simple, clear volumes of the interior vaulting even being comparable to the large basic forms of the exterior —these all bodied forth a unity of architectural concept that was at the forefront of professional thinking of the time.

Robert Mills also laid the foundations for the east and west wings. These were carried on by Thomas U. Walter, "Architect of the Capitol Extension," who built the east wing between 1850 and 1852, and worked on the west wing from 1851 to 1854. This was completed in 1856 by Edward Clark, his successor (fig. 27). The north wing, though begun by Walter in 1856, was not completed until about 1867, the last 2 years being supervised by Clark.[76] All these

[76] From information supplied by Donald J. Lehman, who also notes that Alexander Parris had proposed to the Commissioner of

38

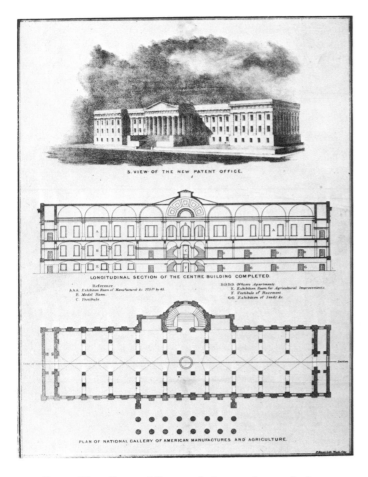

FIGURE 26a. Patent Office; rendering, section, and plan.

FIGURE 26b. Patent Office interior. First floor, west wing, looking southwest.

FIGURE 27. Patent Office, west wing, by Thomas U. Walter and Edward Clark, 1851-56. Photograph taken about 1920.

facades, however, continued the monumental design of Elliot, except for the addition of an extra basement story by Walter, due to an alteration in the grade and a desire to provide more light and space.

The third building constructed in this flurry of government spending was a new Post Office Department. This was also necessitated by a fire, since in December of 1836 the old Blodgett Hotel, being used for the Post Office Department, was destroyed. Robert Mills was again the architect for the new building, which was located just south of the Patent Office, at E and F Streets, between Seventh and Eighth Streets, N.W. The south portion of the structure, with two northward wings at each end, was completed in 1841-42 (fig. 28). Here at last, marble was chosen as the original material, though in the Patent Office it was used in the east, west and north por-

tions. It is said that marble was selected here not for its greater beauty, but because it did not, like sandstone, have to be painted every few years to keep the stone from weathering badly.[77] The north section, with the remainder of the sides, was completed by Walter in 1855–66, although there was a brief suspension of work during the Civil War; after 1865, Edward Clark became the architect, with M. C. Meigs the engineer.

Although completely of marble on the exterior,

Public Buildings, William Noland, that the basement walls of this south wing be thickened. This was apparently done in 1838. For the many hands involved in this building, see also Louise Hall, "The Design of the Old Patent Office," *JSAH*, XV, 1 (March 1956), pp. 27–30.

[77] Bryan, II, 248. This first section by Mills, prior to the northern additions, is reproduced in the lithograph published by Goupil Vibert & Co. (from a drawing by A. Kollner) about 1848. This view, however, is not completely accurate, rendering the sloped parapets as pediments, reducing the size of the chimneys, etc. (Reproduced in John W. Reps, *Monumental Washington* [Princeton: Princeton University Press, 1967] fig. 27, erroneously dated ca. 1869.)

FIGURE 28. Post Office, south portion, by Robert Mills, 1839-42. Photograph taken December 1864.

this building was somewhat less successful than Mills' Treasury or Elliot's Patent Office. The other buildings had strong, easily discernible masses and parts—the colonnade of the Treasury, or the massive porticos flanked by wings of the Patent Office—with details subservient; the Post Office, however, is treated more as a thin wall screen with pilasters giving it some relief, which fails somewhat in contrast with the other more assertive structures. Furthermore, its long sides have no truly prominent features for relief beyond the rather delicate detail.[78]

These three buildings were considerable successes,

especially when the almost total absence of other significant architecture is noted. There are a number of reasons for this success. For one, the construction was left largely to the men who designed the buildings, or to men who understood the style and made no radical changes in completing it in the original concept. There was apparently little meddling or alteration from Congress or committees,[79] so that once the building design was decided on, the architect could proceed with what, in his professional judgement, fulfilled it best. Then too, Mills in particular was an accomplished architect working in the most viable style of the time, which included a happy blend of new construction techniques that lent themselves to large and volumetric forms. As the Patent Office shows, these forms can also stand alone, without any surface decoration. The Greek Revival style not only combined a historically allusive classical style, growing in popularity, with economical building, but was also a style well suited by its very formality to a city with open squares, vistas, and a generally formal relationship of buildings established from the begin-

[78] Interestingly enough, in 1847 this style was called "Italian or Palladian," while that of the Treasury and Patent Office was called "Grecian," by Robert Dale Owen, who had apparently known Mills for several years. (For the chart listing the stylistic terms, see Owen, *Hints on Public Architecture* [New York: George P. Putnam, 1849], p. 98.) Thus the flatter effect may have been a conscious desire, both for a somewhat different style, and perhaps because of the siting of the building with sidewalks on all sides. (The elevation, minus chimneys, is reproduced in the plate facing p. 52 in *Hints*.) The grade changes of the 1870's have, of course, considerably changed the present proportions of the building. See also Historic American Buildings Survey No. DC-219, published in [Harley J. McKee and Thomas L. Fauntleroy], *Washington, D.C. Architecture—Market Square* (Washington: Urban Design and Development Corp. and the Historic American Buildings Survey, 1969), pp. 16–35.

[79] This is except for the unsuccessful attempt by Walter and Young to discredit the structural soundness of Mills' construction of the Treasury.

40

FIGURE 29. The Capitol, about 1830, as completed by Bulfinch.

FIGURE 30. Original design for the extension of the Capitol, by Thomas U. Walter, 1851.

ning. For a city of three story red brick buildings, these four to five-story structures of light stone, with an inherent bigness of scale, were the perfect size to be able to stand out and be imposing, but not overwhelm the surroundings.

The architects, furthermore, did not have the severe financial problems that plagued the early architects of the Capitol, for the Congress was willing to provide what was needed for these obviously essential public structures, and realized that it was best to let the professional architect do what was best. The results repaid their confidence.

The fourth major government construction was, of course, the extension of the Capitol. By 1841, the Congress had grown to 293 members and needed larger meeting and committee rooms, expanded library, and other facilities. A competition for an extension was announced in 1850 and a number of plans were submitted, including ones by Mills and Walter. The Committee on Public Buildings was not satisfied with any of these and had Mills, in his capacity as Architect of the Treasury, make a combination plan. The committee recommended wings to the north and south of the original structure, not on the east or west, as some had proposed. It was President Filmore, however, who finally selected T. U. Walter for the position of Architect of the United States Capitol Extension on June 10, 1851, and Walter developed the scheme of north and south wings connected to the old building by corridors (fig. 30). At this stage, a low dome was still envisioned; the more massive dome was not designed until 1855. The south wing for the House was complete enough to move into in 1857, and the north wing for the Senate in 1859. The new dome was not fully com-

pleted until 1865, although work continued on the interior and exterior of the building for a couple more years.[80]

The wings and dome were an astonishing success (fig. 31). In their size, and the new massing that the building obtained, something of the Greek Revival came through, though of course the details are based on the earlier Thornton designs. Part of the success was due to Walter's care in following the earlier style rather than making any radical departure. It still retained life, however, by being more robust and more massive than the original, thus subtlely distinguishable from the earlier work (figs. 32–35). The north and south ends, utilizing open columned loggias, brought back a feature eliminated from Thornton's first design. Here they are ably used in creating a less abrupt ending to the long wing, and giving a more animated treatment in light and shadow. And the tall dome, in relation to the new wings, was a parallel with the earlier arrangement, but with the more active, broken, and assertive silhouette that the esthetic of "picturesque eclecticism" in American architecture was then evolving, and which later in the century would be carried out in more animated degrees.[81] Walter himself, in 1851, emphasized his desire to complement rather than overwhelm the original Capitol:

The architecture of the exterior of the wings is designed to correspond in its principal features to that of the present

[80] The details of this work are fully examined in Brown, II, 114–142.

[81] For a discussion of this unifying architectural concept that progressed throughout the century and underlies most of the stylistic revivals, see Carroll L. V. Meeks, "Picturesque Eclecticism," *Art Bulletin*, XXXII (September 1950), pp. 226–35, and also the same author's *The Railroad Station* (New Haven: Yale University Press, 1956).

FIGURE 31. The Capitol, as enlarged by T. U. Walter. Photograph taken about 1900.

building, and the disposition of the various parts is intended to present the appearance of one harmonious structure, and to impart dignity to the present building, rather than to interfere with its proportions, or detract from its grandeur and beauty.[82]

This restraint showed an architect of considerable understanding, willing to forgo a personal or assertive building.

The last major construction sponsored by Congress was the City Hall, to which they contributed $30,000 in 1849 in order to complete the building begun in 1820. It stood on a site which on L'Enfant's map was set aside for some large religious structure, a short distance from the national church. Thus, locating the City Hall at this spot followed

the general guidelines of the original plan. This grant of $30,000 brought the total congressional contribution for the City Hall to $40,000, or what they calculated to be one half of the cost of the building. This was made so that the central portion of Hadfield's structure could be erected (though without the originally planned dome), and provide enough space for the District Court and its offices (fig. 36). The eastern half was already occupied by the United States and the west by the city, but when the Federal Government needed more space, it was the convenience of the city that suffered.[83]

The building, as completed, was one of the most handsome in the city. The wings and flanks, treated with a flat, Regency-like plainness relieved only by panels, recessed arches, and string courses, set off the

[82] Thomas U. Walter, *Report of the Architect for the Extension of the Capitol,* House Executive Document 60, 32d Cong., 1st sess. (1851), Ser. 641, p. 3.

[83] Bryan, II, 334.

FIGURE 32. Detail, Capitol west facade, as completed by Bulfinch.

FIGURE 33. Detail, Capitol west facade (Senate wing), as extended by Walter.

two wing porches with Ionic columns *in antis* and the central Ionic portico most effectively. Far less massive than the Treasury or Patent Office, and more distinguished even than the Post Office, Hadfield's building seemed to be a tangible proof that Congress was willing to share some of the city's expenses.

All this construction, it should be emphasized, was undertaken because of actual need, and not from any real largess in response to the criticism of the Southard report of 1835. As will be seen, the other improvements effected by Congress were often also requirements of the government, though a few were motivated by a deliberate desire to take a fair share of local expenses.

Other improvements which in part benefited the city were also begun. These included semipublic buildings, landscaping some of the public spaces, some street paving, and other municipal improvements.

In the 1850's, Congress authorized work on a number of buildings which were long overdue. In 1852,

Congress established the home for Disabled Soldiers, and also the Insane Asylum, in which the insane of the Army and Navy were also cared for. The costs of the asylum were thus legitimately shared by the government.[84] Both of these institutions, however, were well outside the main part of the city. In 1857, Congress made its first appropriation for the care of the deaf, dumb, and blind at the Columbia Institution, relieving the District of much of this burden.[85] And in 1855, the government constructed a brick armory east of Seventh Street on the Mall for the District militia, and also to house a military museum. It joined on the Mall the Smithsonian Institution and the Washington Monument, begun in 1847 and

[84] Ibid., p. 337.
[85] Ibid., p. 342.

FIGURE 34. Detail, Capitol window following Thornton's design, completed by Bulfinch.

FIGURE 35. Detail, Capitol window Senate wing, designed by Walter.

1848, respectively, though these two structures, not paid for by government appropriation, cannot be considered government structures in the same way.

Although the Columbian Institute had improved the west end of the Mall with its greenhouses, this was given up in 1836 and the land incorporated into the Capitol grounds.[86] Then, in the early 1840's, Congress began to see the need for improving the run-down lots owned by the government. These areas were unfenced, piled high with brush and refuse, or cut by gullies or pitted with excavations for clay or gravel. The open land west of First Street was described in 1841 as "a magnificent Sahara of solitude and waste—appropriated as a cow pasture and frog pond, and decorated with a stone-cutter's yard, a slaughter house and pig pens."[87] The Mall was also unimproved, and sewers drained into the swampy land below the President's House. In 1848, some work was begun. A few of the public squares were cleared and fenced, and the Mall from Seventh

Street west to the Potomac was graded and fenced. The following year the area around the Smithsonian was graded and planted, and work was also done on the Capitol Grounds and the President's grounds.[88] In 1851, a group of local citizens urged that Andrew Jackson Downing, the noted landscape architect, be called in to landscape the Mall; this was done, although his death in 1852 cut short his work and he only supervised the planting around the Smithsonian. Some further work was carried on following his plan, but by 1859 this too had stopped. These developments will be discussed later.

Congress also did some paving of streets. Under the Army Corps of Topographical Engineers, streets between K and O, running from Third to Twelfth, N.W., were paved in 1841, and O and P between Twelfth and Seventeenth Streets, N.W., in 1843.[89]

[86] Ibid., p. 325.

[87] Ibid., p. 316, quoting the *National Intelligencer* of Mar. 24, 1841.

[88] Ibid., pp. 323–324.

[89] Ibid., p. 284. What kind of paving this was is not specified.

FIGURE 36. Washington City Hall, by George Hadfield, begun in 1820.

Congress also replaced the old macadam paving on Pennsylvania Avenue with cobbles in 1845, and for the first time paved with gravel that avenue west of the President's House and east of the Capitol. In 1848, some other streets outside of Pennsylvania Avenue were graveled, but this work continued only a few years.[90]

Other municipal improvements were also largely for the benefit or convenience of Congress. Lighting was provided for Pennsylvania Avenue by Congress in 1842, but in 1844 it was decided that the lamps should be illuminated only when the legislature was in session, in order to save money.[91] The water sup-

ply was also improved at long last. Prior to 1850, all water was obtained from springs or pumps, but the increase in population and the need for better fire protection of government buildings made a more reliable water system advisable. In 1850, a study was begun by Col. G. W. Hughes of the Topographical Engineers, sponsored by the government and the city council. This sought to determine the advisability of bringing water from the upper Rock Creek to Washington and (in 1852) to Georgetown as well.[92] A second report in 1853 by Lt. Montgomery C. Meigs advised conducting water from above Little Falls and Great Falls.[93] His plans were adopted and a large appropriation made by Congress in March 1853 to begin the work. It was completed in 10 years, bringing water from Great Falls 14 miles into Washington by pipes, at a cost of over $3,500,000.[94]

Gravel paving was a layer of ordinary gravel ranging from 9 to 18 inches in thickness, which was then rolled to compact it. Macadam paving was composed of small pieces of hard stone, generally granite, broken to sizes no larger than 6 ounces in weight or 2 inches in diameter, laid generally 10 inches thick, but sometimes as much as 14 inches in the center of the roadway and 8 inches in the gutters. This stone was then rolled and, because of its sharp edges, held together far more durably than gravel. It was thus quite different from modern macadam which uses a smaller aggregate and is bound with asphalt.

[90] Ibid., p. 318.

[91] Ibid., p. 295

[92] Ibid., p. 305.

[93] *A Report of Lt. Meigs, with Surveys, Plans, and Estimates for Supplying the Cities of Washington and Georgetown with Water,* S. Doc. 48, 32d Cong., 2d sess. (1853), Ser. 655, (55 pp.)

[94] Bryan, II, 307.

FIGURE 37. Tiber Canal, about 1861.

This was a great help to the city, which now had a completely up-to-date water supply. Sewers, however, were left in a primitive condition and still drained into the Tiber Canal. Though dredged many times, this canal was still barely navigable at high water, and an open marshy sewer at low (fig. 37). The upkeep of the nearly 3-mile length was largely the city's responsibility.

From these improvements by Congress it is clear that they had modified their previous position only slightly. The buildings were needed for the proper functioning of the government and the actual expenses specifically for the city were slight. Although Congress had, in 1836, assumed the canal stock debt, they had taken over only the principal, not the interest or other expenses. And in a way, this assumption made many Congressmen feel that their duty to the city had now been done! No real principle of sharing had grown up, with the exception of the City Hall expenses. While the government's activity encouraged the city, it did not change matters much. The general opinion in Congress still seemed to be that the city should take care of itself and be glad for any of the government buildings that were constructed in its bounds. In 1856, Senator Brodhead of Pennsylvania declaimed:

These demands on the public Treasury—the people's money— for purposes of expenditure in the cities of Washington and Georgetown, are shameful; and the manner in which our money is poured out to these people is shameless.[95]

As usual, the local and national interests, and the duty of Congress, were not understood.

During this same period, the city struggled to meet the needs of citizens in a steadily growing city —for police, schools, care of the poor, and some attempts at improving the city. Its vast street system was still largely unpaved—livestock and pigs still roamed at will—and what paving was done was largely gravel, not macadam or cobbles. The first cobblestone paving was begun in 1845, but up to 1860 only a few of the major streets were thus improved, and it even became the duty of the city to maintain Pennsylvania Avenue, which had been paved by Congress. Although the tax base had been broadened in 1848 to include more than just real estate, expenses also rose so that no benefits were discernible.[96] The only construction of note was the Washington Monument, begun in 1848 from a public subscription started in 1833 by the Washington National Monument Society. Only after much debate and urging did Congress grudgingly let the Society build their monument at the west end of the Mall, where L'Enfant had proposed the equestrian

[95] Green, p. 205.
[96] Bryan, II, 290.

statue to General Washington. This lack of cooperation from Congress is not surprising, seen in the light of their other exertions for the city. The only other major change was the advent of the railroad, with the Washington branch of the Baltimore and Ohio Railroad being brought into the district to a depot at Pennsylvania Avenue and Second Street, in 1835.[97] This was heralded as a boon to communication and commerce, much needed in light of the slow and disappointing progress of the C. & O. Canal. But by 1855 a second line ran across the Mall at the foot of the Capitol, and the number of people killed at the grade crossings was causing considerable complaint. Thus a project orginally urged by the city, and approved by Congress, proved a mixed blessing. Although early legislation had stipulated that no steam engines would be used on the line crossing the Mall, this was soon abandoned and the noise and commotion was bought into the heart of the city.

The financial condition of the city was still insecure, industry was purely local, and the unimproved streets and sewers, and the inadequate street lighting were hardly inducements for outside investment or settlement. The quality of city officials also declined after Mayor William W. Seaton left office in 1850 and the succeeding mayors of the 1850's, lacking Seaton's sense of diplomacy, "tended to view Washington as a national monument for which Congress should bear a large part of the cost, an attitude that created resentment on the Hill and lowered civic morale." [98]

Reports of the period still emphasized, however, the disparity between what the govenment should do and did not, and what the city had to undertake. In 1848, a report to Congress from a committee headed by Mayor Seaton reiterated the familiar facts. By ownership of all the streets and much additional land, and from the original understanding with the proprietors, the government was certainly responsible for grading, making streets, erecting bridges, and constructing necessary public buildings. Since government land was not taxable, the city simply could not do this itself. The cost of improvements to the city made by that time were outlined, and the very few improvements by the government outside its own buildings and its own roads emphasized.[99] Clearly, the 1835 Southard report had brought little change.

Ten years later, in 1858, the attitude of the government was the same. The annual report of the Secretary of the Interior noted, with reference to appropriations for Washington:

> The past legislation of Congress has been examined with some care, to ascertain if possible, whether any fixed or determinate line of policy has ever been adopted in reference to . . . appropriation within the city of Washington. . . . But the search has been in vain. . . .[100]

This was because Congress had appropriated money for a wide variety of things, and the Secretary felt that many government buildings, and attention to Pennsylvania Avenue and the Mall, showed ample concern for the city. While he recommended the government squares be graded, he went on to claim that opening of streets, grading, paving, making sewers, lighting streets, and erecting markets were all municipal duties, and should be paid for by the city. The duty of sharing, and active aid to the city, were concepts no further advanced than decades before.

> Whether the government, as a property holder, should contribute to these ends in proportion to its interests in the city, is a question which addresses itself exclusively to the discretion of the national legislature.[101]

On the eve of the Civl War, 60 years after Congress had moved to the Federal City, Washington was by no means the monumental Capital many hoped it would be. Neglect of Congress and the strained economy of the city combined for these poor results. The economy was stagnant; and especially as the Civil War approached, the heightened crisis over slavery occupied the attentions of Congress. Fearful that the government might move the Capital, the city survived the best it could and did what it was able.

> The spasmodic efforts of the city government at various times to develop and beautify the city met with little encouragement from the inhabitants through investment or otherwise. . . . Congress gave but little attention to the affairs of the District. So when the war came, in 1861, Washington was a shabby town, with little or no architecture to attract attention, other than that displayed in the public buildings. . . .[102]

---

[97] Bryan, II, 117. See also Charles Moore (comp.), *Federal and Local Legislation relating to Canals and Steam Railroads in the District of Columbia, 1802-1903* (Washington: U.S. Government Printing Office, 1903; S. Doc. 220, 57th Cong., 2d sess., Ser. 4430).

[98] Green, p. 208.

[99] *Centennial History*, pp. 192-193. No further reference is given for this report, and a search has failed to discover the original document.

[100] *Annual Report of the Secretary of the Interior for the Year 1858*, p. 16.

[101] Ibid., pp. 16-17.

[102] Carroll D. Wright, "The Economic Development of the District of Columbia," *Proceedings of the Washington Academy of Sciences*, I, (1899), (Washington, 1900), pp. 175-176.

CHAPTER III

The Conservative and Vernacular Tradition in Local Architecture

THE CAPITOL and the President's House, the two most advanced buildings in the Capital in its early years, had no apparent influence on local architecture in Washington or neighboring Georgetown. In fact, the local architecture, with but a few exceptions, showed a continuing conservative and builder-like tradition, seen especially in its domestic architecture. This conservativeness continued in force even after about 1830, when the Greek Revival style began to be adopted throughout the country, creating a new, vigorous movement. In spite of the impressive Greek Revival structures of Washington begun in the mid-1830's, local architecture maintained its conservativeness and these buildings had little effect. Later, this unadventurous spirit would be a factor influencing the acceptability of work by James Renwick and A. J. Downing. These conservative and vernacular bases of the local tradition—and the few structures that stood out distinctly from it—can be seen in a representative selection of buildings from Georgetown and Washington.

In Georgetown, incorporated in 1751, a very large proportion of original buildings can still be found or can be documented. By examining these structures, and then comparing what is known from Washington of the same period, we can come to a good sense of this local tradition and understand why, in many ways, it was inimicable to influences of

a new monumental style, and later, why picturesque forms were slow to be adopted.

Three general aspects of Georgetown architecture can be suggested: a professional architecture, builder architecture, and true vernacular architecture.

The most important dwelling in Georgtown by a professional architect is, without a doubt, Tudor Place, 1644 Thirty-first Street, N.W. (figs. 38–39), designed by Dr. William Thornton, and completed by 1816.[1] It is quite different in style and effect either from the masonry Capitol or President's House, or from the local architecture of brick. The very appearance of its materials is different. Although constructed of brick, the surface is stuccoed to give it a smooth and in a way more monolithic quality than its brick neighbors. The whole building is also conceived in clear volumes: a large central mass connected

---

[1] This important building has been published by Armistead Peter III, the present owner, in his *Tudor Place, designed by Dr. William Thornton* (Georgetown: [privately printed], 1970). The volume includes photographs by Cervin Robinson and a "Commentary on Dr. Thornton" by Frederick D. Nichols which reproduces original studies and plans.

See also Harold Donaldson Eberlein and Cortland VanDyke Hubbard, *Historic Houses of George-Town and Washington City* (Richmond: The Dietz Press, 1958), pp. 123-134. This volume is concerned more with the history of the occupants rather than the architecture itself. Helpful sources, however, are given at the end of each essay.

FIGURE 38. Tudor Place, 1644 Thirty-first Street, N.W., by William Thornton.

FIGURE. 39. Tudor Place, 1644 Thirty-first Street, N.W., by William Thornton.

by loggia-like wings to two-bay end blocks. These end blocks (built between about 1794 and 1805) had been erected earlier and were remodeled by Dr. Thornton. Because of the absence of window detail in these end pavilions, and the thin string course, they have a solid and blocky quality which contrasts sharply with the links which, because of the win-

FIGURE 40. Tudor Place. Circular porch on south façade.

dows, are essentially glazed open loggias.[2] The central portion is given a particularly sculptural treatment because of the circular feature with large Tuscan columns and a hemispheric roof, forming an open semicircular porch (fig. 40). Its form is continued around by an equal mass being scooped out of the house, thus making the porch cylindrical. This dominating feature, as well as the deep sunk arches which frame the ground floor windows, give the central block a plastic and sculptural effect; the conception of the house as solids and voids, conceived and played off one against the other, is very clear. These are, of course, an architect's concerns far more than a builder's. While a builder is primarily concerned with solid walls that support and enclose the structure, with embellishment essentially additive, here we have spatial concepts, the relation of positive to

[2] The west loggia is, of course, glazed in the central opening only; a dining room is located at this point. But studies by Thornton show that his earlier conceptions were to have both links open loggias (see *Tudor Place*, pp. 75–82), and the final scheme of recessed sections to catch shadow is clearly intended to approximate the loggia-conservatory on the east, and yet provide a useable room behind.

negative spaces, with disguised wall surfaces, treated in an original rather than traditional way. Similar concepts are found at the end of the Eighteenth century in the work of John Soane in England, and also Latrobe, and were taken up by Robert Mills in the 19th century—concepts of a new, more austere geometry of building that were also being explored by Ledoux and Boullée in France. Although the flat stuccoed walls that Thornton used give it a certain planar, Regency quality, especially on the north side, the "tholos" porch and open links between body and wings successfully bring elements of space into the three dimensional composition.

Tudor Place was, however, a unique building. It showed no influence from architecture in Washington, and had no effect on the local tradition. This may seem curious, until we examine the nature of the local architecture, which helps explain why a building such as Tudor Place—and later, Washington's Greek Revival structures—had no apparent influence.

The majority of local structures were builder architecture, which had as its basis not the architect's concerns with interior spaces or exterior massing in volume and void, but rather the nature of construction. This meant an emphasis on flat planar wall surfaces that grew out of the mode of building and the concerns of masons. The size and dimensions were largely determined by lot sizes and spanning capabilities of wood members, rather than predominantly architectural concerns. Detail was primarily additive, rather than integral with the architectural conception. Because of this attention to solid masonry walls, there was no interest in plasticity or the sort of concern with volume and void that we saw in Tudor Place.

Even in larger dwellings with some architectural pretentions, these builder elements are dominant. In Quality Hill, 3425 Prospect Street, N.W. (fig. 41), of 1798,[3] the flat wall treatment is clear. Its decorative details, such as the keystone lintels (the doorway is modern), are elements derived ultimately from an earlier Georgian architecture, and are also used in simpler rowhouses. In fact, except for the gable ends, the facade looks very much like two townhouses placed together.

Dumbarton House, 2715 Q Street, N.W. (fig. 42),

FIGURE 41. Quality Hill, 3425 Prospect Street, N.W.

FIGURE 42. Dumbarton House, 2715 Q Street, N.W.

of 1799,[4] while in many ways very close to the Georgian formula of a central pedimented pavilion flanked by two or more bays, has a generally flat appearence. The pavilion projects only very slightly, and the dec-

[3] John Thomson Mason, owner-builder. See Eberlein and Hubbard, pp. 32–39. See also Historic American Buildings Survey No. DC–167, Library of Congress, Division of Prints and Photographs.

[4] The date is not 1747, as occasionally published. See William V. Elder III, "Dumbarton House," reprinted from *Winter Antiques Show Catalogue* (n.d.), courtesy Society of Colonial Dames. Before being moved to its present location in 1915, the stone basement foundations were visible for about 3 feet above the ground rather than buried as presently seen. See Cordelia Jackson, "People and Places in Old Georgetown," Columbia Historical Society *Records*, XXXIII-XXXIV (1932), plate 19, facing p. 138.

FIGURE 43. Laird-Dunlop House, 3014 N Street, N.W.

FIGURE 44. Townhouse facade, from Asher Benjamin, *American Builder's Companion*, 1806, plate 33.

orative elements are almost flush with the wall surface.

A few larger houses, such as the Laird-Dunlop House at 3014 N Street, N.W. (fig. 43), of 1799,[5] make a slight departure from the flat facade that we will see is common in ordinary brick houses, by the use of round-headed first floor windows set within recessed arches capped and joined with brownstone moldings. This treatment at once gives the wall a somewhat greater sense of plasticity, and the "architecturalness" is heightened by this variation on the neo-classic ground floor arcades used in England and France in the late Eighteenth century. For taller buildings, these obviously help provide meaningful divisions for the facade. A variety of recessed ground floor arches became popular in the 1790's, used especially by John Soane in England, as well as a number of architects in the United States.[6] Recessed arches (on capped pilasters) are found, for example, in a

drawing of 1799 by John McComb of New York,[7] and similar arches were used by Charles Bulfinch in Boston in a variety of forms. By 1806 this treatment was being disseminated by Asher Benjamin in the first edition of his *American Builder's Companion* (fig. 44).[8] Even with the relative small scale of the Laird-Dunlop house, and the use of plain brick walls, these arches give it a further touch of sophistication.

Even at Evermay, 1628 Twenty-eighth Street, N.W.

---

[7] Ibid., fig. 163.

[8] Plates 33 and 35. The same engravings are reproduced as plates 51 and 53 of the sixth (1827) edition. A drawing of 1830 by William Small for a house on North Charles Street, Baltimore, also seems to be based quite closely on this Benjamin plate (33 or 51), closer even than the earlier Laird-Dunlop House because of its square-headed windows under the first floor moldings. See Richard H. Howland and Eleanor P. Spencer, *The Architecture of Baltimore* (Baltimore: The Johns Hopkins Press, 1953), plate 54. This gives some indication of the range along the eastern coast that this motif had. It was also adapted by Robert Mills in his "Waterloo Row" of 1815, though more in the manner of Latrobe and Hadfield than the Benjamin model. This row, originally one of the handsomest in Baltimore, is depicted in Howland, plate 44. See also Kenneth Ames, "Robert Mills and the Philadelphia Row House," *Journal of the Society of Architectural Historians*, XXVII, 2 (May 1968), pp. 145–146, figs. 13 and 14.

---

[5] Attributed to William Lovering, "architect-builder." Eberlein and Hubbard, pp. 72–74. The porch is a later addition.

[6] Kimball, pp. 204–206. Latrobe used these recessed arches on more imposing public buildings.

FIGURE 45. Evermay, 1628 Twenty-eighth Street, N.W.

FIGURE 46. Adams-Mason House, 1072 Thomas Jefferson Street, N.W.

(fig. 45), of 1801,[9] on which great care was lavished, the effect is still planar in spite of the exquisitely carved details around the door, in the cornice, and above the windows. Although the central bay is somewhat wider, and emphasized by a roundheaded window above the door, it does not project any from the wall surface.

The development and persistence of this planar quality can best be seen, however, in the smaller dwellings in the builder architecture tradition, both in wood and brick. These achieve much of their pleasing effect from a careful attention to proportions of the facade, placement of windows and doors, and often the use of details, both exterior and interior, that are derived from the Georgian classical vocabulary or, later, from the Adam-Federal taste. Since the builder would combine both the attention to structural logic and appropriate materials, with refinements, proportions, and detailing ultimately derived from the many American and British pattern books available to him, the blend was often particularly felicitous.[10]

Georgetown has a number of wood houses which, in their proportions, plan, and interior detailing, in spite of their plainness, can be considered Federal in style. The Adams-Mason House, 1072 Thomas Jefferson Street, N.W. (fig. 46), of about 1810, has the wide exterior boarding, plain eaves, and undecorated window enframements as seen in more clearly vernacular houses, but the well proportioned three bay facade, and the door (originally at the right) leading into a hall with two rooms off it to the left, is a type very common in small Federal houses.[11] The orientation, with the gable parallel to the street, is also common to Federal buildings. Although the interior is very plain, attractive undecorated Federal mantels give a hint of pattern-book refinement. In the Methodist-Episcopal Parsonage house, 1221 Twenty-eighth Street, N.W. (fig. 47), of about 1816, the facade proportions are even more canonical, the door now given an overlight, and the eaves treated in a slightly more architectural manner.[12]

9 Deering Davis, Stephen P. Dorsey, and Ralph Cole Hall, *Georgetown Houses of the Federal Period* (Cornwall, N.Y.: Architectural Book Publishing Co., Cornwall Press, 1944), pp. 94–97. The short essays are primarily concerned with the history of the builders and inhabitants.

10 The use of pattern books, particularly for technical matters and for architectural detail, was well established in the colonies, especially after about 1750. See Fiske Kimball, *Domestic Architecture of the American Colonies and of the Early Republic* (New York: Charles Scribner's Sons, 1922), pp. 54–63 for the early development of these books. For early 19th century use, see especially pp. 150–152.

11 HABS No. DC-161. Published in [Ellen J. Schwartz and William P. Thompson], *Georgetown Residential Architecture—Northeast* (Washington: Commission of Fine Arts and the Historic American Buildings Survey, 1969), pp. 55–67. This house was "restored" in 1968 and now has a more elaborate cornice, with the central door made into a window again. The siding has also been replaced.

12 HABS No. DC-176. Published in [Daniel D. Reiff and William R. Gwin], *Georgetown Architecture—The Waterfront* (Washington: Commission of Fine Arts and the Historic American Buildings Survey, 1968), pp. 80–92.

FIGURE 47. Methodist Episcopal Parsonage House, 1221 Twenty-eighth Street, N.W.

FIGURE 48. Prospect House, 3508 Prospect Street, N.W.

As Georgetown grew, wood houses were less and less common in the central part of town and the majority of builder architecture was brick, both smaller townhouses and rowhouses.

In the townhouses, the three bay facade of plain brick, sometimes with decorative details, becomes almost standard. Some early examples are quite plain, with no surface decoration other than belt courses and water tables, elements of earlier Georgian architecture, though the cornice is sometimes enriched. Windows are capped with a pattern of diagonal bricks forming a flat arch. An excellent though heavily restored example of this type is Prospect House, 3508 Prospect Street, N.W. (fig. 48), built in 1788.[31] The plain brick facade is relieved by the molded water table and the projecting belt course, as well as the quite rich cornice and the architecturally enframed doorway. A similar though somewhat plainer treatment is found in the pair of buildings at 3001–3003 M Street, N.W., built some time between 1789 and 1792 (fig. 49). Because grade changes have given it an additional basement story, the original water table is found now between the present first and second floors.

More common, however, are townhouses that lack these Eighteenth century belt courses and water ta-

bles, and have a plainness uninterrupted by such horizontal bands. Some such townhouse are extremely plain, as the Harmon House, 3025 P Street, N.W. (fig. 50), of about 1810.[14] This lacks both dormers and any wall embellishment, but its attractive proportions (in part determined by the lot size established in 1751), Flemish bond brickwork, and the plan, are standard. The most common Federal houses of this size, however, use some decorative features, such as keystone lintels over the windows. This is an element commonly found in earlier Georgian brick architecture, particularly in the Philadelphia area in the mid and late Eighteenth century,[15] and in Georgetown is found in Dumbarton House. In the early Nineteenth century, however, it was simplified and often reduced in profile. The doorway also was enriched with a semicircular overlight, though the heavier enframements are avoided. These details can be found both in very small houses, such as the two bay dwelling at 1063 Thomas Jefferson Street, N.W. (fig. 51), and in somewhat larger homes, as the Gannt-Williams house, 2806 N Street, N.W. (fig.

13 Eberlein and Hubbard, pp. 40–43.

52), of 1817.[16] At the same time, however, flat wood lintels with bull's-eye block ends, a more severe treatment than the older masonry keystone form, were common, as in the Riggs-Riley House, 3038 N Street, N.W. (fig. 53), of 1816.[17] Those with more pretention also included a doorway with side lights, such as the Decatur House of 1813,[18] or the particularly fine Linthicum House, 3019 P Street, N.W. (fig. 54), as late as 1829, in which the flat wall surface is almost unbroken by the bull's-eye lintels, the only sculptural enrichment found in the superb doorway.[19]

Occasionally these simple Federal houses were built in rows. Two such remain in Georgetown, Smith Row, 3255–3263 N Street, N.W. (fig. 55), of 1815,[20] and Cox's Row, 3327–3339 N Street, N.W. (fig. 56), of 1817.[21] But here again, (except where later altered), the flat surafce is maintained, the doors treated serverely as archways flush with surface with an inset fanlight, and the only concession to more formal treatment suggested by a row of shallow sunk panels below the second and third floor windows (fig. 57). These serve more to emphasize the flatness of the wall, in their shallowness, rather than give it any plasticity. Some of the panels are still decorated with thin and delicate lead floral swags. The cornice, too, is plain, though bricks set at 45° (appropriate to a builder's architecture) are sometimes used to give added richness.

The planar quality we have seen in both large mansions and smaller dwellings in the builder tradition, with detail conceived as additive, probably also had its roots in the true vernacular architecture which was common in Georgetown. This was manifested in the three basic materials, stone, wood, and

FIGURE 49. 3001-3011 M Street, N.W.

FIGURE 50. Harmon House, 3025 P Street, N.W.

brick. These vernacular structures are all essentially "styleless", in that their forms and details grow out of sheer necessity, the manner of construction and the capabilities and limitations of the materials, rather than an active attempt at achieving a specific style, with its attendant refinements and historically based details.

14 Davis, Dorsey, and Hall, pp. 76–79.

15 Townhouses of about 1759 employing them, with other rich detail, are depicted in George B. Tatum, *Penn's Great Town* (Philadelphia: University of Pennsylvania Press, 1961), plate 14. They are used also in more formal buildings, such as Cliveden (1761) and Mt. Pleasant (ca. 1770). Because of river and coastal shipping, the architectural styles of Philadelphia were spread wide, with Alexandria strongly affected. See Thomas Tileston Waterman, *The Dwellings of Colonial America* (Chapel Hill: University of North Carolina Press, 1950), p. 91. Similar use in Federal buildings is also seen in other coastal centers, especially Baltimore.

16 Davis, Dorsey and Hall, pp. 24–29.

17 Ibid., pp. 50–57; Eberlein and Hubbard, pp. 68–71.

18 Davis, Dorsey and Hall, pp. 36–41.

19 Eberlein and Hubbard, pp. 91–93.

20 Walter and Clement Smith, owner-builders.

21 John Cox, a prosperous merchant and real estate owner, erected the row. See Davis, Dorsey and Hall, pp. 58–61; Eberlein and Hubbard, pp. 63–67.

FIGURE 51. 1063 Thomas Jefferson Street, N.W.

FIGURE 52. Gannt-Williams House, 2806 N Street, N.W.

The earliest stone vernacular building is the "Old Stone House," 3051 M Street, N.W. (fig. 58), built in 1766 by Christopher Layhman.[22] The structure, of rubble stone masonry, has the solid, flat walls, with windows simple rectangular perforations in the wall mass. The four solid walls, with their strong mason-built quality, obviously support floors and the roof, and enclose a compact volume of space. There are, really, no exterior decorations besides the simple wood framing for the sashes; the pleasing effect of variations in light on the rough stone is a result of its mode of construction, from the nature of the materials, rather than any conscious decorative intent. The builder and masonry origins of the forms, its sense of being a simple shelter rather than a sophisticated dwelling, are appropriate to a structure that was built without any conscious effort at design other than arranging small rooms off a central passage that was convenient and compact.

This mode of building is found nearby as well. At Pierce Mill on Rock Creek above Georgetown, both the mill itself, of about 1820 (fig. 59), and its ice house, 1801 (fig. 60), continue this tradition.[23] Especially in the large mill building, the solid, compact masonryness of the walls comes out, its size giving the stone walls an even greater sense of solidity. It is not surprising that this stone vernacular architecture was the form chosen when the lock houses of the Chesapeake and Ohio Canal were erected, beginning about 1829 (figs. 61–63). The written specifications assured that they were all the same,[24] and their use of massive stone lintels and sills at the doors and windows, the random laid walls of considerable thickness (plastered inside directly on the stone), continue this mason-based form well into the Nineteenth century.

Of course, this form of vernacular stone cottage is

22 This building is documented in Cornelius W. Heine, *The Old Stone House* (Washington: U.S. Department of the Interior, 1955).

23 See HABS No. DC-22. Although the date of 1826 is found on the mill building, it is probably as early as 1820. For illustrations of a number of other Rock Creek mills of similar general design, see Allen C. Clark, "The Old Mills," C.H.S. *Records,* XXXI–XXXII (1930), pp. 81–115.

24 A facsimile reproduction of these specifications (which were also published) is found in Ronald F. Lee, "Chesapeake and Ohio Canal," C.H.S. *Records,* XL–XLI (1940), plate facing p. 193. All measured 18 by 30 feet.

FIGURE 53. Riggs-Riley House, 3038 N Street, N.W.

FIGURE 54. Linthicum House, 3019 P Street, N.W.

not unique here, being built wherever stone is readily available. The similarity between these buildings and, for example, stone mills and mill houses of the early Nineteenth century in Maryland and Rhode Island, indicates that the resulting form grows essentially from the nature of the materials.[25]

The wood vernacular houses take a more varied shape. The earliest is at 1222 Twenty-eighth Street, N.W., possbily dating from the 1770's (fig. 64). This diminutive house has the steep roof and sloping dormer that reveal its very early date, elements which come ultimately from northern European medieval sources.[26] Two very similar frame dwellings exist in

[25] Similar small stone houses in Rhode Island are illustrated in H.-R. Hitchcock, *Rhode Island Architecture* (Providence: Rhode Island Museum Press, 1939), plate 34.

[26] Such sloping dormers and steep roofs are found on a number of 18th century structures in the northeastern United States, particularly those that retain strong European influences. For example, in Pennsylvania they are common on the Moravian buildings in Bethlehem of the 1750's and 1760's (see William J. Murtagh, *Moravian Architecture and Town Planning* [Chapel Hill: University of North Carolina Press, 1967], plates 13, 16, 17, 27, etc.). They are also found in 17th and 18th century Dutch houses of northern New Jersey and southern New York (see Rosalie Fellows Bailey, *Pre-Revolutionary Dutch Houses* [New York: Dover Publications, 1968], plates 13 and 34). The sloping dormers found on

FIGURE 55. Smith Row, 3255-3263 N Street, N.W.

17th and 18th century Virginia farmhouses probably come from English examples such as the house at St. Osyth, Essex, illustrated in Hugh Morrison, *Early American Architecture* (New York: Oxford University Press, 1952), p. 142, fig. 110.

FIGURE 56. Cox's Row, 3327-3339 N Street, N.W.

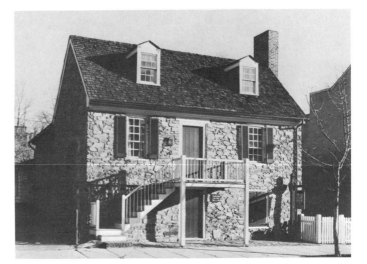

FIGURE 58. Old Stone House, 3501 M Street, N.W.

FIGURE 57. 3339 N Street, N.W., (Cox's Row).

FIGURE 59. Pierce Mill, Broad Branch Road at Tilden Street, N.W.

wide boards are still extant on the north end; there are no exterior decorative details. The aim was simply to erect a snug, weatherproof dwelling of wood, rather than achieving any special stylistic effect.

A second type, not commonly built in Georgetown, was the gambrel roofed dwelling such as the Joseph Jackson House, formerly at 3250 M Street, N.W., of about 1800 (fig. 65) .[28] Though not locally common, this type of roof was found on early and mid-Eighteenth century houses elsewhere in the region, such as at Williamsburg and in southern Mary-

Baltimore, and also are from the end of the Eighteenth century.[27] On the Georgetown example, very

[27] Two early frame houses are on Wolfe Street, Baltimore. See Howland, plate 15.

[28] The house was demolished in 1892. See John Clagett Proctor, "Aqueduct Bridge is Being Removed," *Sunday Star* (Washington), Dec. 17, 1933. (This article, and all subsequent references to others by Proctor in the *Sunday Star,* are from the mounted series, from 1928–53, in the library of the Columbia Historical Society, Washington, D.C.)

FIGURE 60. Pierce Mill spring house.

FIGURE 62. Chesapeake and Ohio Canal, Lock House, lock 22.

FIGURE 61. Chesapeake and Ohio Canal, Lock House, lock 22.

FIGURE 63. Chesapeake and Ohio Canal, Lock House, lock 9.

land.[29] The plainness of the dwelling and lack of all decorative detail emphasizes its vernacular qualities.

Another early wood house, with the more common gable roof, is the Edgar Patterson House at 1241 Thirtieth Street, N.W., built sometime before 1810 (fig. 66).[30] Although now given a high brick basement story because of grade changes, it was originally a simple one story frame building, the entrance at the right bay, with the gable end to the street. Although considerably more sophisticated than 1222 Twenty-eighth Street, N.W., with the gable much less steep, it is essentially a vernacular structure.[31]

A third wood example, considerably larger in size, is located at 3134–3136 South Street, N.W. (fig. 67).[32] This double house has an equally plain exterior, the pattern of clapboarding providing the only relief other than the false parapet ears at the north end. Built about 1800, the house has small, plain Federal mantels, indicating a beginning interest in appropriate decoration.

[29] See Henry Chandlee Forman, *Tidewater Maryland Architecture and Gardens* (New York: Architectural Book Publishing Co., 1956) pp. 96–97, 141, 145, and 148.

[30] See HABS No. DC-177, published in *Northeast*, pp. 2–13.

[31] A somewhat similar building, a one and a half story frame house on a high basement story of brick with gable end to the street, formerly stood at 1046 Wisconsin Avenue N.W.; it was demolished in 1960.

[32] See HABS No. DC-158, published in *Waterfront*, pp. 11–24.

FIGURE 64. 1222 Twenty-eighth Street, N.W.

FIGURE 66. Edgar Patterson House, 1241 Thirtieth Street, N.W.

FIGURE 65. Joseph Jackson Residence, 3250 M Street, N.W.,
(demolished).

FIGURE 67. Brickyard Hill House, 3134-36 South Street, N.W.

A unique collection of early vernacular wood houses, surprisingly enough, forms an ell (fig. 68) to the north of Mackall Square, 1633 Twenty-ninth Street, N.W., built about 1820. Contrary to what might be expected, these three frame buildings are older structures which were kept when the main house of brick was subsequently built. Reading from left to right, they form a compact summary of vernacular wood types.

But the vernacular architecture that was to have the longest life was that in brick. It is difficult to

class brick houses in the category, since if a person were wealthy enough to build a brick dwelling, he would employ a builder who would probably be familiar with some architectural refinements and pattern books, as noted above. The small Foxall House at 2908 N Street, N.W., of about 1790 (fig. 69), may possibly fall in this category, however. But the many

60

early warehouses which existed along the waterfront do partake quite definitely of the vernacular tradition: their walls and eaves are undecorated, the brick walls are broken only by the placement of plain doors and windows, and lintels are either flat brick arches or rough hewn lintels of wood. The size and shape of the structures are in large part determined by the lot size, the capabilities of wood beams used for spanning interior space, height to which brick walls could be conveniently and safely built, etc. Many such plain structures lined the Georgetown shore, and details from Civil War photographs clearly show their appeerence (figs. 70–71). Two small ones of about 1800, originally owned by the Dodge family, still remain at Wisconsin Avenue and K Street, N.W. (figs. 72–73).[33] Significantly, these warehouses utilized part of a stone building formerly on the site for their foundations, thus in a way continuing the vernacular tradition of solid, mason-built walls, unadorned surfaces, and the building conceived as structural and material necessity rather than the result of historically based design or details.

We have seen, then, many of the qualities that distinguish the local architecture—the emphasis on plain flat walls, a tradition of builders' rationalism rather than architects' considerations, detail and decorative features as applied rather than integral. These are not, of course, qualities that builder designed structures must *always* have; Georgian buildings with a projecting central pavilion capped with a pediment could be given considerable plasticity. Also, the late Eighteenth century saw a number of Federal mansions with projecting oval and octagonal bays and eliptical rooms, a concept brought from England and especially France.[34] Federal rowhouses as well were, in many instances, given a much greater sense of plasticity, of inner spaces expressed on the outside, by having a bow front, as built by Charles Bulfinch in Boston around 1800, and later by his many imitators and followers.[35] But these were not variations ever

FIGURE 68. Mackall Square, 1633 Twenty-ninth Street, N.W. Eighteenth and early Ninteenth century frame houses forming ell to north.

FIGURE 69. Foxall House, 2908 N Street, N.W.

used in Georgetown rowhouses, although Dumbarton House was built with two such bays on its north (garden) facade. It was, however, unique in Georgetown.

This vernacular and builder tradition is one factor that explains why, in the 1830's and 1840's, the Greek Revival was so very modest in Georgetown, in spite of the remarkable classical buildings rising in Washington. When we examine some of the George-

---

[33] See HABS No. DC-100, published in [James Philip Noffsinger and Thomas R. Martinson], *Georgetown Commercial Architecture —Wisconsin Avenue* (Washington: Commission of Fine Arts and the Historic American Buildings Survey, 1967), pp. 12–20.

[34] These projecting bays, oval rooms, etc. are discussed at length in Kimball, pp. 145–174.

[35] A number of Boston architects carried on this mode and their buildings are illustrated in Walter H. Kilham, *Boston After Bulfinch* (Cambridge: Harvard University Press, 1946). Bow front rowhouses attributed to Asher Benjamin (54–55 Beacon Street), and one by Alexander Parris of 1816 (the Somerset Club) are reproduced on plate VI. This style was popular in the Greek Revival period; a number of such rowhouses from the early 1840's were built

on Louisburg Square (plate IX). For the continuation of this bow front style into the later Nineteenth century, see Bainbridge Bunting, *Houses of Boston's Back Bay* (Cambridge: Harvard University Press, 1967).

FIGURE 70. Georgetown shoreline, ca. 1863.

FIGURE 71. Warehouses, Georgetown shoreline, 1861. Detail of photograph by George Barnard.

town examples of this period, the continuance of the earlier Federal types and the tradition of flat walls and applied details will be obvious, and help explain why no houses employing a peristyle or temple front were built in Georgetown.

As manifested in detached wood houses, the Greek Revival was very closely tied to earlier styles; such wood houses, however, were very rate. One of the earilest is the Benjamin Miller House, 1524 Twenty-eighth Street, N.W. (fig. 74), about 1845, which has a well proportioned Doric entry porch and pediment. Unfortunately, the owner-builder, Mr. Miller, came to Georgetown in the 1830's from New York City, so that this unique building cannot be considered a local manifestation.[36] A house that follows more closely the local Federal plan, though in wood, is the William Knowles House (fig. 75), 1228 Thirtieth Street, N.W., of about 1858.[37] It is Federal in general form, but with a cornice-and-frieze cap over the facade windows. Instead of dormers, however, a space of flush boarding below the dentiled eaves is treated as a frieze, and small windows are here inserted. The porch, with two fluted Roman Doric columns supporting a roof with large modillions, is, like the attic treatment, somewhat maladroit. A third wood example, though probably from the late 1850's, is 1323 Thirty-sixth Street, N.W. (fig. 76). The doorway is framed with attractive Doric half-columns supporting an entablature, and the windows have cornice-and-frieze caps. The sills are decorated with three guttae-like projections. But the cornice, composed of brackets and inverted modillions, seems more picturesque, indicating the late date.

The paucity of wood detached dwellings in Greek Revival style shows how firmly the brick townhouse type was developed in Georgetown. It is not surprising, therefore, that those Greek Revival manifestations most common are in this idiom. A variety of types can be examined.

Some houses, such as 2904 P Street, N.W. (fig. 77), are quite close to the earlier Federal houses at first glance, but closer inspection shows how Greek they really are. Although the same three-bay width is used, and three stories as in Cox's and Smith Rows, the proportions are somewhat taller, a full third floor replacing dormers. The roof is of much gentler slope which, from the street, is not readily visible at all. The decoration, except for the rather heavy door, is flat and understated, with the cornice rendered in projecting angled bricks. Very often, however, such houses have the third floor treated as a half story, such as at 3050–3052 P Street, N.W. (Fig. 78), where the attic windows are inserted into an entablature course. Again, the gently pitched roof is barely visible from the street, emphasizing the flat wall plane presented on the property line. Details are even plainer in this example with no window enframements at all, a simpler doorway, and a cornice of bricks forming a large scale dentil course. When this solution of small attic windows is carried out in

FIGURE 72. Dodge Warehouses (lower two buildings), 1000-1006 Wisconsin Avenue.

FIGURE 73. Dodge Warehouses, south end.

wood, such as 3003–3005 O Street, N.W. (fig. 79), of about 1845, the result can be particularly felicitous. Here the details are somewhat more minute, the window caps having a dentil band and the cornice a modillion and dentil course directly above the frieze windows. Interestingly, the front is sheathed in shiplap (but not flush) siding, for greater smoothness, while the sides are ordinary clapboards. When this treatment of small frieze windows in an expanded entablature is combined with simple lintels and sills, as at 2823 N Street, N.W. (fig. 80), the contrast with the red brick can be extremely handsome. In this house,

36 HABS No. DC-247, published in [Daniel D. Reiff and Ellen J. Schwartz], *Georgetown Architecture* (Washington: Commission of Fine Arts and the Historic American Buildings Survey, 1970), pp. 2–16.

37 HABS No. DC-163, published in *Northeast,* pp. 110–123.

FIGURE 74. Benjamin Miller House, 1524 Twenty-eighth Street, N.W.

FIGURE 76. 1423 Thirty-sixth Street, N.W.

FIGURE 75. William Knowles House, 1228 Thirtieth Street, N.W.

the Corinthian porch seems to be later, but the Ionic side gallery may be original.

It is thus significant, with these variations on a traditional theme in mind, that when a large mansion was built on an ample corner lot, such as at 2813 P Street, N.W. (fig. 81), the usual three bay facade was maintained, though the height was increased by a third floor plus a basement level, and an ell to the side provided additional space. With such an ample site a more academic Greek Revival building could easily have been built; rather, a large scale and severe version of the traditional solution was used.

During the 1850's and even later, a very common type was the Greek Revival house with cornice caps, plain white sills, and a simple classical enframement for the doorway, but also with an enlarged cornice now supported by brackets. The house at 3031 O Street, N.W., is one such example (fig. 82). This cornice treatment, probably based on enlarged modillions or dentils, would make the transition to Italianate details later much easier.

Even some business blocks adapted the Greek detail to the traditional brick forms. At 3273–75 M Street, N.W. (fig. 83), the ground floor was originally supported by simple cast iron square pillars (preserved in the left building only). Above, the window caps and sills are utterly plain; only the cornice with mutules and guttae, and egg and dart moldings, has any elaboration.

There were no large buildings that adopted the rec-

FIGURE 77.   2904 P Street, N.W.

FIGURE 78.   3050 P Street, N.W.

FIGURE 79.   3003-3005 O Street, N.W.

tangular temple form in Georgetown. Mackall
Square (fig. 84), of about 1820,[38] has a very handsome Ionic porch, but this is attached to a brick
structure that is no radical departure from previous
brick mansions. The Ionic porch that graced the
front of the old Union Hotel on M Street, N.W.,
(fig. 85), is clearly an addition to a Federal building,
perhaps added in 1836 when the hotel was reconstructed after a fire.[39] One structure which, seen in
Civil War photographs of the waterfront, appears at
a distance to be a temple-type building, is not, in fact.
The Bank of Columbia on M Street, N.W., (fig. 86)
has indeed a small classical porch, but also ground

floor arches which seem to link it to the older tradition rather than the new.[40] In fact, it may incorporate
portions of an earlier building, since when sold in

38 HABS No. DC GEO 8–3.

39 The cornerstone of the building (formerly at 2921–29 M
Street N.W.) was originally laid July 4, 1793; the building was destroyed by fire in 1832 but was rebuilt, opening again in March
1836. Later in the century it was further changed by having a
mansard roof added to it, as well as oriols attached to the west
side. See John Clagett Proctor, *Washington and Environs* (Washington, 1949), p. 58.

40 Talbot Hamlin, in *Benjamin Henry Latrobe* (New York: Oxford University Press, 1955), p. 348, feels that Thornton or Hadfield could well have designed the exterior (it being more or less
consistent with their style); Latrobe installed an iron roof on the
building in 1805, "and perhaps had done more."

FIGURE 80.   2823 N Street, N.W.

FIGURE 82.   3031 O Street, N.W.

FIGURE 81.   2813 P Street, N.W.

FIGURE 83.   3273-75 M Street, N.W.

66

1781, the property cost over $25,000, indicating that a substantial structure was already on the site.[41]

The only other buildings which adapted the new Greek orders were Forest Hall, and perhaps one or two churches. Forest Hall was constructed during the 1850's at Wisconsin Avenue and N Street, N.W. (fig. 87). It does not, however, understand the new architecture at all, for the colossal Ionic order, elevated above a high basement story, is clearly just a frontispiece decoratively applied, with the brick flanks of the building clearly exposed. In fact, its extreme flatness, and the use of the Ionic order as pilasters rather than columns or half columns, confirms this attention to continuous flat facades and surfaces. A similar effect is seen in the Chapel of the Sacred Heart, 1500 Thirty-fifth Street, N.W. (fig. 88); though built in 1821, the facade is certainly much later, and has a similar flatness in the use of Ionic pilasters at the front only.

It is therefore clear that the Greek Revival in Georgetown manifested itself in a number of variations of well known forms. New detailing and proportions made the style different, but there was no real change from older forms. With the superb Greek Revival buildings of Washington for emulation, this may be surprising, but there are a number of reasons why the local architecture maintained its own course.

1. Because of the local conservativeness, apparently of both builder and client (often one and the same), the vernacular and builder tradition of plain brick walls was adhered to in the form of buildings, and Greek detail and a variation in the proportions were the only real changes. This lack of interest in experimenting with established types is seen, for example, in the lack of bow fronts, or engaged pilasters on facades. Adhering to the three bay facade was clearly a matter of choice, used even in a house on an ample site (such as Mackall Square). In a sense, the very concept of clear big volumes, while negated in continuous rowhouses, does come out in large detached structures such as 2813 P Street, N.W., and, being of solid brick, does have a certain "Greekness" in solidity, if you will, that is more true to essentials than a small scale Doric cottage in wood.

[41] Recorder of Deeds, Annapolis, Md., Liber A, Folio 624, deed of Apr. 26, 1781, recorded May 5, 1781, conveying lots 25, 26, and 27 from Robert Peter to Bernard O'Neill for £12,500. I am indebted to Robert W. Lyle and the Peabody Room, Georgetown Public Library, for this information.

FIGURE 84. Mackall Square, 1633 Twenty-ninth Street, N.W.

FIGURE 85. Union Hotel, M Street, N.W., ca. 1860.

2. The very nature of the builder tradition is concerned with details and in the accumulation of them into a completed structure. In William Force's *The Builder's Guide: Containing Lists of Prices* . . ., published locally in 1842, every conceivable detail of construction in wood or brick or stone, of interior and exterior detailing, roofing, painting, fencing,

FIGURE 86. Bank of Columbia, M Street, N.W.

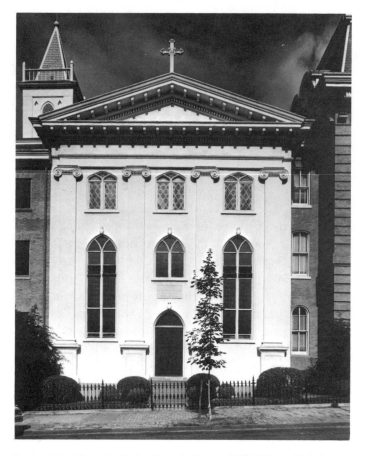

FIGURE 88. Chapel of the Sacred Heart, 1500 Thirty-fifth Street, N.W.

FIGURE 87. Forest Hall, 1256 Wisconsin Avenue, N.W.

and so on, is set out as a unit and given a price.[42] For example, a page of various mantels gives varying

prices as they increase in complexity; one with plain pilasters and a panel frieze with cornice and bed molding was only $3, but if it had reeded pilasters and fret dentils, it cost $15. Columns were also carefully priced; those made from glued planks forming a cylinder cost $0.30 a foot, fluting or reeding, $0.20 a foot, and Tuscan or Doric capitals $2 each, with Corinthian more.[43] Most significantly, Force also mentioned earlier pricelists. The only complete one, for all trades, was published previously in 1804,[44] but it is clear that each trade had its own lists and he mentions specifically those of the carpenters, bricklayers, and painters societies, which he made use of compiling his own work.[45] Clearly, with a frag-

[42] W. Q. Force (comp.), *The Builders Guide: Containing Lists of Prices, and Rules of Measurement, for Carpenters, Bricklayers, Stone Masons, Stone Cutters, Plasterers. . . .* (Washington: Peter Force, 1842), 80 pp. Copy courtesy of the Library, American Institute of Architects, Washington, D.C.

[43] Ibid., pp. 17–18.

[44] John Evans, *Builder's Universal Price Book* (Washington, 1804).

[45] Reference is made to the *Carpenters Price Book* published by the Master Carpenters of Washington, an 1836 pricelist of the Bricklayers Society of Washington, to The Master Painters Society of Washington and Georgetown, and others.

mented approach to erecting a building, and an obviously strong local builder tradition, this mode of construction would yield with difficulty to any change in basic concept.

3. Construction of rowhouses or detached houses of brick simply did not lend itself to ready adaptation to more academic or temple-form buildings, which might be inspired by the Washington public buildings. Wood houses with the gable end to the street, seen only in a few early Georgetown examples, would have a far better chance had the tradition continued. The sloping gable of the Federal house is, on the other hand, an impediment to creating a temple form, while placing columns at the gable end of a wood house, so often painted white in the first place, is almost a logical step. Such is impossible with an equally wide brick house with the gable parallel to the street. Furthermore, the practice of stuccoing brick, which would be a necessity, was not popular; Tudor Place was probably the only residence in Georgetown treated in this manner.

4. In addition, the great public buildings of Washington were in stone, were of immense size, and were clearly governmental and public in their use. It seems likely, therefore, that local tradesmen, merchants and professional men, to say nothing of builders, may have considered it a style inappropriate for a private house. We have seen already how few residences were ever made of stone. It is probably significant that in nearby Alexandria, the two major temple-fronted buildings, the Lyceum (1839) and the Bank of the Old Dominion (1851–52), are both essentially public structures. Furthermore, since the classical buildings in the Capital were very closely linked to new advances in brick vaulting, fireproofing, and other structural innovations, this would remove the style further from private use, both from the lack of need of these advances in smaller buildings, and from the disinclination, or inability, of local builders to radically change their methods.

5. There is also a basic antithesis in adopting this style to use for houses. The best Greek Revival in Washington was of great power and massiveness, with a distinct plastic, sculptural quality. These aspects work very well for large, four- and five-story buildings of considerable lateral extent, but might make a smaller building look stodgy or pompous. And as we have previously seen, local builders were not interested in sculptural or plastic treatment, rather in flat walls and applied detail. This essential difference in the basic tenets of the two modes of

building may have been recognized, and the chance not taken for possible failure. Unlike a country builder in Massachusetts, who may never have seen a real monumental Greek Revival building, local builders could see fine examples only a few miles away, and may have sensed the impossibility of truly imitating them on a small scale.

6. It also seems obvious that the financial resources of Georgetown (to say nothing of Washington) were not such that private citizens could, if they had desired, have built a large temple-form building. We know that trade and shipping had been declining for years, and the C. & O. Canal was one effort to help revive it. But the canal was not completed until 1851, and then extended only half of the distance originally projected. Much of the difficulty arose from the silting up of the river, due in large part to changes in the shape of Mason's Island, after a flood in the spring of 1780, which changed the scouring pattern of the river. A government report of 1835 described this problem and made various suggestions for its correction [46] which were only partially successful in helping Georgetown trade. The financial panic of 1837 also did not help matters. While large estates were constructed up to about 1820, there are no new ones for over 30 years, though smaller row houses or detached buildings, far less costly than estates, are still built.

7. Another reason for the Greek Revival's lack of appeal in Georgetown, far less possible to document, is the fact that Georgetown was a city of merchants and professional men. Talbot Hamlin has pointed out that one of the reasons for the success of the Greek Revival was that it was admired and encouraged by men and architects of considerable learning and taste, with a strong background in Greek and Roman literature and a knowledge of classical languages, who often collected the new architectural publications, such as Stuart and Revett's *Antiquities of Athens* (1762, 1789), which published new archeological discoveries.[47] These men—Jefferson and Latrobe among the most accomplished—also saw in the profound social and political changes in America a link with the ancient democracies of Greece and the Republic of Rome, so that the new style was politically, as well as philosophically and aesthetically,

[46] *Report from the Secretary of the Treasury in compliance with a Resolution of the Senate, with a report concerning obstructions to the Navigation of the Potomac between Washington and Georgetown*, S. Doc. 133 (1835), Ser. 268, 23d Cong. 2d sess., p 5.

[47] Talbot Hamlin, *Greek Revival Architecture in America* (New York: Dover Publications, Inc., 1964), pp. 315–329.

FIGURE 89. 1516-18 Twenty-eighth Street, N.W.

FIGURE 90. Wheatley Town Houses, 3041-45 N Street, N.W.

appropriate. Sympathy with the struggles of Greece to free itself from Turkish rule in the 1820's also con-

tributed. It may well be that Georgetown simply had fewer people with these inclinations, who would wish to body them forth in an architectural statement.

8. Finally, even if there had been more of an inclination to build large, Greek Revival houses, the very climate of Washington was not conducive to the prospects of long term use of a costly estate. The vast debt of the cities, lack of Federal Government concern for local problems, possibility of moving the Capital, poor local economy, and many other reasons discussed above, did not encourage costly private building, unless the wealth was firmly based on shipping or extensive plantations. But even these two sources were on shaky foundations; local shipping had its ups and downs, and, especially from the 1830's on, agitation for abolition of slavery in the District was a constant issue.

These may be some of the reasons why the influence of the important Greek Revival buildings in Washington had so little local effect. And as pointed out, one of the most persuasive was the builder tradition, a factor which continued in strength even in the 1850's, when more picturesque elements became common. A look at a few Georgetown houses during the next decade, up to the Civil War, will show how this tradition continued after the Greek Revival.

At 1516–18 Twenty-eighth Street, N.W., are two houses which, in a way, show the beginning of the trend seen in the 1850's (fig. 89). The dwelling at the left is quite similar to the late Greek Revival type mentioned at 3031 O Street, N.W., with a simple Greek doorway and caps and a projecting bracketed cornice. To the right, in a house with somewhat taller proportions, the Greek doorway is still employed, but now the windows have segmental arches (and two over two light glazing rather than six over six as heretofore) with a light masonry keystone emphasizing the slightly projecting hood mold around the window head. The cornice brackets are somewhat more massive. These changes presage a more picturesque emphasis and a richer polychromy than the red brick and light trim of the Greek Revival.

A townhouse built in 1854 by Francis Wheatley at 3045 N Street, N.W. (fig. 90) carries this trend further.[48] The arched windows (which retain the older 6/6 and 6/9 glazing) have the keystone of the

[48] Mr. Wheatley was the cofounder of a prosperous lumber business. See HABS No. DC-168 in *Waterfront*, pp. 247–248. He is also mentioned in a number of instances in Mary Mitchell, *Divided Town* (Barre, Mass.: Barre Publishers, 1968), an account of Georgetown life during the Civil War.

arch in a tawny sandstone decorated with a fleur-de-lis, similar stone haunch blocks, and molded voussoir bricks which, though flush with the wall, are in the shape of hood molds. The cornice is also elaborated further but here, appropriate to a brick aesthetic, it takes the form of corbelled pseudomachicolation, derived probably from brackets and modillions rather than actual machicolation. Together with the bands of diamond bricks at the second and third floor sill level, the play of light and dark is increased on the facade in spite of its planar qualities everywhere except the door enframement and the cornice. The colors—red brick, buff sandstone, and black shadows in the diamond brick bands—also have a hint of picturesque Ruskinian detailing.

Very conveniently, Wheatley also built the two houses adjacent, at 3041–43 N Street, N.W., in 1859.[49] Here the flat brick walls and tall proportions are animated by handsome cast iron hood molds above all windows, the most elaborate and sculptural at the bottom. The doorway has a boldly projecting pediment and the large modillioned cornice is supported on widely spaced brackets. This shows clearly, if belatedly, a trend to a more animated facade, appropriate for a period when major architects were seeking more varied silhouettes and profiles, less symmetry, and a concern for more natural colors and materials—a movement that had gained particular momentum in the 1840's and 1850's with the publications of A. J. Downing and others. It should be noted, however, that only more plastic details, not bay windows, were employed here to further enrich the facade.

The hood molds and trim being painted white gives a superficial similarity to the trim of light or white-painted wood and stone (or cast iron) in the Federal (or Greek Revival) periods. This is deceptive, since the original color here was probably brown or green, thus giving a somber quality that would be parallel with the tawny stone trim of 3045 N Street, N.W.[50]

Other row houses of a similar type, erected about the same time, sometimes do have a projecting bay, such as at 3107–9 N Street, N.W., (fig. 91). Significantly, however, it is a wooden bay, only one story

FIGURE 91. 3107-3111 N Street, N.W.

high, that is added on in a space which is normally occupied by two first floor windows. In a way, then, the bay is not a radical departure in architectural concept but an added detail, in a different material from the brick wall, which carries on the trend to more picturesque detailing, and, in a limited way, massing.

This examination of Georgetown architecture up to about 1860 has brought out not only the elements inherent in a vernacular and building tradition which would inhibit adaptation of forms based on monumental Greek buildings, but also shows the conservative and somewhat lagging styles which help explain the general lack of interest in architectural advances. As we will see, these same factors are among those that prevented the work of Renwick and Downing in Washington and Georgetown from having extensive effect.

The domestic architecture in Washington by and large followed the same trend of development as we find in Georgetown, though it was somewhat less conservative in some ways. A brief survey of buildings, many of which are directly comparable to types in Georgetown, will point up this similarity.

[49] HABS No. DC-186 (3043 N Street only). Published in *Northeast*, pp. 126–139.

[50] I am indebted to Mr. C. Dudley Brown, A.I.D., for this information. A restoration specialist who has lived and worked on Capitol Hill since 1958, Mr. Brown has observed from work he has done that these dark colors were preferred at least in Washington and Georgetown.

FIGURE 92. The Octagon, 1799 New York Avenue, N.W., by William Thornton.

FIGURE 93. The Octagon, 1799 New York Avenue, N.W.

Just as in Georgetown, Washington had domestic structures that can be grouped into three categories: professional architecture, builder architecture, and vernacular. And similarly, we find that those from the first group had almost no effect on other buildings, though they were of equally high quality as those in Georgetown.

The earliest of these works of professional architecture is the "Octagon," the residence of John Tayloe, at 1799 New York Avenue, N.W., (fig. 92), built in 1798–1800.[51] The most unique feature of this mansion, designed by Dr. Thornton, is of course its novel shape, the plan conforming to the acute angle of the two streets, and given special importance by the projecting central bay. But besides this plastic, volumetric projection and the clear, solid geometry of the house (emphasized by the hip roof, fig. 93), its component parts are not specifically new. As with many three-story Washington houses, the second floor level is marked with a stone string course, helping to give a sense of rhythm to the three stories, each one of a different height. The stone inset panels be-

tween the second and third floor windows are also a feature used in some Federal architecture, an element which was seen in the Georgetown rows. Thus the unique and distinctive aspects—the bay front and ingenious shape—were the features which one might expect to find imitated in a city with so many such sites. But they were not.

A second house in this class is Latrobe's Decatur House at 748 Jackson Place, N.W., (fig. 94), of 1817–18.[52] Here again, the individual features are not particularly different—the bull's-eye lintels and the doorway with elliptical fan light and side lights are not uncommon. The exterior distinction is to be found rather in its generous proportions and scale, and the austere sense of cubic volume, with the hip roof giving it a particularly imposing effect. The major innovation by Latrobe, the vaulted entrance hall and foyer, was visible only to those entering the building.

51 Eberlein and Hubbard, pp. 301–316. For observations on its architecture, see Kimball, pp. 170–172.

52 Eberlein and Hubbard, pp. 259–274. For a discussion of the architecture, see Talbot Hamlin, *Benjamin Henry Latrobe* (New York: Oxford University Press, 1955) chapter 19, and also "Decatur House," special issue of *Historic Preservation* XIX, 3–4 (July-December, 1967), National Trust publication No. 123, esp. pp. 9–23.

Latrobe's house for General Van Ness, however, formerly at Seventeenth Street and Constitution Avenue, N.W., (fig. 95) has none of the local vernacular elements.[53] Built in 1813–17 for a wealthy patron, this mansion had much of the Greek severity that Latrobe admired and espoused. The front had a porte-cochère of four Doric columns on a high plinth supporting a pedimented roof. The body of the house had a three bay central portion with single bay pavilions projecting slightly at the ends and emphasized by parapets, but all tied together by a string course at the first floor level and at the second floor window sill level. Since the whole house was stuccoed, the monolithic and Greek quality was enhanced as the brickwork, inherently read as small units combined for a larger whole, was not at all visible. The severity of the detailing, restricted on the facade to small cornice blocks and square caps over the main floor windows, enhances this austere quality. On the rear (fig. 96), the treatment was similar, but with triple windows on the main floor (a feature that became popular in the Greek Revival), set within large sunk arches in the flanking end pavilions. Unlike the windows of the Laird-Dunlop House in Georgetown, these recessed arches are not mainly moldings that animate the surface, but, by their recessed nature, emphasize the thickness and massiveness of the wall and its forms.

Probably the most astonishing of those early residences is the Custis-Lee Mansion (fig. 97) designed by George Hadfield.[54] Although the north and south wings were built between 1802 and 1804, the central portion, a true temple front of six massive Doric columns with the main portion of the house behind, was not completed until 1817. Although not actually in Washington City, it was within the District when erected and because it was (and is) highly visible from the city (but not from Georgetown) it can be considered here. This is obviously a marked departure from previous buildings, the first truly Greek Revival structure in Washington. Its massive columns, somewhat overpowering and ill-proportioned when experienced at close range, read perfectly from a distance, and viewed from across the Potomac in

FIGURE 94. Decatur House, 748 Jackson Place, N.W., by Benjamin H. Latrobe.

FIGURE 95. Van Ness Mansion, by Benjamin H. Latrobe, facade (demolished).

Washington they form a striking feature near the crest of the high hill. The whole is stuccoed, drafted, and tinted to resemble stone, including the low wings whose windows are framed by the sunk arch motif (fig. 98).

A second building by Hadfield, though not a residence, is on a residential scale and could, but for

---

[53] Eberlein and Hubbard, pp. 359–370. For architectural comments see Hamlin, *Latrobe*, pp. 464–467; also Kimball, pp. 170–174. For extensive information on General Van Ness, see Allen C. Clark, "General John Peter Van Ness, A Mayor of the City of Washington, His Wife, Marcia, and her Father, David Burnes," C.H.S. *Records*, XXII (1919), pp. 125–204.

[54] Murray Homer Nelligan, *Custis-Lee Mansion* (Washington: U.S. Government Printing Office, 1962).

FIGURE 96. Van Ness Mansion, rear.

FIGURE 97. Custis-Lee Mansion, Arlington National Cemetery.

the bars on the windows, be an elegant mansion rather than the Branch Bank of the United States (fig. 99). This was located at Pennsylvania Avenue at Fifteenth Street, N.W., and was completed in 1824.[55] As in many of the previous examples, brick is eschewed, the surface being stuccoed and drafted to resemble stone. Its solid and massive quality is emphasized by the numerous recessed coffers over the windows and the recessed arches on the facade. Like Decatur House, the hip roof emphasized its simple cubic geometry.

---

[55] W. B. Bryan, *A History of the National Capital* (New York: The Macmillan Company, 1914–16), II, 194. The building was demolished in 1904.

But just as in Georgetown, it was the builder architecture which was most common. Washington also had a few larger mansions in this mode, as well as innumerable smaller brick and wood townhouses. Probably the most famous of the larger mansions was Duddington, formerly at E, F, and Second Streets, and New Jersey Avenue, S.E., built between 1793 and 1797,[56] the replacement for the dwelling which L'Enfant had earlier demolished. This building (fig. 100) is quite similar to Dumbarton House in Georgetown of a few years later, with a pedimented central projecting pavilion and keystone lintels. Lacking symmetrical setback wings, its planar quality is even more pronounced. While this harked back to the Georgian past, the Thomas Law House at Sixth and N Streets, S.W., of 1796 (fig. 101),[57] like the Laird-Dunlop house, shows considerable refinement of the builder tradition. Here we also find keystone lintels, a string course at the second floor level (a motif common in Washington to help create a logical division for the tall facade), and also roundheaded windows on the first floor, framed in arched moldings. This is similar to a plate published 10 years later, in 1806, by Asher Benjamin (fig. 102), showing that it was a design generally current at the time to give variety to the planar Federal facades.

But as in Georgetown, it was the simple brick townhouse with flat brick walls and applied details that was the most common. Especially because of the early building codes of 1791[58] which prohibited wood houses, this mode was encouraged. Since these houses are very similar to those built in Georgetown, we can assume that the same builders were active in both localities.

A small, two bay brick house with keystone lintels, formerly at 932 Twenty-seventh Street, N.W., (fig. 103)[59] is almost identical to the house at 1063 Thomas Jefferson St., N.W. Larger houses with this motif were extremely common in the early Nineteenth century. A watercolor of 1817 (fig. 13) depicting the Bank of the Metropolis (built as Rhodes' Tavern

---

[56] Eberlein and Hubbard, pp. 388–394. See also Allen C. Clark, "Daniel Carroll of Duddington," C.H.S. *Records*, XXXIX (1938), pp. 1–48. The house was demolished in 1886.

[57] Eberlein and Hubbard, pp. 371–381. Attributed to William Lovering.

[58] These are quoted in William Tindall, *Standard History of the City of Washington* (Knoxville: H. W. Crew & Co., 1914), pp. 122–123. Because of their strictness they were suspended from 1796–1800; see Saul K. Padover (ed.) *Thomas Jefferson and the National Capital* (Washington: U.S. Government Printing Office, 1946), pp. 196–197.

[59] HABS No. DC-Wash. 42–4.

in 1800–01) at Fifteenth and F Streets, N.W.,[60] shows that the keystone lintel and a shallow cornice was in common use. This form can also be seen in Brown's Indian Queen Hotel on Pennsylvania Avenue, as depicted in a lithograph of about 1832 (fig. 104). Other private houses of two and a half stories with this keystone lintel, such as General Alfred Pleasonton's headquarters of the Civil War (location not ascertained) are quite comparable to Georgetown examples (fig. 105). Even one of the most elaborate of early houses built, the Caldwell-Monroe House at 2017 I Street, N.W., (1802–06)[61] uses this keystone motif (fig. 106), together with stone string courses (a Federal refinement), and a Federal doorway very similar to that found in the Linthicum House in Georgetown. Larger than most Georgetown examples, the use of four bays and three and a half stories keeps the proportions the same as the more common three bay, two and a half story houses. It should be noted, however, that this height was required by the 1791 regulations, which specified that no house on a major street could be less than 35 feet tall.

The use of bull's-eye lintels was also common, both for small houses and large. One surviving example at 614 Seventeenth Street, N.W., (fig. 107), a block west of the President's House, was originally one of a pair constructed here. A detail from an 1879 photograph (fig. 108) shows both clearly, as well as the original doorway. These lintels were also used on larger dwellings, such as the John Marshall House (fig. 109) at 1801 F Street, N.W., of 1825.[62] Changes in brickwork indicate that it was originally a gable roofed, two and a half story (plus basement) house and not three stories; the cornice and bay are also obviously later. It was, nevertheless, an imposing building situated on an ample corner lot. Even so, the traditional house form was continued.

Because of the need for many new brick dwellings, connected rows sprang up quickly. "The Seven Buildings," on Pennsylvania Avenue between Nineteenth and Twentieth Streets, N.W., (fig. 110), built about 1796, were among the first.[63] Except for the rounded end at the Nineteenth Street corner and the stone belt course at the second floor level, the row

FIGURE 98. Custis-Lee Mansion, from the southeast.

FIGURE 99. Branch Bank of the United States, Pennsylvania Avenue at Fifteenth Street, N.W., (demolished).

was very similar to those erected in Georgetown. Though the doorways were quite plain, the keystone lintels added to its decorative features. A very similar row, "The Six Buildings," on Pennsylvania Avenue at Twenty-First Street, N.W., (fig. 111) is even plainer, with flat brick arches over the windows, though the second floor sills are joined by a continuous course.

Similar rows were built at the other end of town, on Capitol Hill. Carroll Row, on First Street at Pennsylvania Avenue, S.E., (fig. 112), built between 1800

---

[60] Watercolor of 1817 by Baroness Hyde de Neuville, showing also the end of the rebuilt Treasury Building (left). From the I. N. Phelps Stokes Collection of American Historical Prints, New York Public Library, Print Division.

[61] Eberlein and Hubbard, pp. 330–341.

[62] Tench Ringgold, owner-builder. See *Waterfront*, pp. 92–93.

[63] Eberlein and Hubbard, pp. 317–329.

FIGURE 100. Duddington, at E., F, and Second Streets, S.E., (demolished).

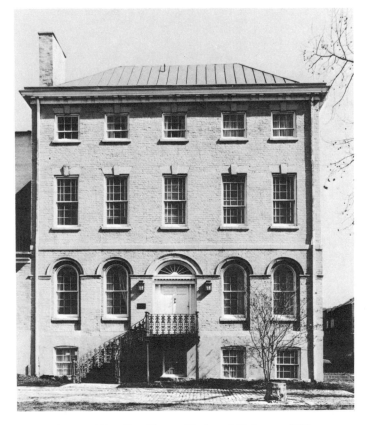

FIGURE 101. Law House, Sixth and N Streets, S.W.

FIGURE 102. Townhouse, from Asher Benjamin, *The American Builder's Companion* (1806), plate 35.

dows above, with one on the second floor being a Palladian light.[64] On the first floor the windows are roundheaded and linked by a molding that is identical to the treatment found in the Laird-Dunlop House of about 1799, in Georgetown.

These brick buildings, mainly on avenues and major streets, are all at least three and a half stories tall; but it is clear from old photographs that the simpler two and three bay brick houses of two and a half stories, so common in Georgetown, were also built in considerable numbers. A view of December, 1856, taken from the south Capitol wing looking southwest (fig. 113), reveals many of these, both isolated and in short rows.

Because there was very little architecture on the site when the Federal City was laid out, the continuity of the builder architecture and the basics of a vernacular architecture are not as close as in Georgetown; but since most of the builders were probably from Georgetown in the first place, this makes little difference. There were, however, a few vernacular buildings, and from those documented, they follow a pattern similar to that of neighboring Georgetown.

Vernacular stone buildings, known from the Eigh-

and 1810, has four dwellings of three and four bays, with keystone lintels and simple arched doorways (but no string courses) at the south end. The north end, however, is given far more importance by a building of seven bays, originally used as a tavern. It has a large entrance door with an elliptical light, giving a central focus, and emphasized by wider win-

---

[64] About 1799–1800 the tavern was erected by Daniel Carroll; by 1810 the rest of the row had been completed. See Charles O. Paullin, "History of the Site of the Congressional and Folger Libraries," C.H.S. *Records*, XXXVII–XXXVIII (1937), pp. 179–180.

FIGURE 103. David Walker House, 932 Twenty-seventh Street, N.W., (demolished) .

FIGURE 104. Brown's Indian Queen Hotel, Pennsylvania Avenue, N.W., Lithograph about 1832.

FIGURE 105. Gen. Alfred Pleasanton's headquarters, Washington. Photograph taken April 1865.

teenth and early Nineteenth century around George-town, were rare in Washington. Although there was sparse settlement in the area before 1791, no stone structures have survived, and the only reference to one found was to "Lear's warehouse" of about 1800 which was located at the foot of Twenty-fifth Street near the water.[65] The only extant early stone build-ing, dating from about 1833, is the lock house for the Washington Canal at Seventeenth Street and Constitution Avenue, N.W.; it follows the standard lock house form (fig. 114) .

Early vernacular wood houses are more common. Probably the earliest known example is the David Burnes House (fig. 115) , formerly at Seventeenth Street and Constitution Avenue, N.W., of about 1740.[66] This building, the early home of General Van Ness' father-in-law, was conscientiously preserved on

a corner of the Van Ness property even after his man-sion was completed. The early house has a very steep gable roof and wide boards, suggesting its early vernacular origins. Another vernacular example that

[65] John Ball Osborne, "The Removal of the Government to Washington," C.H.S. Records, III (1900) , p. 143.

[66] See Teunis S. Hamlin, "Historic Houses of Washington,"

Scribner's Magazines, XIV, 4 (October 1893) , pp. 475–491, for a contemporary description and illustrations, and also James Frank-lin Hood, "The Cottage of David Burnes and its Diningroom Mantel," C.H.S. Records, XXIII (1920) , pp. 1–9. The building is mentioned also in Eberlein and Hubbard, pp. 353–358.

FIGURE 106. Caldwell-Monroe House, 2017 I Street, N.W.

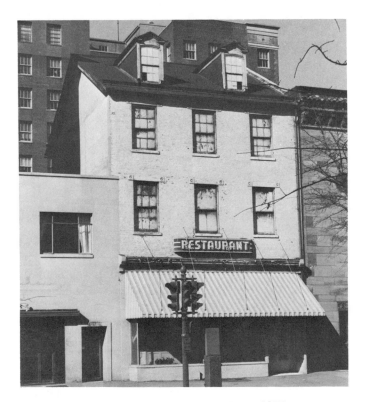

FIGURE 107. 614 Seventeenth Street, N.W.

dates from before 1790 is a gambrel roof house (fig. 116) that was located in the small settlement of Hamburgh, and formerly stood at 412 Twentieth Street, N.W.[67] Like the Joseph Jackson House in Georgetown, this was not locally a common style, though was known elsewhere in the region.

Although the original building code of Washington in 1791 prohibited wood houses, this was relaxed in 1796, and many small generally nondescript frame houses sprang up. In 1818, the size was limited to no more than 320 square feet (about 16 by 20 feet) and the eaves could be no higher than 12 feet, thus restricting them to two stories.[68] Originally, they could be no closer than 24 feet to any other dwelling.

Such houses are now very rare. Two examples which seem to date from the early Nineteenth century can be illustrated however. One is at 1639 P Street, N.W., (fig. 117), north of the President's House. Though now somewhat modified, the two bay facade and general style are appropriate to the period. A pair of similar frame houses, one two bay and the other three bay, are found east of the Capitol at 208–210 Fifth Street, S.E., (fig. 118); they are certainly within this tradition, though now leaning more toward Federal proportions. Old photographs, however, show a large variety of early wood houses, all devoid of achitectural distinction. A view from the Capitol in 1861 looking northwest (fig. 119) shows a number just at the end of Pennsylvania Avenue. One, near the center, appears to be a double house not unlike the Brickyard Hill House in Georgetown.

No brick warehouses or other truly vernacular brick structures survive from the early years, but we can assume here too that they were similar to those built in Georgetown. But this vernacular tradition in brick was certainly present. When local residents erected in 1815 a temporary Capitol building at First and A Streets, N.E. (fig. 120) for the use of Congress following the British invasion, it had many of the marks of vernacular architecture—flat wall surfaces, almost no detailing, large wall areas, and relatively small windows. There was only a token effort at more elaborate treatment, seen in the large windows in the center of the south and west facades. And as

[67] HABS No. DC-10-6 (Wash. 120–1), view from the southeast. It is illustrated and discussed in John Clagett Proctor, "Days Before Capital Was Laid Out," *Sunday Star*, Sept. 10, 1933. The house was demolished in 1935.

[68] Proclamation of President Monroe, Jan. 14, 1818, quoted in Force, p. 74.

we have seen, Washington's ordinary brick houses by builder architects maintain this tradition of flat, planar surfaces.

With this tradition of conservative architecture, similar to that in Georgetown, it is not surprising that none of the distinctive mansions had any noticeable effect on the local architecture. The reasons are probably similar to why the Greek Revival, in the 1830's and 1840's, was not more vigorously adopted in Georgetown. But several specific features are certainly paramount.

As buildings conceived by professional architects as an overall artistic concept, they were not amenable to meaningful borrowing. Even less than a temple front motif or classical orders, these buildings (except for the Lee Mansion) relied for their distinction most on arrangements of solid and void rather than specific features that possibly could be borrowed. The sunk arches, for example, would be meaningless used improperly. As works of trained architects, with considerable knowledge and experience, it was simply not within the reach of anyone not comparably trained to really imitate their work.

Furthermore, except to an extent for Decatur House, each building had a vivid sculptural and geometric quality which would not lend itself to builder adaptation.

Finally, some, like the Octagon and the Custis-Lee Mansion, depended very much on their site. It would be preposterous, for example, to place a huge Doric portico on any normal city lot.

During the 1830's and 1840's we find that local Greek Revival buildings in Washington follow many of the same principles as seen in Georgetown. Many of the same types are found, but also a class of larger buildings decorated with brick pilasters which are the culmination of the builder adaptations of the Greek Revival.

The essentially Federal type house, with dormers and gable roof but with plain lintels, and sills, and a classical door enframement, is found in two examples on the south side of F Street near Fifteenth (fig. 121, at far left). Next to them are two others which combine the ground floor arches (as in the Thomas Law House) with a stone string course and inset stone panels, but the form is still Federal, showing that there were some mixtures of elements.

Houses clearly in the Greek Revival style, however, were built in abundance, both with and without the frieze window motif. One very attractive ex-

Figure 108. 612-620 Seventeenth Street, N.W. Photograph taken November 25, 1879.

Figueg 109. John Marshall House, 1801 F Street, N.W.

ample of the former type (since altered) stands at Twentieth and F Streets, N.W., (fig. 122); though five bays wide and thus quite formal and symmetrical, the same general forms were used for more modest houses (fig. 123). Such buildings are similar in many ways to comparable, if more elaborate, houses constructed in Baltimore in the 1840's.[69] A detail of an 1861 pho-

[69] For example, in Howland, plates 39 and 40, and other illustrated examples.

79

FIGURE 110. "The Seven Buildings," Pennsylvania Avenue between Nineteenth and Twentieth Streets, N.W. Photograph taken in 1865 (demolished).

FIGURE 111. "The Six Buildings," Pennsylvania Avenue at Twenty-first Streets, N.W., (demolished).

FIGURE 112. Carroll Row, First Street at A Street, S.E. Photograph ca. 1880 (demolished).

tograph of the area northwest of the Capitol (fig. 124) shows a number of these Greek Revival houses scattered among the older Federal and frame dwellings; they were also found in the area of Fourteenth and F Streets, N.W., (fig. 125). As in Georgetown, many Greek Revival houses had full-size windows at the third floor rather than frieze windows. The most famous house of this type in Washington is probably the Petersen House (The House Where Lincoln Died) at 516 Tenth Street, N.W., built in 1849 (fig. 126). And this same formula could be handsomely adapted to larger structures as well as seen in the W. B. Moses building (fig. 127), begun in 1851.[70] That this simplified Greek treatment of plain lintels and sills set off against bare walls was of considerable popularity is attested by "Philadelphia Row," 124–154 Eleventh Street, S.E., (fig. 128), a group of 16 houses erected in 1856 to the east of the Capitol. Although the cornice brackets show leanings to more picturesque treatment, the format is still essentially Greek Revival.

Brick pilaster strips were also occasionally used to augment the classical nature of some Greek Revival structures. One particularly good example is the building at the corner of F and Fifteenth Streets, N.W., (fig. 121, right side). Here, the first floor level is composed of what appears to be tall stone piers and lintels, and the handsome entry has two fluted Doric columns supporting a frieze block with cornice and sloping parapet. Above this solid base are three levels of windows with projecting caps, divided into three unequal bays by four tall pilaster strips with caps. The fifth floor is neatly hidden behind the wide entablature, with small frieze windows. But in spite of the pilaster strips and Greek detailing, the obvious facadism and the thinness and flatness of the features affirm the essentially decorative, not architectural, role of these elements. The architectural concept is not much different from the smaller Federal or Greek Revival townhouse types.

And the architecture was still, basically, conservative. For example, in the building erected in 1849 for the St. Vincent's Orphan Asylum at Tenth and G Streets, N.W., (fig. 129), the form is still that of a (much enlarged) Federal house, with an attempt to tie the very tall facade together by using a second

FIGURE 113. Brick Federal houses, southwest of Capitol. Detail of photograph taken December 1856.

FIGURE 114. Lock House, Constitution Avenue at Seventeenth Street, N.W.

floor string course and tall pilaster strips (without bases) with an entablature. But the thin facadism is unrelated to the sides and emphasizes its decorative, added-on quality.

When discussing why the Greek Revival was not adapted more completely in Georgetown, it was pointed out that one possible reason was that the temple form, or the use of peristyles, was appropriate

[70] This was located at Seventh Street and Market Space; it was occupied by the W. B. Moses firm until 1865. The building was demolished in 1885. See John Clagett Proctor, "Historic Market Space and its Early Business Houses," *Sunday Star*, Oct. 24, 1943.

FIGURE. 115. David Burnes Cottage, Constitution Avenue at Eighteenth Street, N.W. Photograph taken in 1886 (demolished).

FIGURE 117. 1639 P Street, N.W.

FIGURE 116. Frame House, Hamburgh Village (demolished).

FIGURE 118. 208-210 Fifth Street, S.E.

FIGURE 119. Frame houses, northwest of Capitol. Detail of photograph taken June 27, 1861.

FIGURE 121. F Street (south side) at Fifteenth Street, N.W. Photograph taken April 1865.

FIGURE 120. "Brick Capitol," First Street at A Street, N.E. (demolished).

only for a large public building. Those structures built in Washington which use these elements confirm this, as they are all churches or public halls. The earliest one documented is the Ryland Methodist Church (fig. 130), built in 1844, which formerly stood at Tenth and D Streets, S.W.[17] Though only 40 by 50 feet, its corner location and elevation on a basement story makes the temple quite convincing.

[71] John Clagett Proctor, "Ryland Methodist Church to celebrate its Centenary," *Sunday Star*, Oct. 17, 1943.

FIGURE 122. 1925 F Street, N.W. Photograph taken 1865.

FIGURE 123. I Street, Between Eighteenth and Ninteenth Streets, N.W.

FIGURE 124. Greek Revival rows northwest of Capital. Detail of photograph taken June 27, 1861.

FIGURE 125. F Street, N.W., looking east from Fifteenth Street.

FIGURE 126. The Petersen House, 516 Tenth Street, N.W.

FIGURE 128. "Philadelphia Row," 124-154 Eleventh Street, S.E.

FIGURE 129. St. Vincent's Orphan Asylum, Tenth and G Streets, N.W. (demolished 1901).

FIGURE 127. W. B. Moses Building, Seventh Street and Market Space, N.W., (demolished).

The facade has a portico of four Tuscan columns and the side is divided into five bays by windows set in recessed arches, familiar from the work of Hadfield and Thornton. A second church, St. Matthew's Catholic Church formerly at Fifteenth and H Streets, N.W., (fig. 131), though larger and originally built with a steeple, is very similar in effect and style.

A third example is somewhat anomalous. Willard Hall, formerly at Fourteenth and F Streets, N.W., (fig. 132), was originally built in 1807 as a Presbyterian church; but when it was sold in 1859, the temple portico with two Doric columns *in antis* was appar-

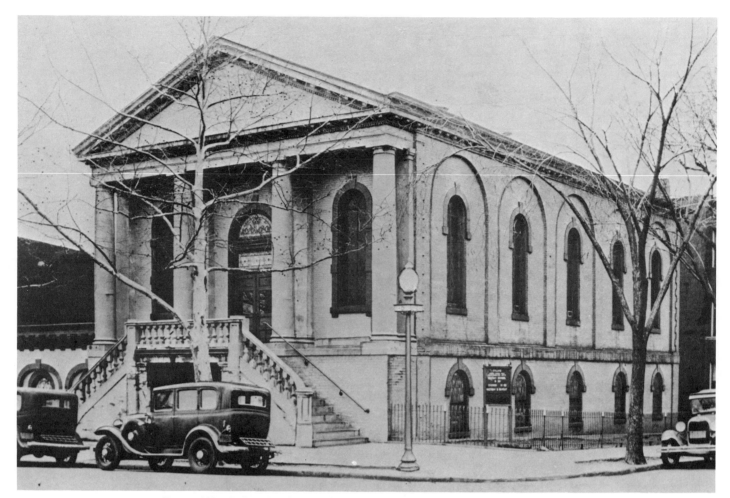

FIGURE 130. Ryland Methodist Church, Tenth and D Streets S.W., (demolished).

ently added.[72] As can be clearly seen (also in fig. 125 at the extreme right), the pedimented facade extends back only one bay so that the Greek frontispiece is very clearly simply added on, immediately destroying its sense of temple-shape and volume, though naturally still being an attractive, if false, facade.

It is clear, then, that this temple form, used apparently only for public structures, was not a style adopted for private residences.

As in Georgetown, the rowhouses of the post Greek Revival took on more picturesque characteristics while maintaining their essentially planar quality. An example to indicate the extent of similarity is two houses at 120–122 Fourth Street, S.E., (fig. 133) which are generally parallel to the houses at 3041–45 N Street. The similarity of style is quite striking, and the fact that these on Capitol Hill probably date from about 1868 (120 Fourth Street) and the early 1880's (122 Fourth Street) only reaffirms the persistence of the conservative builder tradition.

We have seen, then, aspects of the local architecture, and some of the probable reasons, that help explain why the architectural climate of Washington and Georgetown was not very conducive to the adaptation or imitation of the grand Greek Revival buildings erected in the 1830's, or for any major architectural adventures. Even in Washington, where there were many large tracts of open ground in the heart of the city, not just a few empty lots, the builder tradition held sway. This local architectural climate, together with the social, political, and economic problems examined earlier are all factors in the slow growth of architecture in the Capital.

---

[72] "The front and pillars . . . together with other additions, were added prior to the Civil War." John Clagett Proctor, "Old Willard Hall was Center of Community Affairs," *Sunday Star*, Aug. 16, 1936.

FIGURE 131.   St. Matthew's Catholic Church, Fifteenth and H Streets, N.W., (demolished) .

FIGURE 132.   Willard Hotel and Willard Hall, Fourteenth and F Streets, N.W., (demolished) . Photograph taken 1899.

FIGURE 133.   120-122 Fourth Street, S.E.

CHAPTER IV

James Renwick and A. J. Downing in Washington

It HAS been shown that the generally slow development of Washington was due to a combination of factors—political, social, economic, and psychological. Many of these elements also figured in the surprisingly negligible influence that the important Greek Revival government buildings had on local architecture. As noted, one prominent factor in this appears to have been the inapplicability of the monumental classical forms to domestic architecture, both for associational and for economic reasons. Peristyle and temple portico buildings, other than government structures, were simply not erected, except occasionally for churches.

In contrast to this, the buildings erected by James Renwick, Jr., and Andrew Jackson Downing (in collaboration with Calvert Vaux, his architectural partner) would appear to be eminently suited to inspire a whole series of followers. The Smithsonian Institution building, as we shall see, was designed to be flexible, adaptable, and cheap; and Downing's villas, specifically adapted to southern climates, were informal, could be fitted to a variety of sites, and could be added onto with ease. But these buildings—together with Downing's Mall plan and Renwick's other structures—had a very limited effect, almost as slight as that of the Greek Revival. The reasons include many we have seen before, as well as some new ones. By examining the buildings of Renwick and the work of Downing, and the influence they did have, these can be clearly understood.

James Renwick's first building in Washington was that for the Smithsonian Institution. The origin of this unique institution is complicated, but it should be at least summarized since it brings out again the reluctance of Congress to spend anything on a project with nonutilitarian ends.

When James Smithson, the British scientist, died in 1829, he left his fortune largely to a nephew, but with the stipulation that if this relative should die without issue, then the whole amount of his property was to go "to the United States of America, to found at Washington, under the name of the Smithsonian Institution, an Establishment for the increase and diffusion of knowledge among men." [1] When his nephew did indeed die unmarried, the United States was notified of its windfall, and after several years in English Chancery Court, the decree of May 9, 1838, turned over the sum of $508,318.46 to Richard Rush, the American envoy. Additional accrued interest brought the sum to about $550,000. [2] This fund was immediately invested in state bonds until a decision could be arrived at how to implement the will. [3]

---

[1] A. Hunter Dupree, *Science in the Federal Government* (New York: Harper & Row, 1964), p. 66. The origin and development of the Smithsonian Institution is thoroughly recorded in many government reports, some noted below, as well as in the *Annual Reports* of the Board of Regents (1846ff.) and a number of special-

A controversy immediately arose as to the use of the funds and the nature of the institution to be established. Some Congressmen wanted to found an agricultural college; John Quincy Adams introduced a bill in 1839 to establish an astronomical observatory. Letters of opinion were solicited from distinguished American scholars as to what they might suggest; most favored a national university.[4] The city of Washington even petitioned Congress in 1840 urging swift adoption of some plan (they did not really care which!) to carry out the will "as soon as practable," hoping to avert any movement to use the funds for other purposes.[5] Even the local National Institution attempted, in 1841, to absorb the bequest for its own scientific activities. But by 1844, bills in the Senate (June and December) sponsored by the Library Committee at last characterized the Smithsonian Institution. The building was to be "plain and durable, without unnecessary ornament, and to contain provisions for cabinets of natural history and geology, and for a library, a chemical laboratory, and lecture-rooms."[6] Its location was to be on the Mall west of Seventh Street, with the cost of the building limited to $80,000. In 1846, Robert Dale Owen, Senator from Indiana, who took a very active interest in the Institution, introduced a bill which was similar, except he put the cost limit at $242,129, the exact amount of accrued interest.[7] It was generally agreed that the original capital of the bequest should be maintained, the interest only being used for the work of the Institution.

Thus the nature of the Institution was generally established, leaning somewhat toward popularization of scientific knowledge, one of Owen's interests. These considerations were important, of course, in designing the building. After the Smithsonian Institution was established by an act of Congress on August 10, 1846 (and approved by President Polk), a governing body of Regents was established [8] and a Building Committee formed, with Owen as its chairman.

The day-by-day activities of this committee are fully documented.[9] It appears from these records that on the day after the Executive Committee was chosen (September 8, 1846), Owen submitted plans for the building prepared by his brother, David D. Owen, M.D., as well as a plan and drawing by Robert Mills. It was decided, however, that the Building Committee should visit major cities, examine appropriate public buildings, and consult their architects. This the committee did, visiting Philadelphia, Trenton, New York City, Boston, and Cincinnati, consulting with virtually all the major architects then working in the United States.[10]

The architects were requested to send in plans by December 25, but before that date the Regents "unanimously selected" on November 30, 1846, two projects by James Renwick, Jr. (figs. 134–135), out of 13 plans already in hand. His design in the Lombard or Norman style was preferred. It was thus clear that the long meeting Owen and his colleagues had had with Renwick in New York had produced favorable results. On January 20, 1847, presumably after studying all the other submissions, Renwick's Norman

ized studies. See especially in Dupree, pp. 66–70 and 76–90, and in George Brown Goode (ed.), *The Smithsonian Institution 1846–1896* (Washington, 1897), pp. 1–80 and 115–156.

[2] The financial account of the London attorneys for the United States, Messrs. Clarke, Fynmore and Fladgade, are outlined in astonishing detail in *Smithsonian Bequest: Report to the President,* May 4, 1840, H. Rep. 277, 26th Cong. 1st sess., Ser. 370, pp. 118–144.

[3] Arkansas state bonds, at 6 per cent interest, took almost the whole amount. They were not, however, a sound investment, and by 1843 almost $80,000 in interest remained unpaid. John Quincy Adams, active in insuring that Smithson's will was faithfully administered, was careful to see that the full sum was recovered. The investment is set out fully in *Letter from the Secretary of the Treasury, transmitting Statements relative to the Smithsonian Fund, &c.,* Feb. 19, 1844, H. Doc. 142, 28th Cong., 1st sess., Ser. 442.

[4] Extensive correspondence of Adams with European astronomical observatories, and replies from a number of American scholars, are given in H. Rpt. 277, 26th Cong., 1st sess., Ser. 370, especially pp. 72–89.

[5] *Memorial of the Corporation of the City of Washington on the Subject of the Smithsonian Bequest,* Feb. 4, 1840, H. Doc. 51, 26th Cong., 1st sess., Ser. 364.

[6] Goode, p. 248.

[7] Ibid.

[8] The Regents consisted of a Chancelor, a Secretary, and an Executive Committee, which was designated to procure plans. Owen had been chairman of the Organizing Committee of the Smithsonian Institution, and he and Alexander Dallas Bache were instrumental in assuring that it had a strong board of Regents (to which they were both elected). See Thomas Coulson, *Joseph Henry* (Princeton: Princeton University Press, 1950), p. 176.

[9] For example see *Smithsonian Institution. Report of the Board of Regents . . . May 3, 1847,* S. Doc. 211, 29th Cong., 2d sess., and especially in the *Report of the Board of Regents of the Smithsonian Institution . . . January 6, 1848,* S. Misc. Doc. 23, 30th Cong., 1st sess., Ser. 511 [1], the "Report of the Building Committee," pp. 4–155.

[10] This list is quite impressive. It includes John Notman, James Renwick, Sr., James Renwick, Jr., Richard Upjohn, Isaiah Rogers, Ammi B. Young, Thomas U. Walter, and others. They missed John Haviland in Philadelphia, but left communication for him. Robert Mills was, of course, in Washington. S. Doc. 211, 29th Cong., 2d sess., pp. 6–7.

FIGURE 134. Norman design for the Smithsonian, by James Renwick, 1846. (From Owen, *Hints on Public Architecture* [1849], facing p. 104.)

plan, "as amended," [11] was adopted by the Regents, who also awarded $250 prizes to four other contestants (Wells and Arnot, John Notman, John Haviland, and Owen J. Warren). Renwick's plan was further altered, however, since on January 28 it was again approved, "as amended and reduced," following suggestions of the Building Committee. Authorization was then given to enter into construction contracts.

It is clear that during this whole time the nature and style of the proposed architecture was under careful study, and that Renwick—already the favorite since November 1846—and Owen had had long discussions about it. Owen wanted to publish a treatise on the subject, in part to explain how they had

arrived at the style of architecture chosen, and on February 5, 1847, the Regents authorized publication of his *Hints on Public Architecture*,[12] which was "prepared by Doctor Owen, with the assistance of Mr. Renwick." [13] This joint authorship is more or less implicit, given Owen's lack of architectural background, and since much of Renwick's previous New York architecture (such as Grace Church, the Free Academy, and Calvary Church) is illustrated as models in the book which was finally published in 1849.[14]

It is worth noting the basic arguments of Owen and Renwick since many of their points are similar

---

[11] One of the recommendations appears to have been adding the battlements when it was decided that the roof would be too visible from Washington. Goode, p. 251, note 1.

[12] S. Doc. 211, 29th Cong., 2d sess., p. 31.

[13] Goode, p. 255.

[14] Robert Dale Owen, *Hints on Public Architecture, containing, among other Illustrations, Views and Plans of the Smithsonian Institution* (New York: George P. Putnam, 1849). These are illustrated facing pp. 58, 71, and 92, and on p. 97.

FIGURE 135. Gothic design for the Smithsonian, by James Renwick, 1846. (From Owen, *Hints on Public Architecture*, facing p. 99.)

to those held by Downing, and emphasize the common-sense advantage, economy, and adaptability of the style chosen, surely encouraging factors for imitators.

Many of Owen's ideas coincided with the growing interest in more picturesque, irregular, and adaptable architecture, with a greater emphasis on a rational plan derived from functional needs; structure honestly expressed; decoration derived from natural (plant) forms, or from actual necessity (as parapets to deflect rain); and a more free and creative use of past styles.[15] He applies these ideas to his discussion of the nature of architecture, and the choice of the Twelfth century Norman style for the Smithsonian.

After noting that architecture must be adapted to local climate, materials, and the best technical advances, he observed that an indigenous school of architecture may well be based on some former style, but emphasized "its privilege to originate as well as to adopt."[16] He felt that there were four basic conditions for a "national style:"[17]

First, it must have flexibility. Discarding rigid rules and canons (as our government had done . . .), the external forms should follow the internal functions.

Second, for a republic, the architecture must not be elaborate or expensive.

Third, the pleasing effects of the architecture should be due more to "justness of proportion, to graceful outline, to skillful grouping and artistical management of masses, than to gorgeous ornament or costly decoration."[18]

Fourth, decorative features can often be derived from indigenous plants (as the corn and tobacco cap-

---

[15] Many of the basic tenets of the "picturesque" were spelled out in Sir Uvedale Price's *Essay on the Picturesque* (1794); it has been fully studied by Christopher Hussey in *The Picturesque* (London: G. P. Putnam's Sons, 1927). As an underlying path of development in 19th century architecture, see Carroll L. V. Meeks, "Picturesque Eclecticism," *Art Bulletin*, XXII, 3 (September 1950), pp. 226–235. He discusses five basic aspects: Roughness (natural materials, rough textures, etc.); irregularity (variation and asymmetry in forms); variety (especially of the silhouette, implicit in the above); and intricacy (forms and relationships complex and lavishly conceived). Many of these, of course, appear in the Smithsonian building.

The greater informality, interest in natural materials, more convenient plans, and so on, were early popularized by J. C. Loudon in his *Encyclopaedia of Cottage, Farm and Villa Architecture*

(1833), and in America spread widely by A. J. Downing in his *A Treatise on the Theory and Practice of Landscape Gardening* (1841) which had a chapter, number XIX, on "Rural Architecture." See also the same author's *Cottage Residences* (1842).

One of the most important theoretical works in this new emphasis on the use of natural materials, honestly expressed structure ("truth" in construction), returning to nature for decorative forms, an emphasis on bold and irregular silhouettes, adaptation for current use of grand (medieval) styles of the past, etc., was John Ruskin's *Seven Lamps of Architecture* (1849). For an excellent study of many of these issues, see James Early, *Romanticism and American Architecture* (New York: A. S. Barnes & Co., 1965).

It is obvious, of course, that the Greek Revival style in architecture was far from unadaptable. The freedom with which porticos and peristyles could be successfully combined to meet various needs shows this. We have also seen how the structural logic of construction, vaulting and fireproofing, is exposed and apparent in a number of Greek Revival buildings, such as the Treasury Department and the Patent Office. But while these are factors which are taken further and developed in the 1840's by the picturesque movement, others, such as a more animated silhouette, greater irregularity of plan, less formalized detailing, greater choice of building materials, etc.—these are essentially new developments.

[16] Owen, p. 6.

[17] This desire to create a "style of the times" or a particularly Nineteenth century style was to plague advanced architectural thinkers throughout the century. Even Owen noted (pp. 1–2) that *iron*, as a new material, could well transform modern architecture. In a way, the period of Romantic experimentation of the Nineteenth century, especially 1840–80, was necessary to establish the viability of using (traditional) materials honestly and undisguisedly, and allowing the form of buildings to derive from their plan and function, not from an exterior conceit (like a rectangular temple). Until this was assimilated, no amount of urging, as in the writings of Viollet-le-Duc (1854ff.) and Henry Van Brunt (1870's), would prompt the use of iron for architecture in a nonhistorical manner. While many realized that Joseph Paxton's London Crystal Palace (1851) of iron and glass presaged a new era of building, it took half a century for people accustomed to historically based styles to be able to accept it as architecture purely derived from structure, materials, and need. While "truth" in construction and use of materials was at first advocated on ethical and philosophical (and for Ruskin, religious) grounds, it finally became accepted on functional and aesthetic grounds as well. Thus, quite apart from the actual architecture built, the evolution of architectural thought—bodied forth especially by A. J. Downing in a historical vocabulary of forms—is a Nineteenth century contribution of immense importance.

[18] Owen, pp. 8–9.

itals by Latrobe in the Capitol); the Smithsonian would also have such native decorations.

Owen emphasized, of course, many of the basic romantic tenets, such as the necessity of "truth" in architecture (as in morality): "every important feature in a true architecture should have, as it were, selfproclaimed reasons for being what it is." [19] Although ornamentation is a natural proclivity, it should be based on actual use (as a drip mold over a window) and not be "misused" decoratively as in so many Greek Revival buildings.

Throughout the study, Owen uses Girard College in Philadelphia, by Thomas U. Walter, as the example of poor architecture because of the great waste of money in the costly peristyle, the inefficient system of containing the vault thrusts by iron bands, the inflexibility of plan, poor lighting on the first floor, and so on. With Owen's interest in freer organization, he finds "Arch Architecture" the most adaptable, and especially the Twelfth century Lombard or Norman style. Its buttresses economically conteract vault thrusts; its plainness of detail, and flexibility of plan were ideal. While adapting a Greek temple for modern use is almost impossible, and very costly,[20] the use of the Lombard style for the Smithsonian (which, as we have seen, already had specific rooms and functions designated), was a perfect solution. Not only was the style "bold and varied and lofty and aspiring," [21] but also very adaptable. Towers were necessary for chimneys, forge and furnace flues, two freight elevators, main stairways that would not cut into large exhibition spaces, and for private stairways. Treating them as towers not only indicated their separateness of function, but also avoided occupying prime space. The great variety of rooms for exhibits, lectures, research, and study, required a complex arrangement and special lighting that could be ill fitted into a fixed exterior form. The Norman style allowed a central block with wings, also expressing the various different room uses. The buttressing expressed the arching inside, and also enabled the general wall thickness to be economically reduced. With such a plan, and his feeling that in all "true architecture" the "external form should be the faithful interpreter of internal purpose," [22] it is clear that

FIGURE 136. Norman design for the Smithsonian, from the southeast. (From Owen, *Hints on Public Architecture,* facing p. 108.)

a rectangular temple-type buliding like Girard College would be inadequate.

There are, however, three other important reasons for Owen's choice of the Lombard style.

The style was philosophically appropriate. "Its entire expression is less ostentatious, and, if political character may be ascribed to Architecture, more republican." [23] There was to be no elaborate tracery or carving.

The style also allowed more personal expressiveness (which, as we have seen, was highly prized by Congressmen in the early Nineteenth century). Thus, while Owen advocated this style, he hoped that at the same time there would be "no servile reproduction of any one example," but rather "that American genius should labor in that prolific field, and exercise a discretion neither tame-spirited nor presumptuous, in selecting and rejecting; in combining old forms and features, and originating new."[24]

[19] Ibid., p. 12. Similar ideas of the need for the form of objects to derive from their function are expressed throughout the writings of the Nineteenth century American sculptor and critic Horatio Greenough.

[20] Ibid., see Ch. IV.

[21] Ibid., p. 30.

[22] Ibid., p. 48.

[23] Ibid., p. 75.

[24] Ibid., p. 77. Though he advocated this Norman style as possibly the best adapted to be a "National style," if treated creatively, it did not find many followers. But it is interesting to note that 25 years later, H. H. Richardson *would* inaugurate a style, based on somewhat similar Romanesque forms, that in its general acceptance, high level of success even by modest builders, and very wide distribution for a quarter of a century, would indeed approach the nature of a national style.

Finally, the Lombard or Norman style was economical. Owen studied the cost per cubic foot for a number of buildings and found that the Girard College Greek temple cost 83½ cents, the Treasury Building in Washington, 42½ cents, but the Smithsonian building only 17½ cents per cubic foot, showing the value of the more flexible style, the use of buttresses, and the elimination of expensive fluted columns, sculptured capitals, and carved entablatures.[25] This was also probably the reason for rejecting Renwick's more elaborate (and expensive) Gothic design though it fitted the same ground plan.[26]

This summary of the main arguments by Owen, with the assistance of Renwick, shows clearly why the style—which today, ironically, many consider to be very elaborate—was chosen.

Bids were solicited in early 1847, and James Dixon & Co. was awarded the contract on March 8, 1847.[27] Robert Mills had been appointed Superintendent of the work on February 17,[28] and he and the Building Committee spent most of March studying the durability and accessibility of local building stone. One distinct advantage of the Norman style was that any good local freestone could be used—it did not have to be costly white marble—and after exhaustive scientific tests on dozens of samples and numerous trips to local quarries, a lilac-gray sandstone, which hardened and turned a bit pinkish on exposure, was selected. It is not certain when the change to the darker red Seneca sandstone (which had also been tested) was made, but it was well after the foundations of the building had been started.[29]

The building location on the Mall had been selected by March 20, 1847; the cornerstone was laid May 1, and by April 1849, the east wing was also completed.[30] Work progressed slowly in 1850 since it was decided to fireproof parts of the central portion; but by 1852 all the exterior work was completed, with only the interior of the central block unfinished. The "valuable services" of James Renwick were discontinued, and the interior work was taken over by Capt. Barton S. Alexander, U.S. Corps of Engineers. His work began in June 1853, and was at last completed in the spring of 1855. It took a few more years to provide all the necessary furnishings and equipment.[31] Some of the delay was due to changes made inside at the behest of Dr. Joseph Henry, the first Secretary, who had left Princeton to join the Institution in December 1846, and who had particularly strong ideas about the function of the Institution. He specifically felt that it should sponsor important original research, mainly in the sciences, and publish the results in a scholarly manner, rather than duplicate existing educational efforts or become a mere popularizer of knowledge. The incorporation of a library, a museum, and popular publications he gradually managed to eliminate in large part so that the small annual interest could be spent most effectively.[32] Many of the rooms were now used for lodging visiting scholars and for more laboratory space.

25 Ibid., p. 98. Others, with special problems of foundations, etc., cost even more than Girard College. It should be pointed out, however, that Walter was required to abandon his own original design, and to build a lavish Corinthian temple, by the Hellenophile trustee Nicholas Biddle.

In all fairness to Walter it should be noted that his building, finished in 1843, was indeed highly successful in many ways. Its gigantic size and scale, exquisitely carved details, and fine white marble made it one of the most impressive Greek Revival structures in America. The plan, while regular, was skillful; the lighting of the third floor (by skylights) very successful; and, contrary to popular belief, the peristyles were ample enough to let in adequate light and still provide some protection from the weather.

26 Illustrated facing p. 99.

27 S. Misc. Doc. 23, 30th Cong., 1st sess., Ser. 511 1, p. 56. The contract (pp. 58–62) and the building specifications (pp. 62–74) by Renwick are of considerable interest, providing a minute description of the entire building.

28 In H. M. Pierce Gallagher, *Robert Mills* (New York: Columbia University Press, 1935), pp. 189–198, is an undated letter Mills sent to Owen during an early stage of the Smithsonian development. It appears from this that Mills had originally also designed a Norman building ("I have introduced buttresses . . .") as Owen preferred. His discussion of this style and period, based on wide reading, shows how fully he could become acquainted with the style from published sources. Two books known to have been in his library were John Carter, *The Ancient Architecture of England, including the Orders during the British, Roman, Saxon and Norman Eras* (London, 1795–1807), and John Britton, *The Architectural Antiquities of Great Britain* (London, 1807–26) (Gallagher, p. 24). The letter may date from September 1846, although in it he also mentions that he had previously prepared plans in 1840 and 1841 "at Mr. Poinsett's request." (p. 93). The idea of wings seems to have been Dr. David Owen's. Thus, it was not as curious as might first appear that Mills, most noted for his superb classical buildings, should be the Superintendent Architect of a Norman edifice.

29 S. Misc. Doc. 23, 30th Cong., 1st sess., Ser. 511 1 gives full details on their investigations and tests up to 1848. The gray stone was still being quarried in October 1847, and was probably used for foundation work. There had been some concern that the veins were not extensive enough; perhaps this proved to be the case. The most significant parts of the experiments are reproduced in the appendix of *Hints*, pp. 113–119.

30 Goode, p. 256.

31 Ibid., p. 259.

32 Henry was interested in putting the Institution on a truly professional course. His plans for the Smithsonian are summarized

Renwick's Smithsonian building, as completed in 1855, was a unique building for the Capital (fig. 137). It was, in fact, "the first great public building in the United States of full picturesque irregularity and asymmetry." [33] When seen from an angle, as from the southeast or northwest (as in the published lithographs), the asymmetry of its eight major towers and many chimneys, its numerous recesses and projections, all appear in their most striking manner and created the varied, animated silhouette desired. As Renwick and Owen planned, the vertical accents are maintained and repeated throughout, not only by these towers but also by the many tall windows, unbroken vertical moldings and piers, the many buttresses, and the slender proportions of the towers themselves. Furthermore, a very strong sense of plasticity—part of the romantic and picturesque irregularity—is achieved as well, obviously intended from Renwick's renderings. Each main facade has a pro-

jecting central feature, with the north entrance having an additional porte-cochère. The entrance doorways, because of their deep splays, emphasize the thickness of the stonework at these points. The many buttresses, of course, assist this feel of multiple planes and volumes of mass as do the thick moldings, the machicolation, and the battlements. And two of the most effective plastic devices, projecting bays, are employed, at the north of the west wing (in the form of an apse) and above the south entrance (as a corbelled oriole). The cloisters which link the three major masses (the wings and the central block) also act as a foil, their openness and lightness contrasting with the more massive and solid main sections. Thus, in details as well as treatment of masses and wall surfaces, this rugged plasticity is clearly shown, helped, of course, by the shadow which is caught by the many breaks and recesses. This treatment fulfilled admirably many of the new advanced ideas of what architecture should be, and it is astonishing to think that the structure was said to contain a total of 90 rooms, eight of which were of considerable size.

Somewhat surprisingly, this rich exterior effect is achieved with very little carved detail. There are no

in Coulson, pp. 177–178. See also Wilcomb E. Washburn, "Joseph Henry's Conception of the Purpose of the Smithsonian Institution," in Whitfield J. Bell et al., *A Cabinet of Curiosities* (Charlottesville: The University Press of Virginia, 1967), pp. 106–166.

[33] Early, p. 85.

FIGURE 137. Smithsonian Institution, ca. 1864, from the northwest.

gargoyles, buttress pinacles, elaborate tracery, open-work spires, crockets, iron cresting, bas reliefs, rows of jamb statues, or other such features. Rather, as Owen insisted, Renwick has achieved an effect of richness with very limited details, and these being principally architectural features of considerable simplicity. As stated, it was the general massing that was most important.

But when we look at the building in elevation, we find, somewhat to our surprise, that much of the animated silhouette and the apparent asymmetry disappears (fig. 138). In fact, we find that the building is remarkably symmetrical. The main rectangular block has a central feature of two towers, like the facade of some cathedral. Though the east tower is shorter, its tall pointed roof helps give the facade an asymmetrical balance. The east tower is somewhat more massive above the eaves, while the west one becomes more slender. The five windows of the main block on each side of this feature are also symmetrically placed. Each corner of this central portion of the building has a tower, and while each is somewhat different in size and outline, all are clearly of a secondary size. The wings to the north and south, though one is treated as a chapel (west) and the other as a miniature fortress (east), are both the same height, and each has one projecting element higher than its general roofline.[34] When we examine

the plan (fig. 139) this symmetry appears even more striking; from the plan one would never imagine it to be the markedly picturesque edifice depicted in the published lithographs.

This symmetry, of course, is necessary; were the building completely and actually very asymmetrical, the effect would be chaotic and distressing. Finding one's way when inside would be impossible; the cost would also surely have been far greater. By combining the picturesque silhouette, especially seen upon approaching from various angles, with an actual overall regularity and order, Renwick achieved the best of two seemingly exclusive systems.

We have seen above many of the reasons which Owen and Renwick felt dictated such a building. But certain other factors should be kept in mind why such a building was actually constructed.

First, the Smithsonian Institution building, prominently located in the center of the Capital, and housing an organization dedicated to the "increase and diffusion of knowledge," was to be a model for a new, inexpensive, appropriate, and yet still impressive style of architecture for the United States. It would hopefully be adopted throughout the country. The style was supposed to break with the classical styles of the past, which Owen and presumably Renwick felt were extravagent, expensive, and no longer expressive of the American Republic.[35] The Greek Revival was by that date out of favor in many places. In the 1840's, A. J. Downing thought very little of imitative Greek temples for houses and his attitude was widely spread through his publications. By the 1850's the Greek Revival style was largely outmoded in advanced centers.[36] Thus, besides being an embodiment of the latest advanced architectural thought, the Smithsonian building was the latest style as well. Renwick may have been particularly willing to erect this Norman (not Gothic) essay since his Gothic Grace Church in New York (1843–46) had been criticized at the time for a

---

[34] The east wing and the connecting links, as noted below, have been rebuilt, changing somewhat the original balance. The original roof on the east wing was much lower.

[35] Thus, when the Smithsonian building is called "a romantic red brick [sic] building" of unlikely design for such a prominent spot (John W. Reps, *Monumental Washington* [Princeton: Princeton University Press, 1967] p. 42), the whole point of it needing to be highly visible as an educational and didactic structure is missed.

[36] See Ellen W. Kramer, "Contemporary Descriptions of New York City and its Public Architecture ca. 1850," *Journal of the Society of Architectural Historians*, XXVII, 4 (December 1968), p. 279. The author finds that by the early 1850's "Classical Revival pretentions to architectural beauty were no longer valid," and quotes a critical description of Greek Revival banks in *Putnam's*, February 1853, p. 132.

FIGURE 138. Smithsonian Institution, north facade.

number of reasons—the overly rich and showy details, the "untruthful" spire of wood (rather than stone like the body of the church), the too thin interior columns, and so on.[37] And since, in each period of viable architecture the architect feels that the latest advanced style is better, for any number of reasons, than what went before, it would have been surprising indeed if an enlightened and enthusiastic patron and a successful and erudite architect had attempted to build in a style no longer considered viable. Thus the building was to be itself didactic—of the best architectural style, of economical building, and truthful construction and decoration.

Second, the imposing structure was to give a special architectural lustre and importance to the fledgling Institution. Owen wanted to "dignify and make conspicuous" the work of the organization, and W. W. Seaton, mayor of Washington and one of the Regents, wanted another important building to ornament his city and be an attraction, perhaps, to other learned societies.[38] Although Joseph Henry thought that money spent on "a pile of bricks and mortar" rather than research and publication was essentially wasted, the building did indeed give the Institution a distinct image.[39] As George Grown Goode (Assistant Secretary of the Smithsonian) wrote in 1896, "scarcely any one can doubt that Doctor Owen was right and that the usefulness of the Smithsonian Institution has been materially aided by the fact that its building has for fifty years been one of the chief architectural ornaments of the national capital."[40]

With these reasons for its very existence so largely didactic, we may ask why Renwick's Smithsonian building gave rise to no imitators in Washington. As so often the case, the primary reason was probably that there was little occasion for one. Other institutions that were founded—orphanages, schools, hospitals, etc.—did not have the immense sum of over $200,000 to spend on a building and had to content

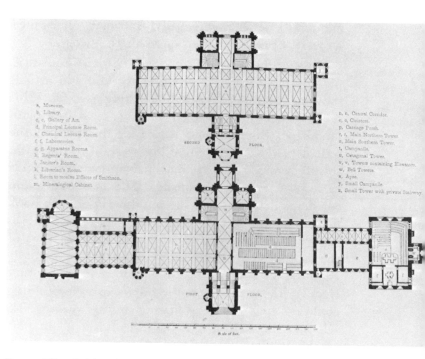

FIGURE 139. Smithsonian Institution floor plans. (From Owen, *Hints on Public Architecture,* facing p. 105.)

themselves with even more utilitarian forms. Washington in general was still struggling financially, and there was neither the occasion nor the money. The next major government building was not to be built for almost 20 years.

Another reason is that while Owen wanted to make a sharp break with the expense, excess, and lavishness of a Girard College, the Greek Revival buildings then being constructed in the Capital (such as the Treasury Department or the Patent Office) were actually far less objectionable. They had considerable internal flexibility, no excessively rich detailing, and little waste space. Since it was also logical and expedient to continue these buildings in the style in which they were started, there was no reason for the government to change. Therefore, the Norman style found no immediate use in government buildings either.

A third reason why this style was not adopted is that it may have been too different from what people were used to. The Greek Revival in Washington, after all, had the background of the Capitol and the President's House, and before that the Georgian style itself which was full of classical bits and pieces —pediments, pilasters, entablatures, and cornices. To local people, who we have seen were essentially conservative in their architectural thinking, the new style may have seemed impressive, but not familiar

[37] Ibid., pp. 275–276.

[38] Goode, p. 250.

[39] Joseph Henry wanted a plain building (for one-tenth the cost) that would be inexpensive to maintain, so that more money could be spent on research and publishing. He frequently deplored the large "Norman castle." His biographer asserts that "had he been left to his own devices he would probably have rented a second floor of some premises on a quiet street" for himself and his staff (Coulson, p. 188). See also Washburn, "Influence," pp. 105–106. But as Coulson concludes, "In his opposition to the building, Henry may have been in the wrong. He was either insensitive to or ignored the psychological influence which a large impressive building exercises upon the minds of men." p. 188.

[40] Goode, p. 251.

enough to be adopted readily. And many of its merits were, of course, based on aesthetic theory.

Fourth, the style of the Smithsonian—romantic, picturesque, part of a new architectural and artistic movement—was in the wrong setting (see fig. 137). A classical building can, if need be, exist in a plain landscape. But the very nature of this picturesque style demanded a congenial landscape of rolling hills, thickly wooded groves, diagonal approaches, and a variety of trees and plantings. The lithographs and woodcuts that illustrate the building in Owen's book make this quite clear (fig. 140). The building is framed by trees set about the grounds; one view, of the southern gateway,[41] shows the structure virtually engulfed in a dense forest of tall pines and other trees. Without this romantic framework the building could not help but be a bit anomalous. Downing also felt that the setting of a building was a major part of the architectural effect, and that the style of a proposed home, for example, should be adapted to the nature of the surrounding landscape. The Re-

---

[41] Owen, p. 109; see also plates facing pp. 19, 43, and 75. See also fig. 155.

FIGURE 140. View of proposed Smithsonian Building. (From Owen, *Hints on Public Architecture,* facing p. 75.)

gents speedily set about to remedy this defect, as we shall see below, but it obviously takes decades even so for trees to reach proper size.

A fifth reason, as suggested above, may be that while the building was indeed far cheaper than an elaborate Greek temple or a Gothic pile, it was still far more expensive than plain brick, the material favored locally. In a building tradition less accustomed to working in stone, brick would remain the logical solution even for large buildings.

Sixth, just as the association of the Greek Revival with public buildings seems to have limited its local use for domestic structures, so the Smithsonian building may have appeared to be a style appropriate only for learned institutions, and not adaptable to houses. Of course, we know that Gothic had been used successfully by Alexander Jackson Davis for dwellings in the 1830's[42] when it was also gaining favor for churches, but in Washington no such precedent existed for domestic use of the new Norman style. With the sense of associationalism strong, this vigorous Norman building may have sealed off its use for noneducational buildings.

A seventh possible reason is, as we saw with the Greek Revival, that this was not a structure amenable to adaptation by builders. Its details, elements that could be borrowed and reapplied, were very limited. Its essence was massing, silhouette, and plasticity, all aspects that needed an architect and an overall conceptualization of building. It could not, therefore, spawn convincing imitations, especially when the Smithsonian stood as a physical reproach to lesser works. Were the style imported by pattern books, fanciful moldings and pinacles might have been adapted by an ingenious builder. But compared to the real thing, constructed in their midst, the efforts now would be only ludicrous.

Finally, of considerable importance to the value of the building was its internal arrangements—the careful study of lighting, access, public and private circulation, fireproofing in parts of the building, and so on. Most of these features were not visible in the exterior form and thus could not be as readily influential.

These seem to be some of the reasons why this very prominent building, praised at the time and for many years after, was not influential. Its mere presence, of course, would be no guarantee of this if

---

[42] Edna Donnell, "A. J. Davis and the Gothic Revival," *Metropolitan Museum Studies,* V (1934–36), pp. 183–233.

other factors—economic, social, artistic—were not amenable also.

It might be pointed out that Renwick's Smithsonian building as it stands today is not exactly as it was built. On January 4, 1865, a disastrous fire [43] destroyed the roof and all the second floor of the main block, the interior of the two large north towers, and the south tower. The wings were not damaged. Under a new Building Committee, Adolph Cluss (a prolific local architect), was put in charge of rebuilding the damage. It was also found upon inspection that other parts of the structure were defective, so that some additional reconstruction was necessary. This work was completed by the summer of 1867. [44] In 1884, the east wing was reconstructed, changing it from the Secretary's residence to executive offices. This necessitated raising the roofline considerably and inserting new floors. At the same time, the east

[43] Interestingly enough, it seems to have been caused by an accident not unlike that which destroyed H. H. Richardson's Chamber of Commerce Building in Cincinnati. Workers in the Smithsonian attached a stove to a ventilating duct, thinking it was a chimney flue, and the attic was set on fire.

[44] Goode, p. 261. This work cost an additional $150,000.

connecting link was remodeled and raised to three stories. Thus, the original balance was somewhat changed. The pointed roof of the east facade tower, destroyed in the fire of 1865, was at last restored in April 1970.

The Smithsonian Institution building was probably Renwick's most important structure in the Capital; but it was his other buildings which had some influence on Washington's architecture. Three other projects by him can be considered: the W. W. Corcoran mansion which he remodeled, Oak Hill Cemetery chapel, and the Corcoran Art Gallery.

William Wilson Corcoran was the most famous and generous of the Washington benefactors. Born in Georgetown, his early wholesale auction and commission business had failed in 1823; however, after forming the banking company of Corcoran and Riggs in 1840, he prospered, and by 1847 was able to liquidate all his earlier debts, with interest. Especially after very successful government bond sales in 1848, he became one of the wealthiest and most influential men in the Capital.

Corcoran's house at 1611 H Street, N.W., (fig. 141),

FIGURE 141. Corcoran Mansion, 1611 H Street, N.W., (demolished 1922).

facing Lafayette Square, had originally been erected in 1819 by Thomas Swan, U.S. District Attorney for the District of Columbia.[45] At this time it was probably a three story, three bay gabled house similar to many others built in Washington. It was owned by Daniel Webster from about 1841 to 1843, and was then bought by Corcoran, who embellished the grounds and had it enlarged and redecorated by James Renwick. Corcoran, who was always interested in local improvements, would have followed the progress at the Smithsonian closely, and had possibly met Renwick there in 1846 or 1847. Since Renwick was also quite at home among the wealthy class of New York and had a wide acquaintance,[46] he may also have been recommended by some of Corcoran's New York colleagues.[47]

Renwick added the west wing (a parlor and picture gallery) in 1849, and the east wing (a dining room and library) in 1850. The extensive remodeling also included the set-back fourth floor (apparently servants rooms) and the overall trim of window frames, quoins, cornices, and balustrades. The house was also extended to the north.[48]

Obviously, with an older house as the basis of his work, Renwick was not able to do more than change and enrich the detailing when he added the wings. Thus the central block (and wings) still have the traditional flat brick walls, with the richer ornamental detailing applied to them. Certain features, such

as the carved brownstone floral rinceaux over the fourth floor windows (fig. 142), are very close in effect to elements he would use in the segmental pediments on the Corcoran Art Gallery 10 years later (fig. 143). But in general, there is little new about the design of the house. A somewhat Italian flavor is given by the general symmetry, flat roofs, classical window enframements, double-arched fourth floor windows, and some of the detailing; but the departure from local practice is not radical. The house does not, for example, have any of the rich plasticity or irregularity of the Smithsonian; the bay windows, of a different material, appear as separate units added on to the flat brick walls, rather than a projecting mass of the main fabric. Thus, while the mansion was made far more richly ornamented, it did not influence others to adopt a new style.

The second building that Renwick designed for Mr. Corcoran was the chapel for Oak Hill Cemetery, in Georgetown. This cemetery, laid out by one George de la Roche [49] on land acquired by Corcoran in 1848, was in imitation of the new garden cemeter-

[45] John Clagett Proctor, "Lafayette Square Historic," *Sunday Star* (Washington), Nov. 31, 1937, gives the date as "about 1825," but Mr. Donald McClelland, Coordinator of Special Projects, Renwick Gallery, Smithsonian Institution, has data that indicates that it was built in 1819.

[46] At his death he was a member of the Century Club, the Union Club, the New York Yacht Club, and the Larchmont Yacht Club. "James Renwick," (obituary), *New York Tribune*, June 25, 1895, p. 9.

[47] Original material on Renwick is very scarce. In W. W. Corcoran's *A Grandfather's Legacy* (Washington: Henry Polkinhorn, printer, 1879), in which he publishes over 500 pages of letters, there is none from (or to) Renwick, either regarding his house, Oak Hill Cemetery chapel, or the Corcoran Art Gallery. Corcoran's unpublished papers and letters are particularly unhelpful. Mr. Donald McClelland, at present working on a monograph on the Corcoran Art Gallery (now the Renwick Gallery of the Smithsonian Institution), has found only a few letters between Renwick and Corcoran, and these deal with purely mundane matters, such as the delivery of materials. Numerous contemporary photographs from the Corcoran collection, however, often with annotations, give dates of when the wings of the house were completed, and the notation that James Renwick was indeed the architect. I am much indebted to Mr. McClelland for this information.

[48] Photographs showing the rear of the house and portions of the yard are in the files of the Washingtoniana Collection, D.C. Public Library. The house was demolished in May 1922.

[49] "Oak Hill Cemetery has been laid out with great taste by the engineer, Mr. de la Roche. The surface is by nature varied by hills and valleys, around and through which there are formed fine graveled serpentine and circular walks." From "Communications. Oak Hill Cemetery," *National Intelligencer* (Washington), Dec. 23, 1851, p. 3. This one column notice of the new cemetery (signed "W.") also mentions "lakes," though this must be utter fancy; ponds may originally have been contemplated.

FIGURE 142. Detail, Corcoran Mansion.

FIGURE 143. Detail, west facade pavilion, Corcoran Art Gallery.

FIGURE 144. Oak Hill Cemetery and chapel, Georgetown.

ies then becoming extremely popular, following the examples of Mt. Auburn in Cambridge, Mass. (1831),[50] Laurel Hill in Philadelphia (1836), and Greenwood in Brooklyn (1838), the most famous prototypes. The land for the cemetery was conveyed gratis to the Oak Hill Cemetery Co. (chartered May 3, 1848) by Corcoran in May 1849. The wooded grounds were laid out in terraces and curving walks that led down to Rock Creek. The original forest, which contained many fine old oaks, was embellished further with flowering trees; "rustic iron benches" were placed in shaded areas. These grounds (fig. 144), a favorite local resort for pleasant afternoon excursions, were highly praised at the time for their romantic beauty and superb setting.[51]

Renwick designed a small chapel for this picturesque spot (figs. 145–146); the cornerstone is dated 1850, so the designs were obviously prepared while he was remodeling Corcoran's house. The diminutive structure, measuring only 27 by 45 feet (including buttresses), is made of grayish Potomac gneiss in random laid courses, with red Seneca sandstone trim and tracery. Five buttresses project on each side and two on the front and back.[52] The excellent proportions, clear sense of volume, and absence of distracting minute detail allow the tiny building to still have considerable dignity. As we can see, many of the latest ideas of romantic architecture are called into play.

George F. de la Roche (1791–1861) was a civil engineer who also practiced architecture on occasion; his most well known work was the old U.S. Naval Observatory. He became connected with Oak Hill Cemetery when asked by Cororan to survey and lay out the grounds. He is also credited with the Italianate gatehouse (called "Norman" in the above article), now enlarged and remodeled somewhat though maintaining the original effect. See HABS No. DC-249, p. 7, published in [Daniel D. Reiff and Ellen J. Schwartz], *Georgetown Architecture* (Washington: Commission of Fine Arts and the Historic American Buildings Survey, 1970), pp. 69–84.

See also the extensive, florid account of the cemetery, its plantings and sculptural monuments, in M. E. P. Bouligny, *A Tribute to W. W. Corcoran* (Philadelphia: Porter & Coates, 1874), pp. 11–13.

[50] Mt. Auburn Cemetery, founded by a group of local businessmen, is almost entirely situated in Watertown, Mass.; however a corner of it is in Cambridge, and this is the customary designation.

[51] See also contemporary newspaper descriptions in John Clagett Proctor, *Washington and Environs* (Washington, 1949), pp.

538–543, and the article "Local Matters. Modern Building," *Georgetown Advocate*, Dec. 7, 1852, p. 3. See note 135 below.

[52] The *National Intelligencer* article of 1851 mentioned above (note 49) only refers in passing to the "neat little Gothic chapel of red sandstone [sic]."

The chapel is described and discussed in detail in HABS No. DC-172, published in *Georgetown Architecture*, pp. 82–96. The Potomac gneiss of which it is mainly constructed is a dark gray fine grained stone with considerable mica content. Some of the blocks have a green or yellow cast, giving the ashlar a subtlely rich effect.

FIGURE 145. Oak Hill Cemetery chapel, by James Renwick, 1850.

FIGURE 146. Oak Hill Cemetery chapel.

The materials are natural and local; walling is left in a rather rough "natural" texture; there is a careful juxtaposition of natural colors (the red sandstone trim, the rich gray ashlar, the purple-gray slate) for harmonious effect; and there is an "honest" sense of structure, the exterior buttresses supporting the five roof trusses within. At the entrance the detailing is based on plant forms, appropriate especially for a chapel placed in a luxuriant, rural setting.

The stonework may possibly hark back to the Eighteenth century vernacular tradition of small stone houses that we have examined previously. It is, at any rate, the sort of parallel that would be eminently apropriate to the romantic mind. The same sense of rightness of materials and their honest treatment is found in both. But the actual design is based on the simple rural English chapels of the thirteenth and fourteenth centuries (see fig. 147) which Augustus Welby Pugin, the great English advocate of a return to a more "Christian" form of architecture for churches, proposed among other more elaborate examples.[53]

Recently constructed chapels in England modeled on these ancient examples were published approvingly by Pugin as well (fig. 148). These simple country churches were, of course, quite appropriate models for a rural cemetery chapel, which would not want to imitate types found commonly within cities. We unfortunately know nothing else about the genesis of this building, since just as with the other work for Corcoran, nothing of value is recorded in letters or papers. And since the cemetery recordkeeping, such

[53] Phoebe Stanton, in her *The Gothic Revival and American Church Architecture* (Baltimore: Johns Hopkins Press, 1968) notes (pp. 65–68) that Renwick's knowledge of Augustus Welby Pugin's writings, such as his *Contrasts, or a Parallel between Noble Edifices of the Middle Ages, and Corresponding Buildings of the Present Day* (1836; second edition, enlarged, 1841) or his *The True Principles of Pointed or Christian Architecture* (1841) "can be asserted because of his close transcription of a typical Pugin formula in his Oak Hill Cemetery Chapel." In view of Renwick's wide reading, this is probably true. A chapel of similar proportions, but without a bellcote, is prominently situated on the bridge in Pugin's plate "Catholic Town in 1440" from his *Contrasts*, p. 105 (1841 ed.) Other similar examples are found in his *Apology for the Revival of Christian Architecture* (1843) in which the frontispiece shows three ancient chapels of approved design (Jesus Chapel, Pomfret; North Gate, St. Marie's, Oscott; and St. Austin's, Kenilworth). Approved new designs of chapels based on these ancient models are found in *The Present State of Ecclesiastical Architecture in England* (1843), plate IX, and plate V (2nd essay).

For examples of other American chapels which are also in this spirit, see Stanton, fig. III-7 (St. James the Less, Philadelphia, 1846–49), and especially fig. VI-14 (Church of the Ascension, Westminster, Maryland, ca. 1845, by Robert Cary Long, Jr.).

as it was, did not begin until October 1851 (when the sale of lots began), well after the chapel was completed, there is nothing in the cemetery records.[54]

This chapel did have at least one obvious local imitation, Grace Protestant Episcopal Church (1866–67) located on South Street near Wisconsin Avenue (fig. 149), just below the Chesapeake and Ohio Canal.[55] Built as a mission church for the canal and waterfront area, this small structure is close to Renwick's chapel in general outlines and style, in its use of prominent buttresses and a bellcote (here with a bell), and with a similar handsome use of Potomac gneiss. Both also have an open, rather plain, interior.[56] It is not, however, quite as successful as Renwick's chapel. Nearly twice as large as the Oak Hill chapel,[57] the exterior lacks the sense of bold unity and simplicity of Renwick's building. The great number of facade openings (three doors and three windows), arranged somewhat casually, are of different sizes and shapes (figs. 150–151). The flanks are also less successfully handled, with two levels of windows, the lower ones almost roundheaded, those above too narrow and small in comparison for good effect (figs. 152–153). While it seems probable that Oak Hill was the inspiration, the anonymous architect was simply not as skillful in giving a sense of unity to a small, yet hopefully dignified, structure of this nature.[58]

Before leaving our consideration of Renwick's work at Oak Hill, it should be pointed out that the gates, heretofore unattributed, were also probably designed by him (fig. 154). Both the main carriage and pedestrian gate, and the carriage gate further to the

FIGURE 147. Detail, frontispiece of A. W. Pugin's *An Apology for the Revival of Christian Architecture in England* (1843).

FIGURE 148. The Hospital of St. John, Alton, Staffordshire; detail of chapel. Plate V, second essay, from Pugin's *The Present State of Ecclesiastical Architecture in England* (1843).

[54] The cemetery records were kept with considerable nonchalance from 1851 to 1866, when irregularities of all sorts (including thousands of dollars in uncollected bills and a number of unclaimed bodies) prompted an investigation by the lot holders, at which time the lack of any real records became apparent. See *Report of the Investigating Committee* (Georgetown: Courier printer, 1869), Rare Book Room, Library of Congress.

[55] See HABS No. DC-101, published in [James Philip Noffsinger and Thomas R. Martinson], *Georgetown Commercial Architecture —Wisconsin Avenue* (Washington: Commission of Fine Arts and the Historic American Buildings Survey, 1967), pp. 32–46.

[56] It does not, however, have the red Seneca stone trim. The buttresses have caps of cast iron.

[57] This church measures 38 feet 8 inches by ca. 70 feet, versus 27 feet 2 inches by 45 feet 2 inches for Renwick's chapel.

[58] A second chapel, that at the estate of Green Hill near Washington (where L'Enfant died), is very close to the Renwick building in shape, except for the lack of side buttresses and the narrower windows. The date, however, has not yet come to light so any discussion of it would be only speculation. See *Sunday Star*, Apr. 5, 1936.

FIGURE 149. Grace Protestant Episcopal Church, South Street and and Wisconsin Avenue, N.W.

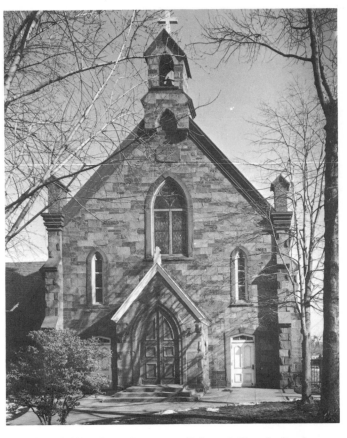

FIGURE 150. Grace Protestant Episcopal Church, facade.

east, have large gate pillars almost identical in design to those illustrated by Owen as designed for the Smithsonian grounds (fig. 155).[59] They also appear to be about the same size. It may even be that these very pillars were originally made for the Smithsonian grounds, first laid out by the Regents in 1849, but when Downing began work in early 1851, were considered redundant. We know that in December 1851, the gates and fences at Oak Hill were still in the process of being erected.[60] A number of other considerations, besides the closeness in design, suggest the possible reuse. The style of machicolation, paneling, and the capitals of the engaged columns are much closer to the Smithsonian Norman style than to the Gothic chapel or the Italianate gatehouse. Furthermore, the chapel is predominately gneiss, and gray in color, while the gatehouse is brick.[61] Red Seneca sandstone is used only for trim on the chapel and gatehouse, so that the pillars do not really match

[59] Owen, p. 109.

[60] *National Intelligencer,* Dec. 23, 1851.

[61] Originally, the gatehouse was a story lower and had a wood belfry. While it may have been stuccoed, the style would still have been more Italianate than Norman.

FIGURE 151. Oak Hill Cemetery chapel, facade.

FIGURE 152. Grace Protestant Episcopal Church, south side.

FIGURE 154. Oak Hill Cemetery gates, west entrance.

FIGURE 153. Oak Hill Cemetery chapel, south side.

FIGURE 155. Proposed gates for Smithsonian Institution, south entrance, published in Owen, *Hints on Public Architecture,* p. 109.

any of the other structures either in style or dominant material. Finally, the gate pillars and foundations are of red sandstone, while all the footings of the connected fencing are gray granite. Since the fence design (Egyptian papyrus or lotus) and manufacture (tubular, not squared) are also very different from the gates, it may well be that the two gateways were a convenient reuse of elements originally designed by Renwick for the Smithsonian.

Next to the Smithsonian building, Renwick's other most famous Washington building is the Cor-

coran Art Gallery (fig. 156).[62] Mr. Corcoran, a collector of painting and sculpture (especially contemporary American), retired from business in 1854 to devote his full time to personal affairs, philanthro-

---

[62] The building was later used for the U.S. Court of Claims and is sometimes called by this name. But when erected, it was usually called the "Corcoran Art Gallery" and is so distinguished from the new gallery, called "The Corcoran Gallery of Art," located at Seventeenth Street and New York Avenue, N.W. It was designed in 1897 by Ernest Flagg.

FIGURE 156. Corcoran Art Gallery. Photograph, 1880's.

pies, and particularly to his art collection. This soon outgrew the wing of his house in which it was kept and he decided to build a public gallery for it, with James Renwick the architect. Located on a somewhat restricted corner lot at Seventeenth Street and Pennsylvania Avenue, N.W., the building was begun in 1859. When the Civil War broke out in 1861 the work was stopped and it was seized by the government for the Quartermaster General's headquarters. By this time,[63] however, the exterior, except for the niches and statues and other minor embellishments, war largely complete. After being returned to Mr. Corcoran in 1869, the work was finished by 1871, and in 1874, with the organization of the gallery completed, it was opened to the public.

The gallery was designed in 1859 by Renwick,[64] with the assistance of R. T. Auchmuty, a relative working in his firm.[65] It was in the "Second Empire mode," ultimately based on the French Renaissance style. The general form of the gallery was that of a rectangle with four slightly projecting corner pavilions with straight-sided mansard roofs; the facade had a central pavilion topped with a curved mansard. The ground floor (for sculpture) was treated as a basement story, with heavy vermiculated quoins at the pavilion corners, and a wide belt course between it and the second floor. This second level (for paintings) was lighted from above, and so statue niches could be inserted around on the exterior, corresponding to the windows below. During the War

[63] A photograph taken during the Civil War shows the exterior complete except for sculptural details. This view is from a collection of photographs (Library of Congress, Prints and Photograhs Division, lot 5341) which seems to have been made in the fall and early winter of 1864, judging from dated placards, the Smithsonian before its fire, and so on.

[64] The elevation and a second floor ceiling plan (plasterwork) were published in the October 1859 issue of *The Architects' and Mechanics' Journal.*

[65] The development and decoration of the building will be dealt with fully in Mr. McClelland's forthcoming monograph on the building.

these niches were left empty (fig. 157), but between 1879 and 1884 they were filled as originally designed. The corner pavilions were emphasized by unfluted composite pilasters supporting segmental pediments; the central facade pavilion had full round fluted columns supporting a triangular pediment, and framing a large Palladian light, with a decorative tympanum above it. The metal roof cresting was augmented further shortly after 1884 by connecting links between the pavilion roofs.

"The exterior of the building is of fine [Baltimore] brick, ornamented with Belleville freestone. . . . A Mansard roof surmounts the building,

adding to its general stateliness." [66] The central pavilion pediment (fig. 159) was to contain a relief "representing the genius of painting, surrounded by figures of the sister arts;" [67] this was never inserted, however, and in its place a bronze relief portrait of Mr. Corcoran was installed sometime between 1881 and 1884. The artistic theme was emphasized, however, by niches which were to contain statues of noted artists, sculptors, and architects. These were gradually filled until all were occupied by 1885. [68] Flanking the central Palladian window are two other artistic emblems within wreaths, a palette and brushes to the left, and sculptors' tools to the right.

The other major decorative features consisted of floral swags above the second floor niches. roundels with the interlaced initials "WWC" in the pavilions, and floral rinceaux in the segmental pediments (fig. 160). When the relief of Corcoran was inserted, two small bronze sculpture groups were also added

[66] Bouligny, p. 40. The building measures 104 feet on Pennsylvania Avenue and 124 feet on 17th Street.

[67] Corcoran, *Legacy*, p. 535.

[68] These were carved in Carrara marble by a Mr. Moses Ezekiel, an American sculptor living in Rome. The facade had Phidias, Raphael, Michelangelo, and Dürer, representing sculpture, painting, architecture, and engraving. The west side had Titian, DaVinci, Rubens, and Rembrandt, "and it is the intention to add those of Murillo, Canova and [Thomas] Crawford." Joseph Moore, *Picturesque Washington* (Providence: J. A. & R. A. Reid, 1884), pp. 251–252. The statues were subsequently sold by the Public Buildings Commission when the building was purchased by the government in 1901. The building has since been carefully restored (though most of the niches have been turned into windows) and will open to the public as the Renwick Gallery in 1972.

FIGURE 157. Corcoran Art Gallery. Photograph ca. 1864.

FIGURE 158. Corcoran Art Gallery. Photograph ca. 1880.

FIGURE 159. Corcoran Art Gallery, elevation published in *The Architects' and Mechanics' Journal*, October 1859.

107

FIGURE 160. Detail, Corcoran Art Gallery, east pavilion.

FIGURE 161. Detail, Corcoran Art Gallery, central pavilion.

above the paired columns of the facade. It should be pointed out also that these columns (as well as the pilasters) have composite capitals made up of ears of corn above a ring of acanthus (fig. 161). The fluting, however, is standard.

This use of "American" and "natural" forms for at least some of the decoration is seen also inside, where some of the galleries were "enriched with panel ornaments and mouldings, representing American foliage." [69] The building was also lighted by 285 gas jets which could all be ignited at once,[70] presumably by electric spark starters. The building was built to be fireproof, the floors being constructed of iron girders and brick arches.

Local enthusiasm for the gallery and its

collection [71] was considerable, due to the generosity of Mr. Corcoran, the beauty of the building, and the excellence of his art collection. A contemporary newspaper also noted that the gallery was "the only one in the United States expressly designed and constructed as a great art gallery," [72] all others being in buildings converted from other purposes. It has obviously been carefully planned, for the illumination of the galleries by skylights and light wells was very successful, and the formal entrance and grand staircase leading up to the huge main picture gallery at the north of the building are still impressive spaces. Some of the newer architectural innovations were indeed used: iron and brick vaulting; considerable use of elaborate cast iron columns, capitals and balustrades; and the "American" capitals and details mentioned above. The exterior too, using brownstone and brick, was of local materials rather than being of more expensive marble.

But unlike the Smithsonian building, where Renwick adopted a past style very freely and with originality in order to fit it to a new and different use,

---

[69] Corcoran, *Legacy*, p. 534. The west gallery, first floor, however, has tall composite columns of an ornate Corinthian-Ionic form. They appear to be of cast iron.

[70] Bouligny, p. 41.

---

[71] The collection is described as of 1874 in some detail in Bouligny, pp. 45–81. It included, among other works, a copy of Hiram Powers' famous Greek Slave, placed in its own octagonal room (the walls of which were covered with red hangings to enhance the color of the marble). Corcoran also owned a superb collection of Thomas Coles.

[72] *Washington Daily Chronicle*, May 19, 1869, quoted in Corcoran, *Legacy*, p. 535.

here the style is much more conservative, based rather on the Pavillion de l'Horloge of the Louvre, designed in 1624 by Lemercier,[73] and the New Louvre of 1852–57, by Visconti and Lefuel.[74]

An interest in French architecture grew in this country especially after the 1844 and 1848 international expositions in Paris, when many visitors could see the Louvre and Tuileries, and bring home published lithographs of them.[75] The extensions of the Hotel de Ville (Godde and Lesueur, 1837–49) [76] were also continued in this style which harked back to the late French Renaissance. It was the impressive New Louvre, however, that helped spread the fame of this Second Empire style the most.

Compared with the Pavillion de l'Horloge (fig. 163), Renwick's facade has a number of similar elements, though is in no way a copy. The central section in both has a pedimented pavillion with a high arched mansard above. The flanking pavilions—adjacent in Lemercier's facade but separated by one slightly recessed bay in Renwick's design—both have segmental arch pediments and straight sided mansards. The detailing of statues in niches, sculptured cartouches, swag surrounds, and engaged columns and pilasters is similar, but treated more freely by

[73] R. T. McKenna, "James Renwick, Jr. and the Second Empire Style in the United States," *Magazine of Art*, XLIV, 3 (1951), p. 99, fig. 6. This important article is one of the few published studies on Renwick's architecture and deals with his use of the Second Empire style in the Corcoran Art Gallery, as well as the New York Charity Hospital (1858–61), the proposed Vassar College Buildings (1860) and also those actually built (1861), and later work.

[74] Henry-Russell Hitchcock, *Architecture: Nineteenth and Twentieth Centuries* (Baltimore: Penguin Books, 1963), plate 68. This book also discusses fully the origin and development of the Second Empire "mode;" see pp. 131–135 and 166–170 especially.

[75] McKenna, figs. 2–3.

[76] Hitchcock, p. 133 and plate 22A.

FIGURE 162. Facade, Corcoran Art Gallery, 1970.

Renwick, who also used vermiculated rustication not found in the Seventeenth century example.

It is probable, however, that it is the New Louvre (fig. 164) that Renwick took more as his model. The use of a central high arched mansard and corner pavilions connected by lower sections is here fully developed; a shortened and more abbreviated version is used by Renwick. Furthermore, the paired columns which support a small group of sculptures on an impost block is found prominently here in the central pavilion, as are the prominent heavy quoins, not found in the earlier facade of Lemercier.

Renwick's gallery, however, does not have the rich

FIGURE 163. Louvre, Paris, Pavillion de l'Horloge, 1624.

FIGURE 164. The New Louvre by Visconti and Lefuel (1852-57).

plasticity of the New Louvre. There, the masses of the corner pavilions, central pavilion, and connecting wings are clear and volumetric; in the Corcoran Gallery, the pavilions do not stand out boldly enough from the wall plane to make this apparent, so that actually the pavilion roofs almost seem perched on the corners a bit willfully. In a similar way, the "plastic enrichment" of statues, appliqués, columns and pilasters, appears to be added to the surface, both because these features are more or less on the same plane, and because in themselves they are only moderately plastic. Thus, the facade and the side is more flat, somewhat like the Seventeenth century Pavillion de l'Horloge, rather than the New Louvre.

This can be accounted for in several ways. First, as a self-trained architect, Renwick's approach would be from the outside appearance, the concept of facades on paper, inward. The interior plan would have the exterior facade wrapped around it, instead of it all being conceived as a three dimensionally plastic unit. In working with new elements—the French vocabulary of niches, columns, reliefs, etc.— these would be added on the surface like so much decoration, their relief being provided by their own modeling rather than any basic concept of architectural volumes.

A second reason may be that Renwick surely drew his inspiration from lithographs or engravings of the French models, and naturally the massiveness and sense of volume that is apparent (in the New Louvre) when seeing it in three dimensions, and in changing sunlight, would be lost. For designs on paper,[77] this borrowing from a print would simply reinforce the drafted quality of the ostensibly plastic detail.

Thirdly, the use of brick walls is within a common tradition of flat surfaces. For all the niches and pavilions, the brick rectangle is not lost sight of, and as we have seen in other contexts, the details are superimposed on this basic unit.

But since this was one of the earliest such buildings in the United States, the lack of full comprehension of the essential plasticity of the Second Empire style can be understood. When used in the next stage of development with greater knowledge, as in

Bryant and Gilman's Boston City Hall (1862–65), this is in large part overcome.[78]

The choice of this Second Empire style by Corcoran and Renwick is understandable. It was a style that Renwick had used successfully earlier in the New York Charity Hospital (1858–61), though with far less ornamentation.[79] This would certainly be a style approved by Corcoran, who was familiar with European architecture (and who, in 1862, moved to France for the duration of the Civil War), and was a style becoming internationally popular, beginning in England in the early 1850's. Since the French were also noted for their artistic interests and great art collections, this may have seemed the only logical style.

The Corcoran Art Gallery, one of the first major American buildings in the Second Empire style, thus inaugurated this mode in Washington, and probably encouraged the use of mansards generally. Unlike the Smithsonian, there are at least two major buildings which can be considered as inspired by its style.

We have seen earlier, in discussing the Greek Revival, that the very existence of a building in the city does not mean that it will be emulated. A great number of other elements—political, social, economic, and so on—are really deciding factors.[80] It is the same with the Corcoran Gallery. It could not be emulated until a building of similar size, with funds for comparable embellishment, needed to be built by the government or some wealthy body, and an architect (not just a builder) assigned to build it. Such circumstances arose after the Civil War when the Department of Agriculture (founded in 1862) erected its new building on the Mall, west of the Smithsonian Institution, in 1868 (fig. 165). Adolph Cluss was the architect.

The building, "designed in the Renaissance style

---

[77] It is perhaps significant that the published drawing of the Gallery shows it only in elevation (not perspective) so that the details on the surface are delineated, but no sense of volume or different planes is achieved.

[78] We will also see this second "plastic" phase effected in Mullett's State, War, and Navy Building, begun in 1871.

[79] McKenna, fig. 8. This is even less "decorated" than the Corcoran Gallery. It was, however, based on the older Tuileries rather than the more plastic New Louvre. Since the Vassar College building (first designs, 1860, figs. 9–10) was specifically requested to be based on the Tuileries, not the New Louvre (Hitchcock, p. 167), this desire for plain surfaces may have been the intent of cost-conscious Americans rather than an actual preference by Renwick for the flatter surfaces. But it is worth noting that even in Booth's Theatre of New York (1869; McKenna, p. 101), elaborated flat surfaces are still used.

[80] This has been discussed in another context by Norris K. Smith. See his "Frank Lloyd Wright and the Problem of Historical Perspective," *Journal of the Society of Architectural Historians*, XXVI, 4 (December 1967), pp. 234–237.

of architecture," was of pressed brick with brownstone used for the basement course, belt courses, window frames, cornice and other trim.[81] Although in no sense a copy of the Corcoran Gallery, this source of its design seems obvious. It was, first of all, about the same size and height,[82] used the same color scheme of red brick walls and brownstone trim, was also capped by a flat sided mansard, and had roof cresting very similar to that on the Corcoran. It also is conceived flatly, with the decoration either applied on the surface (the two reliefs on the ground floor facade, the two columns on the first floor, and the decorative floral swags around the end pavilion roofs), or worked into the brick itself. The walls are articulated by flat brick piers which, as we shall see below, are a vernacular structural motif. Lacking bases or capitals, that is how they are to be read here, rather than as pilasters.

The essential differences between the two buildings are slight. The proportions are somewhat different, though the west side of the Corcoran Gallery (fig. 166) and the facade of the Agriculture Building (fig. 167) do follow the same pattern; both have a five bay central portion between the two higher end pavilions. The Agriculture Building also has dormers in the mansard (a feature used in the New Louvre), and there is far less sculptural and architectural enrichment here than in the Corcoran Gallery. But the sense of flat walls of brick with drafted details applied to its is present in both.[83]

This simplified Second Empire style was chosen undoubtedly because of the pleasing success of the Corcoran Gallery, the latest large building then still being worked on. And since the Agriculture Build-

[81] Data from the 1868 Annual Report of the Department of Agriculture, quoted by John Clagett Proctor in "Another Landmark of Capital Passes," *Sunday Star,* Sept. 14, 1930.

[82] The Corcoran Gallery covered 12,896 square feet; the Department of Agriculture (170 feet by 61 feet) covered 10,370 square feet. Ibid.

[83] The interior of the building was richly paneled and decorated, using many fine woods (such as walnut, mahogany, satinwood, curly maple, and birdseye maple), with some gilding, frescoed ceilings, and so on. The price was somewhat less than the Corcoran Gallery, but then it was not fireproof, being constructed of brick and wood only (Public Buildings Commission, *Public Buildings in the District of Columbia* [Washington: U.S. Government Printing Office, 1918], p. 283). Its assessed value in 1916 was $140,000, though the original cost may have been higher. The Corcoran cost a total of about $250,000 (Moore, p. 252) though by 1861 when essentially completed on the outside, it had cost only about $150,000. In 1869 it was claimed that $50,000 was needed to complete the interior for the collections (Corcoran, *Legacy,* p. 35). The additional $50,000 may have been for the eleven Carrara marble statues.

FIGURE 165. Department of Agriculture. Photograph ca. 1890.

FIGURE 166. West side of Corcoran Art Gallery.

FIGURE 167. North facade of Department of Agriculture Building. Photograph by Bell & Bro., 1869.

ing was carefully aligned with the Smithsonian, and had a French parterre to the north, a formal style was appropriate.[84]

The second influence of the Corcoran Gallery was the remodeled Odd Fellows' Hall at Seventh Street between D and E Streets (fig. 168). Although built originally in 1845 (and dedicated in 1846), the building was completely remodeled in 1872–75,[85] and was given a facade based on that of the Corcoran—a central pavilion flanked by two corner pavilions, connected by one bay. This facade is also two floors tall, but above a ground floor of open bays for shops. As appropriate for the 1870's, the proportions are considerably attenuated, the windows taller, the cornice more sharp and abrupt. But just as the Corcoran Gallery facade, here the wall is quite flat, in spite of pilasters and moldings. It continues the line of the street unbroken. The animation is found in the roofline only; the rear of the building had plain flat brick walls.

Beginning after the war, the mansard began to appear also on residences; but since this feature began to be used on houses throughout the United States as early as the 1840's and 1850's, and was published in architectural books, their use in Washington cannot be attributed to Renwick's gallery. Naturally, through familiarizing people with this roof, it may have helped in its adoption.

From these examples, it is clear that the buildings of Renwick in Washington had only modest success in influencing local architecutre. The Smithsonian, which Owen had such high hopes for as a seminal and influential work of architecture, had no imitators. Oak Hill Chapel, perhaps because of its somewhat special use and small size, also found few imitators; after the war, far more elaborate Gothic and ultimately Romanesque churches were constructed. Even the Corcoran Art Galley had less effect than one would think. It is sometimes supposed that Alfred B. Mullett's State, War and Navy Building to the south of the gallery was built as a sort of pendant to the Corcoran (see figs. 233–234); but its vastly different size and materials, and more advanced style, are on quite a different plane of architectural conception. It was, in fact, based on one of Mullett's own earlier designs, for the Boston Post Office and Treasury, rather than the existing local examples, as might be supposed. As suggested, much of the lack of influence was due to the local situation: little occasion for large, expensive public buildings; lack of adequate funds; the apparent reluctance of local builders to attempt adaptations of the styles; and, as we shall see when we examine what the style of large buildings just after the Civil War generally was, an alternate local style which builders favored more than these somewhat elaborate examples.[86]

---

[84] The building was demolished in 1930.

[85] John Clagett Proctor, "Odd Fellows' Hall Noted Old Show Place," *Sunday Star*, Nov. 17, 1929, and Proctor, "Order of Odd Fellows . . .," Ibid., Mar. 29. 1936. The remodeling cost $60,293 and was thus obviously an extensive job. The building was demolished about 1925.

FIGURE 168. Odd Fellows' Hall. (From Hutchins and Moore, *The National Capital, Past and Present* [1885], p. 236.)

---

[86] It is possible that Renwick designed yet another building for Mr. Corcoran. In his *New-York Times* obituary of June 25, 1895, some of his major buildings are listed, including "the Corcoran Art Gallery and Corcoran Building, in Washington." A "Corcoran Building," built for the use of the government by 1848 is mentioned in "The Sessford Annals," Columbia Historical Society *Records*, XI (1908), p. 336: "A large building, five stories high, at the corner of F and Fifteenth Streets, having forty rooms, has been put up by Mr. Corcoran, intending to accommodate some of the offices attached to the Treasury." Since a Greek Revival building, almost certainly not by Renwick, stood at the southeast corner in the 1860's, this must have been near the northeast corner, the actual corner being occupied even today by the Federal Style house drawn in 1817 by Baroness Hyde de Neuville. A preliminary search at the National Archives has failed to discover any photographs of a "Corcoran Building" at this location.

Andrew Jackson Downing was undoubtedly one of the most famous—and popular—architects and landscape designers in the 1840's. Not only were his books on architecture (suited particularly for building in the country and suburbs, from tiny cottages to large villas) of great influence, but his writings on landscape gardening also revolutionized the taste of America. His first major publication, *A Treatise on the Theory and Practice of Landscape Gardening* (1841), had a chapter on "Rural Architecture;" the book made him famous almost immediately. Although much of his theory, and some of his architectural designs, were based on work already becoming popular in England,[87] he essentially reworked it all, adding considerably from his own observation and thought, to make the designs distinctly his own and fully adapted to American needs and climate. In landscape design, he also drew on his own considerable experience as a nurseryman and student of landscape of the northeastern United States.[88] His most famous architectural volume, *The Architecture of Country Houses,* appeared in 1842 and went through many editions; it affected the design of houses throughout the whole country. When Downing became editor of the *Horticulturist* in 1846, he was able to publish an article each month on various aspects of landscape gardening, which reached a wide audience for years.

Downing's mark on Washington was twofold: as a landscape designer and as an architect. Not only did he draw up a master plan for improving the Mall and supervise a portion of it, but he also designed three local villas.[89] Again, as with Renwick, so well known for his public buildings, one would expect that Downing's influence would have had a considerable impact on the Capital. But the actual results are surprising.

When the site of the Smithsonian was selected on the Mall in 1846, it was realized that some form of landscaping would be necessary. Although the area had been, in the Eighteenth century, a mixture of farms, woods, and swamps, the land had been rapidly cut over by earlier settlers for wood and was thus almost bare. The terrain was plesantly rolling, however, and the letter of Robert Mills to Owen, probably of 1846, quoted above, also comments on the Mall: "These grounds are beautifully diversified into hill and dale, well adapted to the culture of humid and dry plants and if laid out with judgement and good taste would, for its extent, admit of a good variety of rural scenery."[90]

The decision to improve the Smithsonian grounds, up to that time barren, dates from March 26, 1847, after Congress had conveyed the land from Ninth to Twelfth Streets to the Institution.[91] That spring the grounds were enclosed with a wooden fence and in 1849 the Regents finally laid out the grounds, using 150 species of trees and shrubs, with ornamental gateways.[92] The Commissioner of Public Buildings had also recognized, in 1849, the need to landscape this area, including the grounds of the Washington Monument, and had recommended to Congress that an appropriation be made for this purpose.[93] Most important at this time, he pointed out to a jealous Congress that this was a national and not just a local concern:

> The improvement of the public grounds in the city of Washington, although gratifying to its citizens and calculated to give increased value to property, should not be regarded, as some are disposed to do, as a mere local objective. These public grounds are the property of the nation, and were reserved at the founding of the city, as a means of beautifying and adorning the national capital.[94]

In 1850, a small appropriation was made and preliminary planting on the whole Mall was possible. Though no record of the nature of these arrangements is available, it can be assumed to have been an informal design, as would be familiar from Downing's publications. As had been pointed out, Renwick's building needed this sort of setting, with tall

---

[87] In his chapter on "Rural Architecture" in his *Treatise,* Downing lists on the last page of the essay a number of English sources which he had consulted: Loudon, *Encyclopaedia of Cottage, Farm, and Villa Architecture;* Robinson, *Rural Architecture and Designs for Ornamental Villas;* Lugar, *Villa Architecture;* Goodwin, *Rural Architecture;* and Hunt, *Picturesque Domestic Architecture, and Examples of Tudor Architecture.*

[88] He joined his brother Charles, already an established nurseryman, in partnership in 1834.

[89] The problem of Downing as an architect will be discussed below.

[90] Gallagher, p. 197.

[91] John Clagett Proctor, "The Tragic Death of Andrew Jackson Downing and the Monument to his Memory," C. H. S. *Records,* XXVII (1925), pp. 248–261.

[92] Goode, p. 263.

[93] Ignatius Mudd, *Annual Report of the Commissioner of Public Buildings for the Year 1849,* H. Doc. 30, 31st Cong., 1st sess., Ser. 576, p. 7.

[94] Ignatius Mudd, *Letter from the Commissioner of Public Buildings transmitting his Annual Report for 1850,* H. Ex. Doc. 47, 31st Cong., 2d sess., Ser. 599, p. 12.

trees and spiky evergreens, to complement its picturesque silhoutte.

Some people, however, felt that a far more comprehensive scheme for the landscaping was called for. With this end in mind, A. J. Downing was contacted in October 1850, by a number of local gentlemen: Joseph Henry (Secretary of the Smithsonian), Walter Lenox (mayor of Washington), and Ignatius Mudd (Commissioner of Public Buildings), at the urging of W. W. Corcoran and with the approval of President Fillmore.[95] Downing came to the Capital in November of that year to examine the entire Mall, and found it "admirably adapted to make a landscape garden and a drive."[96]

It should be noted, however, that this was a project eminently attractive to Downing from the beginning. Apparently in the mid-1840's he had first been interested in encouraging a "national agricultural bureau at Washington," for educational purposes.[97] Later, writing in the *Horticulturist* in 1848, he had also discussed public parks and grounds at length, pointing out that while well known in France, Germany, and England, such parks were unknown in the United States.[98] Such parks would provide pleasant open air retreats for city dwellers, especially in summer; give genteel ladies a place to stroll about healthfully, instead of languishing indoors; and provide a meeting place for friends and family. By thus establishing handsome public parks, "you would soften and humanize the rude, educate and enlighten the ignorant, and give continual enjoyment to the educated."[99]

The didactic and educational aspect, hinted above, was very strong. In a later essay of 1849 he wrote:

> Such a garden might, in the space of fifty to one hundred acres, afford an example of the principal modes of laying out grounds,—thus teaching practical landscape-gardening. It might contain a collection of all the hardy trees and shrubs that grow in this climate, each distinctly labeled,—so that the most ignorant visitor could not fail to learn something of trees.[100]

If only one great city, such as New York, would begin such a public garden, other locations would soon imitate it, as they had Mt. Auburn Cemetery.

This idea of the need for large public parks, and for some city in the United States to set an example, was reinforced by Downing's visit to England in 1850 where he visited the London parks and wrote an enthusiastic essay on them for the *Horticulturist,* just prior to his invitation to Washington.[101] He concluded his essay with a challenge to his readers: "Is New-York really not rich enough, or is there absolutely not enough land in America to give our citizens public parks of more than ten acres?"[102]

Downing's invitation to plan the Mall and President's grounds thus appeared to fulfill his dream of creating a healthful pleasure ground, beautifully landscaped, in the heart of a city to inspire others; and at the same time to be scientifically instructive. He worked on the Mall plan during the winter of 1850–51 and sent the completed design (fig. 169), "showing proposed method of laying out the Public Grounds," to the Board of Regents in February 1851.[103] On March 3rd, he sent a document which explained the plan and set forth many of his aims and

[95] The development of the Mall plan by Downing has been examined by Wilcomb E. Washburn in "Vision of Life for the Mall," *AIA Journal*, XLVII, 3 (March 1967), pp. 52–59. Unfortunately, no sources or documents are footnoted and there is no bibliography. A few sources are referred to in the text, however. Downing's "Explanatory Notes" for the plan are reproduced on pp. 54–55.

[96] Ibid., p. 52. The quote is from the diary of Joseph Henry. A contemporary account of this visit is found in Ignatius Mudd's report of 1850: "At the suggestion . . . of several prominent gentlemen of this city, and by the approbation of the President, I invited A. J. Downing, esq., of Newburg, New York, to examine and inspect the public grounds with reference to their more decorative and artistic improvement. Mr. Downing, who is a gentleman of the first accomplishments in the art of landscape formations, readily accepted the invitation, and, upon a recent visit to Washington for that purpose, made a thorough examination of their surface, soil, and features. From his own observations, and the plats and profiles furnished him from this office, he will be able to submit at a convenient period a general plan for improving the public grounds, which I shall probably communicate to Congress." *Report of 1850*, p. 9.

[97] *Rural Essays*, p. xliii, according to his friend George William Curtis.

[98] Ibid., "A Talk about Public Parks and Gardens" (October 1848), pp. 138–146.

[99] Ibid., p. 142. The success of Mt. Auburn, Laurel Hill, and Greenwood cemeteries is cited as evidence of their acceptability and appreciation by the public. He suggests that such public parks could even be erected by public subscription if necessary.

[100] Ibid., "Public Cemeteries and Public Gardens" (July 1849), pp. 157–158. Downing also suggested having band concerts, refreshment booths, and botanical displays.

[101] Ibid., "The London Parks" (September 1865), pp. 547–557. The five major public parks of London comprised over 1,000 acres and were laid out, he reports, in both flower gardens and open fields with lakes and streams, "like districts of open country," with a variety of landscape features.

[102] Ibid., p. 557. His reference is to Bowling Green in New York City.

[103] The original map, "Plan showing proposed method of laying out the Public grounds at Washington February, 1851," is drawn on heavy paper, and is now in the Map Division, Library of Congress. It is signed in the lower right corner, "A. J. Downing." The map here illustrated is the tracing made in 1867 by Brevet Brig. Gen. Nathaniel Michler (Engineering Division, War Department)

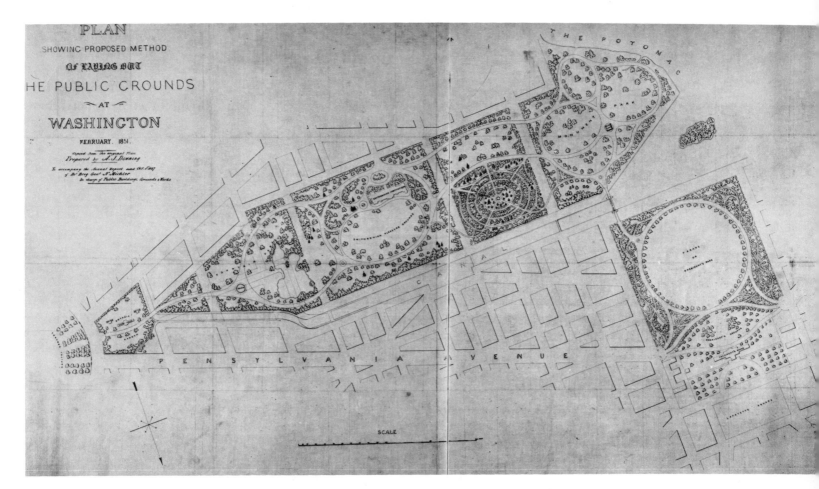

FIGURE 169.   Downing's Plan for the Mall, 1851. Copy by N. Michler, 1867.

theories.[104] He first outlined the purpose of the plan, combining the beautiful with the didactic:

> 1st: To form a national Park, which should be an ornament to the Capital of the United States; 2nd: To give an example of the natural style of Landscape Gardening which may have an influence on the general taste of the Country; 3rd: To form a collection of all the trees that will grow in the climate of Washington, and, by having these trees plainly labelled with their popular and scientific names, to form a public museum of living trees and shrubs. . . .[105]

His design for the Mall was in a number of sections or, as he called them "distinct scenes." This was necessitated by the three major cross streets cut-

ting the Mall, but was also induced by his desire to adapt the grounds to two existing structures (the Smithsonian building and the Washington Monument) and to have, as it were, instructional units. The Monument grounds would have American trees, well grown, but spaced out to allow vistas of the adjacent river. Next (eastward) would be the "Evergreen Garden," 16 acres of evergreen trees, plants and shrubs (130 species) which would thrive in this climate.[106] Footpaths would allow complete and close inspection. Next came the Smithsonian Park or "Pleasure Grounds," to be "an arrangement of choice trees in the natural style," with the area around the Institution building "thickly planted with the rarest trees and shrubs, to give greater seclusion and beauty to its immediate precincts." [107] Across the next street to the east would be the "Fountain Park," which would be dominated by a large fountain and a handsome irregular pond fed

who was in charge of the buildings and grounds at that time. This plan, drawn on linen, is in the Map and Cartographic Division, National Archives, and is identical to the Downing plan except for being somewhat more crisp and linear in its delineation (especially noticeable in the foliage), and without the numerous cracks, tears, and creases of the Downing original.

[104] A. J. Downing, *Explanatory Notes to Accompany the Plan for Improving the Public Grounds at Washington*, Mar. 3, 1851. Manuscript in the National Archives, Record Group No. 42, LR, Vol. 32, No. 1358½. It should be noted that neither the plan nor the notes discusses Lafayette Square.

[105] Washburn, "Mall," p. 54.

[106] Downing considered this important since it was during the winter months that Congress met and great numbers of visitors came to the Capital.

[107] Washburn, "Mall," p. 55.

from it. The final area to the east, the botanical garden, already contained greenhouses. The last section of the plan was the President's Park, connected to the Mall and its carriage roads by a suspension bridge, and having both a large grassed parade ground at the center and sinuous forest paths around the borders. By a large Roman-inspired triumphal arch of marble at the end of Pennsylvania Avenue, these more formal grounds could easily be reached from the city itself. The arch also provided access to the President's House by a separate private drive.[108] Some of the features are visible in a lithograph published in 1852, which is more or less accurate (fig. 170).

These varied areas of planting covering the gently rolling topography of the Mall were unified by a carriage drive which wound from the base of the Capitol through the various areas to the Potomac. Circular drives and paths were created so that the plantings, buildings, and other features (lake, fountain, Potomac, and so on), could be approached from a number of picturesque angles. By connecting the Capitol with the President's House via these peaceful carriage drives, one of the original purposes of the Mall was met as well.

In summarizing the notes, Downing explains the value of this sort of a park, echoing ideas he had arrived at earlier. Such a park, laid out carefully, would influence "the public taste" just as had Mt. Auburn; the Mall "would undoubtedly become a Public School of Instruction in every thing that relates to the tasteful arrangement of parks and grounds, and the growth and culture of trees." [109] It would also, obviously, "embellish and give interest to the Capital," and provide a welcome relief from the "straight lines and broad Avenues of the streets of Washington."

[108] This arch is reproduced on the cover of the March 1967 issue of *AIA Journal*.

[109] Washburn, "Mall," p. 55.

FIGURE 170. "Washington, D.C., with Projected Improvements," Lithograph drawn by B. F. Smith, Jr., published in 1852.

As noted, some of the work on the Mall, of draining, grading, and filling, had been begun before Downing was brought in. In 1850, $12,500 had been appropriated for improving the Mall, some grading and fencing was begun, and about 2,000 small trees were planted.[110]

President Fillmore approved the Downing plan (at least that part west of Seventh Street, which included the Smithsonian grounds) on April 12, 1851; in May, Downing returned to Washington to supervise work on the Mall. He was assisted locally by W. D. Brackenridge, botanist of the Wilkes Expedition of 1838, and also by John Saul, a Washington horticulturist of considerable repute.[111] He had the work previously begun under Mr. Mudd halted. "Mr. Downing thereupon assumed the care of these grounds, and has made great progress in their improvement." [112]

Soon, however, there was controversy. Some apparently felt that Downing should spend more time in Washington supervising the work. There also seem to have been differences with Mr. Mudd as to who was to have jurisdiction over the Mall. This was ultimately resolved after Downing sent a vigorous letter of protest to the President. He pointed out that he (Downing) did not have to be continually present, at least at the early stages when the rough work was progressing, in order to give "personal attention to the removal of every load of earth;" his supervisors were perfectly adequate for this. Furthermore, having been assured by Mr. Corcoran that his (Downing's) control, and final judgement would be complete, he insisted that this should be fully understood, or he would have nothing to do with the project. Finally, a meeting with Mr. Fillmore and his cabinet affirmed this position.[113] The Commissioner of Public Buildings would regain control only after Downing's work was completed.

Even so, Downing's work on the Mall ran into problems again. In early 1852, when more funds were requested for the work, difficulty arose in Congress. Some felt that he was being paid too much;[114] others that money spent on a park was wasted. A motion to limit the appropriation was, however, defeated.[115] But then, as if the project were doomed from the start, on July 28 of that year Downing himself was killed in a steamboat disaster on the Hudson, at the age of 36.[116]

At Downing's death, work on the Mall was continued by Mr. Brackenridge for about a year; but without Downing's energy and conviction, it was bound to languish. Although Fillmore approved the completion of the eastern part of the Mall in 1853, interest in the work seemed to decline slowly. In 1854, the Commissioner of Public Buildings reported that when Brackenridge resigned, the care of the President's grounds "was assigned to Mr. Watt, the gardener at the President's and the general oversight of them, and all that had been under Mr. Brackenridge [i.e., the rest of the Mall] was given to me." He seemed optimistic, however, indicating that "many thousand trees and shrubs" would be planted that autumn.[117] By 1859, however, it was clear that the work was near an end. In the report of the Secretary of the Interior it is noted:

> Several of these [public reservations] have been tastefully enclosed and improved, and Congress has annually made appropriations to keep them in order. For the present year, however, the means allowed fall greatly below the amounts usually appropriated, and the Commissioner of Public Buildings reports them entirely inadequate to preserve the improvements which have been made, as good taste, or even necessity, demands.[118]

In the report of the Commissioner of Public Buildings it is stated further: "on account of the death of this distinguished gentleman [Downing] the work

---

[110] Mudd, *Annual Report of 1850*, p. 9.

[111] Proctor, "Downing," p. 252. Brackenridge was in charge of the Botanical Gardens.

[112] William Easby, *Letter from the Commissioner of Public Buildings, Transmitting his Annual Report [for 1851]*, Feb. 20, 1852, H. Ex. Doc. 79, 32d Cong., 1st sess., Ser. 641, p. 14. Mr. Easby replaced Ignatius Mudd upon the latter's death. The work which Downing had ordered halted consisted of "cutting road-ways and filling in low places" on the Mall and on the grounds below the President's House. This is certainly the last sort of work Downing would have wanted done without his supervision. "After completing the enclosures around these squares which Mr. Mudd had commenced, my charge of them ceased," adds Mr. Easby.

[113] Washburn, "Mall," pp. 53 and 56. See also *Rural Essays*, p. xlix, and Sarah Lewis Pattee, "Andrew Jackson Downing and his Influence on Landscape Architecture in America," *Landscape Architecture*, XIX, 2 (January 1929), p. 82.

[114] He was receiving $2,500. *Rural Essays*, p. xlviii.

[115] Washburn, "Mall," p. 56.

[116] See "Dreadful Calamity on the Hudson River. Burning of the Steamer Henry Clay. Melancholy Loss of Life . . .," *New York Daily Times*, July 29, 1852, p. 2. This article, while describing the disaster, does not list Downing among the missing. The following day, however, he was listed. "The Henry Clay Catastrophe. Forty-seven Bodies Recovered . . .," Ibid., July 30, 1852. The notice mentioned that he had been on the way to Washington. The disaster is discussed by George William Curtis in his "Memoir of the Author," in *Rural Essays*, pp. xi–lviii.

[117] B. B. French, *Report of the Commissioner of Public Buildings*, October 5, 1854, H. Ex. Doc. 1, 33d Cong., 2d sess., Ser. 666, p. 601.

[118] *Report of the Secretary of the Interior, 1859*, p. 14.

was suspended." [119] His urging to complete the unimproved parts of the Mall provoked no response. The Smithsonian grounds, as they existed in 1862, are shown in a well known photograph by A. J. Russell (fig. 171).

The Mall was then disregarded for about a decade. One last effort was made in 1867 by Brig. Gen. Nathaniel Michler, then Commissioner of Public Buildings, who reported in that year that "only one portion of [the Mall] has been tastefully laid out in accordance with the plan proposed by Mr. Downing in 1851. . . . A great deal of additional work has to be executed before perfecting the system adopted." [120] He also wanted the carriage drives completed, and urged the use of gates and lodges where they crossed the transverse streets.

> By some such plan, beautiful and continuous drives could be had between. . . . [the President's House] and the Capitol, free from all the dust and noise and bustle of the busy streets of the city.

His pleas were to no avail. His report of 1868 again pointed out that the work was far from complete. Referring to the 50 acres of the Smithsonian grounds, he observed:

---

[119] J. B. Blake, *Report of the Commissioner of Public Buildings*, Oct. 13, 1859, S. Doc. 2, pt. 1, 36th Cong., 1st sess., Ser. 1023, pp. 843–844. He claims that only a "comparatively small part remained to be finished." This does not, however, seem to have been quite accurate.

[120] N. Michler, *Report of Brevet Brigadier General N. Michler, Major of Engineers, United States Army, in Charge of Public Buildings, Grounds, Works, &c.*, Oct. 1, 1867, H. Ex. Doc. 1, 40th Cong., 2d sess., Ser. 1325, p. 525.

FIGURE 171. Smithsonian grounds. Photograph by A. J. Russell, 1862.

> Only one portion has been tastily [sic] arranged in accordance with the design of Mr. Downing, and a great deal of work remains to be executed before perfecting it. The part lying immediately south of the Smithsonian building has yet to be graded and drained, walks and drives to be spread over its surface, and trees and shrubbery to be planted.[121]

Although some insignificant work had been done on the President's grounds, the rest of the Mall was going to ruin, and he bitterly complained:

> Appropriations have been earnestly urged upon Congress, but scarcely a sufficient amount has been granted to keep even a proper watch over and for the preservation of such improvements both useful and ornamental, as have already been made.

It appears that the portion of the Mall actually worked on by Downing was that part around the Smithsonian. The rest of the Mall, from Third Street to the river, was indeed graded and thousands of dollars spent on trees, but this was effected after his death, more or less following his master plan.[122] But even the Smithsonian grounds that had been his major effort were never really complete. Although in 1895 his plan was "still in use" (see fig. 172), because of his early death "many trees planted for temporary purposes were allowed to remain, and to injure or destroy more hardy species, intended to be permanent in the final effect." [123] Thus the "proper execution" of the plan was never accomplished. In fact, it was in part consciously abandoned: when the grounds of the Agriculture Building were laid out, about 1870, a formal rather than informal scheme was adopted (fig. 173).

We can clearly see, therefore, that the preliminary reasons for the failure of Downing's Mall plan was due to very familiar factors: difficulties of the designer with his subordinates and rivals; lack of understanding and support from Congress; fickle appro-

---

[121] N. Michler, *Report of the Office of Public Buildings, Grounds, and Works*, Sept. 30, 1868, H. Ex. Doc. 1, pt. 2, 40th Cong., 3d sess., Ser. 1368, p. 895.

[122] George S. Boutwell, *Expenditures in the District of Columbia. Letter from the Secretary of the Treasury*, Feb. 19, 1870, H. Ex. Doc. 156, 41st Cong., 2d sess., Ser. 1418. This accounting gives an indication of the extent of the work done by 1858. The land was completely graded from Third Street to the Potomac; a wooden fence was erected around the Mall; over $30,000 was spent on planting trees and some further grading; roads and walks were finished around the Smithsonian (only). These expenses came to $66,904.52 by 1858. The amount spent on continuing this work on the unimproved portions, from 1858 to 1870 amounted to $2,500, although about $57,000 was also spent for trees, tree-boxes, and rent of carts for "public grounds," which may have included the Mall also. But by comparison, the refurnishing of the President's House (act of December 1865) was to cost $160,000.

[123] Goode, p. 263.

FIGURE 172. Smithsonian grounds and Mall, looking east. Photograph ca. 1890.

priations; and, after Downing's death, a lack of compelling vision to carry the project through.

But there is, perhaps, an even more significant reason, within the very nature of the Mall project, which even had it been fully laid out might well have limited its influence.

It is first necessary to examine the actual nature of the Downing concept, besides the factors of open green space and didactic planting, for these could be met in a formal arrangement as well as informal.

The first major point is that the Mall connects the Capitol with the President's House in a less formal manner than the direct linear and visual link of Pennsylvania Avenue. L'Enfant's boulevard, lined with trees and (formal) gardens, was obviously a contrast with Pennsylvania Avenue, to be lined with buildings of uniform height. Downing does the same thing, but in a Nineteenth century vocabulary. For a creative artist to do otherwise would have been an anachronism, especially when the value and popularity of informal grounds had been proved. Sensi-

FIGURE 173. Agriculture building and grounds. Photograph ca. 1875.

119

bility had changed considerably since 1790 and so Downing's link was both faithful to the original concept, but also to new ideas. In fact, he well understood the idea of the formal avenue versus the informal Mall, since he terminated Pennsylvania Avenue at the east side of the President's Park by a Roman triumphal arch—surely a concession for Downing!—yet made the gateway from the Mall a suspension bridge, both "honest" in its novel structure, and "picturesque" in its curve and sweep.

Did, then, Downing violate the original intent of the Mall? In essence, he did not. Both L'Enfant and Downing desired the green Mall to contrast with the regular grid of streets around it. Our eyes are used to the strong formality of the McMillan treatment of 1901 which increased the length of the Mall about 40 per cent, and bypassed one of the original purposes, an alternate link with the President's House. L'Enfant intended it to turn at the Potomac, where his equestrian statue was to be located, and connect with the President's grounds. Downing effects this by his suspension bridge, and the happy expedient of the tall Washington Monument whose circular colonnade, as originally designed, would act as a pivot. Today, of course, this link is lost and the symmetrical cross axis, though barely visible from either end of the Mall,[124] does not achieve the same end. Thus, ironically, Downing was closer to L'Enfant in his essential treatment than was the McMillan plan.

It is also worth pointing out, in this context, that the Mall was not (in Downing's plan) a chaos of woods and groves. He carefully kept the central portion quite open by the use of meadows, roadways, and spaces in the plantings, and emphasized this opening along the center by the fountain near the east end.[125] It should also be observed that the Smithsonian building (and the later Agriculture Building) take this central vista into account—a vista less formal than L'Enfant's, but still present. When the cornerstone of the Smithsonian was laid, the building stood 300 feet south of the real axis of the Mall, thus leaving an open corridor 600 feet wide. This is certainly comparable to the L'Enfant concept which had a 400 foot wide boulevard with trees, and with gardens flanking it. Even after the Washington Monument was begun 2 years later and

it was found that it could not, for structural reasons, be placed on axis, the new centerline, further south, still left the Institution 200 feet. Thus, the idea that the Smithsonian "encroached" on the Mall is based on the extra formal scheme established in 1901, not that of L'Enfant, or even Downing.[126]

In addition to this less formal linking of the Capitol and the President's House which both L'Enfant and Downing effected, a second major desire was to make a contrast with the formal grid system of the paved city. This was a point raised often by Downing. For example, in July 1849, he wrote, regarding such a large informal park in New York, that the variety of landscape, trees, and shrubs, the rolling ground and refreshment cafes, would make it a perfect "holiday-ground for all who love to escape from the brick walls, paved streets, and stifling atmosphere of towns."[127] Similarly, in September 1850, one of the best recommendations of the London parks were the varied landscape features which made "these parks doubly refreshing to citizens tired of straight lines and formal streets."[128] This is echoed in his explanatory notes for his Mall plan:

> The straight lines and broad Avenues of the streets of Washington would be pleasantly relieved and contrasted by the beauty of curved lines and natural groups of trees in the various parks.[129]

We may well ask, then, why Downing's plan, even if politics, economics, and fate had allowed it to be completed, probably would have had little chance of becoming truly influential.

First, the link between the Capitol and President's House was not really needed. Had there been a real desire for a less congested, more open connection, Congress might well have pushed this approach. But we have seen that the political links (which such a park connection would symbolize in part) were tenuous. Furthermore, Pennsylvania Avenue served perfectly well and since, by 1850, it was hardly an oppressively built up and formal avenue, the proposed contrast by the Mall approach was not needed.

---

[124] But which the McMillan plan obscures because of the strong vista to the Lincoln Memorial.

[125] The only real departure is the Evergreen Garden which, however, is made oval in shape so as to intrude into this axis as little as possible.

[126] In Reps, p. 42, it is said that the Smithsonian building "encroached" on the Mall, as did the botanical gardens at the foot of the Capitol.

[127] *Rural Essays,* p. 158.

[128] Ibid., p. 548.

[129] Washburn, "Mall," p. 55. These factors show clearly that Downing was conscious of the need for open parks for recreation; that he understood the possible oppressiveness of the L'Enfant grid of streets; and also saw the contrast between the formal Pennsylvania Avenue and the informal Mall approach to the President's House.

Second, the very idea of the Mall as a grand park for the populace, while perhaps needed in New York, was here premature. There were, alas, far too *few* paved streets completely lined with walls of brick. Furthermore, because of the many vacant lots (and the generous width of the streets) the grid pattern was far less noticeable or oppressive.

Third, there were already ample "breathing" spaces within the city; not just the vacant lots of unimproved land, but in the numerous squares and circles provided by the L'Enfant plan. The need for a vast park was simply not present. And too, within a mile of the center of Washington were hills covered with forests and farms (fig. 174) and a river still harboring marshes and water fowl. Thus the natural park on the Mall, valuable in a built-up city, was here simply an imitation of the actual natural country easily visible around the Capital. This would prevent its local adoption, and by contrast, somewhat diminish its impact for visitors. Even Georgetown, twice as old as Washington, had ample estates on its borders

FIGURE 175. View of western Georgetown. Photograph by William M. Smith, November 11, 1865.

and, toward the western edge, large areas of unimproved land between buildings (fig. 175). As with the major buildings, the actual need for such a proj-

FIGURE 174. Washington, Georgetown, and surrounding country. Boschke map of 1861.

FIGURE 176. Francis Dodge House, published in Vaux, *Villas and Cottages* (1857).

ect had to be present before it could succeed, no matter how successful the design.

During the same period that Downing was concerned with the Washington Mall, he designed two —and probably three—houses for local residents. These, like his Mall plan, were completely unique for Washington at the time and, considering their immediate popularity and the fame of their architect, they are important to investigate for their effect on local architecture.

At the outset, however, we should note just how much Downing actually had to do with their design. Downing, of course, had absolutely no architectural training; his knowledge of architecture (as much of his landscaping theory) was derived from published English sources (especially J. C. Loudon and P. F. Robinson), and also from executed designs by the Americans A. J. Davis and John Notman. With these designs in mind, and combined with his own inclinations (specifically, simplification of detail, compact and efficient plan, and exterior verandas among others) he would prepare a rough sketch which his friend Davis in New York City would then turn into a finished design.[130] He readily acknowledged this debt; in his *Treatise on . . . Landscape Gardening* he includes a note of thanks to J. C. Loudon, Davis,

and Notman "for architectural drawings and Descriptions." [131] He also often included works erected by his friends (including Richard Upjohn and Gervase Wheeler) and even recommended them as appropriate architects to employ! Many of his designs, however, were essentially all his own, only rendered into publishable form by Davis or some other friend.[132]

This practice changed, however, when he formed a partnership in 1850 with the young English architect Calvert Vaux. During the last 2 years of his life, from which these houses date, Downing appears to have been the dominant creative member of this partnership.[133]

The two houses which Downing and Vaux designed for Francis and Robert Dodge of Georgetown still stand at Thirtieth and Q Streets, N.W., (Fig. 177) and Twenty-eighth and Q Streets, N.W., (fig. 180), but each is greatly altered. Fortunately, Vaux published them in his *Villas and Cottages* of 1857 (figs. 176 and 178) and in that volume they bear the legend "D. & V." (Downing and Vaux). Vaux explains that the buildings so marked "have a special interest as the latest over which the genial influence of the lamented Downing was exercised."[134] Since it was Downing who provided the cost estimate, and in a contemporary newspaper account was solely credited with their plans, it is clear that he was active in their conception.[135] Beause of his preoccupations

---

[130] This problem is carefully discussed in George B. Tatum's introduction to the Da Capo reprint of *The Architecture of Country Houses* (New York, 1968). See especially pp. viii–xii. One such sketch which Davis worked up is discussed in Donnell, p. 191.

[131] *Treatise,* section IX, pp. 368–417.

[132] Clay Lancaster, "Builders' Guides and Plan Books . . .," *Magazine of Art*, XLI, 1 (January 1948), p. 19. Here he asserts that in *The Architecture of Country Houses*, "not a few [of the designs] were by the author himself," for example, design 25.

[133] When Downing did not find a satisfactory architectural partner in the United States, he engaged Calvert Vaux while on a visit to England in 1850. Vaux, born in 1824, had trained in the office of N. L. Cottingham in London. Vaux was clearly a man of talent for after Downing's death in 1852 he continued working in both landscape and architectural design. As is well known, he and Frederick Law Olmsted entered the competition for New York's Central Park together in 1857, with their design being selected. They later planned other parks together throughout the United States. Vaux also continued his architectural career, designing (with F. C. Withers) a number of buildings for Gallaudet College near Washington, beginning in 1866. Other structures, designed by himself, include perhaps his most famous work, "Olana," the residence of the painter Frederick Church on the Hudson. Vaux died in 1895.

For Vaux's continuing work in landscape architecture, see Albert Fein, "The American City: The Ideal and the Real," in Edgar Kaufmann, Jr. (ed.), *The Rise of an American Architecture* (New York: Praeger Publishers, 1970).

[134] Calvert Vaux, *Villas and Cottages* (New York: Harper & Bros., 1857), p. x.

[135] "Local Matters, Modern Building," *Georgetown Advocate,* Dec. 7, 1852, p. 3. I am indebted to Mrs. Mary Mitchell for calling this reference to my attention.

in Newburgh, he did not supervise the construction of the houses, leaving this to local craftsmen.[136] Because the two buildings are almost mirror images,[137] they can be discussed together.

The *style*, that of the Italianate Villa, was new to Georgetown. Downing felt that this style was one of the best modern modes:

> The *Italian style* is, we think, decidedly the most beautiful mode for domestic purposes. . . . It is admirably adapted to harmonize with general nature, and produce a pleasing and picturesque effect in fine landscapes. . . . It has intrinsically a bold irregularity, and strong contrast of light and shadow, which give it a particularly striking and painter-like effect.[138]

This asymmetry, which expressed the freer interior arrangements, was also a more "honest" expression; it also enabled the silhouette to be treated with considerable originality (see figs. 179 and 181).

Downing also felt that this style was specially suited to a southern climate:

> So many appliances of comfort and enjoyment suited to a warm climate appear, too, in the villas of this style, that it has a peculiarly elegant and refined appearance. Among these are *arcades*, with the Roman arched openings, forming sheltered promenades; and beautiful *balconies* projecting from single windows or sometimes from connected rows of windows, which are charming places . . . to enjoy the cool breeze—as they admit, to shelter one from the sun, of a fanciful awning shade. . . .
>
> All these balconies, arcades, etc. are sources of real pleasure in the hotter portions of our year . . . while by increased thickness of walls and closeness of window fixtures the house may also be made of the most comfortable description in winter.[139]

As suggested above, these villas also included all the latest technical improvements (for ventilation and heating) and a careful study to suit it to the local climate.

The style was also of didactic value:

> Our rural residences, evincing that love of the beautiful and the picturesque, which, combined with solid comfort, is so attractive to the eye of every beholder, will not only become sources of the purest enjoyment to the refined minds of the possessors, but will exert an influence for the improvement in taste of every class in our community.[140]

[136] Ibid. T. Cissel was the "architect" (builder); A. Barber the master mason; Messrs. Soult (?) & Brown of Washington, the plasterers; and W. H. Godey the painter.

[137] Vaux was careful to point out, however, that "although these two houses have their principal features in common, neither is a servile imitation of the other."

[138] *Treatise*, p. 385. For an excellent discussion of Downing's architectural theories, see Early, esp. pp. 54–71.

[139] *Treatise*, pp. 387–388. It will be noted that the shady verandas are on the north side of the house in both cases, rendering them even cooler in summer.

[140] Ibid., p. 408.

FIGURE 177. Francis Dodge House, Thirtieth and Q Streets, N.W.

FIGURE 178. Robert Dodge House, published in Vaux, *Villas and Cottages*.

Since the building supposedly also expressed the character of the owner—here, perhaps, the sober, restrained, unostentatious manner of two brothers of a shipping family, who had made their fortune from hard work—it was morally truthful also.

FIGURE 179.   Robert Dodge House. Photograph ca. 1930.

FIGURE 181.   Robert Dodge House, facade. (From C. H. Pepper, *Everyday Life in Washington* [1900], p. 371.)

FIGURE 180.   Robert Dodge House Twenty-eight and Q Streets, N.W.

The most significant stylistic effect, however, was its clear sense of volumes, echoing the units of space within. These extended this way and that, the loggias being a transitional volume between open and enclosed space, the bay windows expressive of a plastic outswelling. Furthermore, it was a style based not on ancient classical orders, or their subsequent close variations, but on solid geometrical forms, ostensibly

the vernacular buildings of Italy in the Seventeenth century and later.[141]

The *plan* was the second most significant departure. Rather than the standard long central hall with two rooms off either side (or one side only) which was almost uniform locally and remained popular for many years (figs. 182–183), here a square central hall has the rooms radiating off it pinwheel fashion (fig. 184). The spatial experience is thus quite different, giving the building greater flexibility in circulation as well. This was a plan that Downing arrived at gradually. In his *Cottage Residences* (1844), two designs, Nos. 2 and 6, show steps toward this (figs. 185–186). The first, except for the expansion of the rear hall, is a slight departure from the standard central hall plan. The second, by throwing together the drawing room and library on one side, including a porch and vestibule as part of the sequence of entry spaces, and having only one room on the other side of the hall, shows a further experimentation with the arrangement and flow of space. The new "centrifugal" plan allowed greater freedom, and

---

[141] These were based in large part on the buildings depicted in the painting of the Seventeenth century masters Nicolas Poussin and Claude Lorrain. For a valuable discussion of the origin and development of the Villa style, see Carroll L. V. Meeks, "Henry Austin and the Italian Villa," *Art Bulletin,* XXX, 2 (June 1948), pp. 145–149.

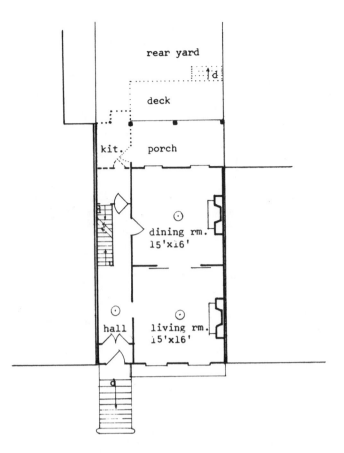

FIGURE 182. Wheatley Town House, 3043 N Street, N.W., plan.

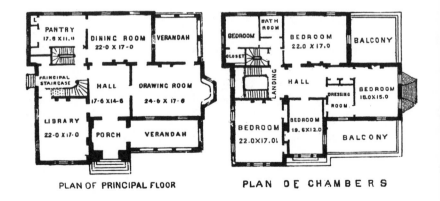

FIGURE 183. James I. Barrett House, 1400 Twenty-ninth Street, N.W., plan.

these variations are reflected on the ouside. This is a far cry from Thornton's efforts only 35 years earlier, when he attempted to fit two oval rooms inside Tudor Place while keeping the exterior a rectangular cube.

A third major innovation for a suburban villa was the *siting*. The very shape—irregular, with windows on all sides, and wings here and there—presumed an open country setting. As might be imagined, the grounds were of great importance.

> Surburban villa residences are, every day, becoming more numerous; and in laying out the grounds around them, and disposing the sylvan features, there is often more ingenuity, and as much taste required, as in treating a country residence of several hundred acres. In the small area of from one half an acre to ten or twelve acres, surrounding often a villa of the first class, it is desirable to assemble as many of the same features . . . which are to be found in a large and elegant estate. To do this, the space allotted to various purposes, as the kitchen garden, lawn, etc., must be judiciously portioned out, and so characterized and divided by plantations, that the whole shall appear to be much larger than it really is, from the fact that the spectator is never allowed to see the whole at a single glance. . . .[142]

142 *Treatise*, p. 117.

The example given by Downing, his figure 26, is a design by John Notman (fig. 187). But the extremely limited sites of both Dodge houses—less than an acre each—may have necessitated a restricted plan more like that illustrated by Vaux (fig. 188), which he warns should not have any very large trees —only shrubs, evergreens, and "a few fruit trees." [143]

This clearly does no justice to Downing's sense of design, though in less capable hands such grounds would become a parody of tightly twisting paths and

143 Vaux, design 14; plan illustrated p. 202.

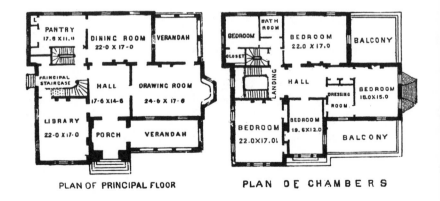

FIGURE 184. Robert Dodge House, plan. From Vaux, *Villas and Cottages.*

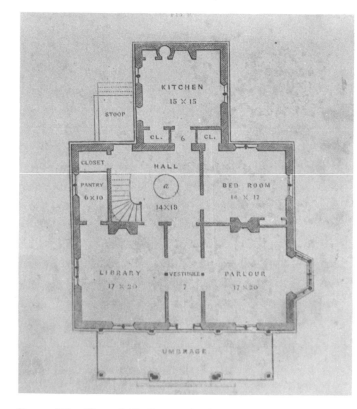

FIGURE 185. Plan of "A Cottage in the English, or Rural Gothic Style," from Downing, *Cottage Residences* (1842), plate facing p. 50.

improper planting (fig. 189). Downing specifically warned in his *Treatise* that an ample size was needed for really good effect:

> The error into which inexperienced improvers are constantly liable to fall, is a want of *breadth* and extent in their designs; which latter, when executed, are so feeble as to be full of *littleness*, out of keeping with the magnitude of the surrounding scene.[144]

This ampleness of conception clearly found best expression in ampleness of ground.

Probably more characteristic of Downing's plans for restricted sites would be the design No. 16 which Vaux published (fig. 190), even though the placement of the house at one side was by chance. [145]

The surroundings were very important not only for the enjoyment of the resident, but also for the setting of the architecture iself.

> *Architectural beauty* must be considered conjointly with the *beauty of the landscape* or situation. Buildings of almost every description, and particularly those for the habitation of man, will be considered by the mind of taste, not only as architectural objects of greater or less merit [as the facade of a townhouse], but as component parts of the general scene; united

[144] *Treatise,* p. 332.
[145] Vaux, design 16 (D. & V.) ; plan illustrated on p. 218.

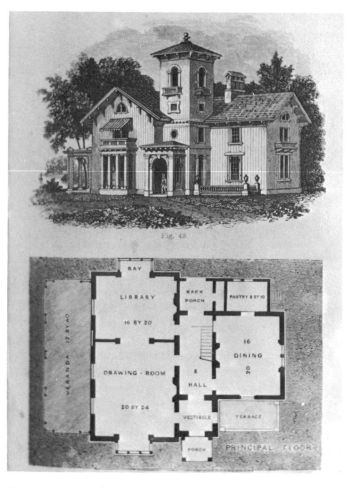

FIGURE 186. "An Irregular Villa in the Italian Style, Bracketed," from Downing, *Cottage Residences* (1842), plate facing p. 124.

with the surrounding lawn, embosomed in tufts of trees and shrubs. . . . Their effect will frequently be good or bad, not merely as they are excellent or indifferent examples of a certain style of building, but as they are happily or unhappily combined with the adjacent scenery.[146]

These factors—the form of the building, its efficient plan, and its setting—were fully appreciated by a local newspaper reporter who examined the Francis Dodge house in 1852.[147] He admired the "gracefulness of outline" and the "harmony of proportions to please the imagination," noting that "outwardly, symmetry is made to exist in the midst of variety." He also approved of the efficient interior plan, its compactness, the separation of private and public stairways and, of course, the latest technical advances—gas lighting, speaking tubes, ventilators,

[146] *Treatise,* p. 370.
[147] See note 135 above. He observed that Robert Dodge's house, to the east, was very similar. (This building is recorded in HABS No. DC-246, published in *Georgetown Architecture*, pp. 18–36.) The identification of the style (Swiss? Venetian?) was somewhat difficult for the reporter, but he liked the results nonetheless.

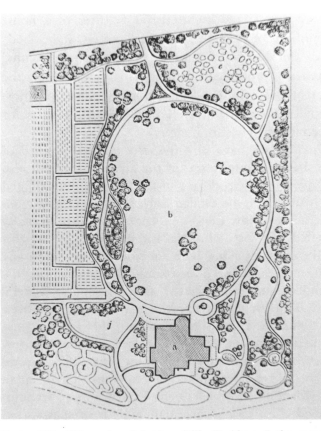

FIGURE 187. "Plan of a Suburban Villa Residence," the grounds of Riverside Villa, Burlington, N.J., by John Notman. From Downing, *Landscape Gardening* (1841), p. 118, fig. 26.

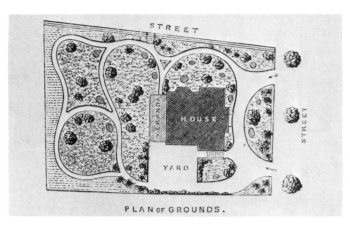

FIGURE 188. "A Picturesque Symmetrical House, " Newburgh, New York. From Vaux, *Villas and Cottages,* design No. 14; plan p. 202.

hot and cold water, the bathroom, hot air furnace, and the dumbwaiter between dining room and kitchen. He fully realized the advantage of the cool, hollow brick walls, and the two shaded verandas. His concluding words are most significant:

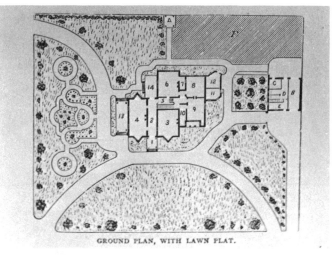

GROUND PLAN, WITH LAWN PLAT.

FIGURE 189. Ground plan for an "Ornamental Cottage," design XIII from *Hobbs's Architecture.*

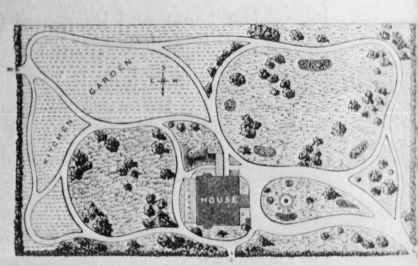

PLAN of GROUNDS.

FIGURE 190. Grounds for "A Picturesque Square House," Newburgh, New York. Designed by Downing and Vaux. From Vaux, *Villas and Cottages* (1857), design No. 16; plan p. 218.

Fifteen or twenty thousand dollars spent in the erection of a building of this character is well applied for the benefit of the community in which it will stand, as it constitutes a fine model in the introduction of a new style of building.[148]

The Dodge villas, however, had no real imitators. Only one or two similar villas were built along Boundary Street (Florida Avenue). The only one of which a photograph could be found, the Christian G. Schneider home of 1864 (fig. 191), looks much like one of the dozens of designs for frame villas in

---

[148] *Georgetown Advocate,* Dec. 7, 1852.

FIGURE 191. Christian G. Schneider Residence, Florida Avenue, N.W.

the 1840's, such as in figure 186. It is perhaps thinner and more meager than those by Downing.[149]

There are a number of reasons why the Dodge houses probably had little effect. Primarily, the essential volumetric character of these villas contrasted with what we have seen was the local vernacular predilection for flat surfaces. The silhouette was also extremely different and the loggias, as an integral part of its spatial treatment and composition, were not elements that could be readily added to a different style dwelling.

Secondly, the plan was quite different from any heretofore built in Georgetown. The opening up of space in a dynamic way is, of course, something that becomes almost standard 15 years later, when large sliding doors separate parlors and dining rooms; but this early it was a considerable novelty to have this interior complexity of space.[150]

A third reason may be that now there were many other factors that the new architectural thought deemed important which were hardly adaptable with any success by builders. Many such factors are treated by Downing (and others) and fitted into the more theoretical and "natural" interpretation of the dwelling: it should reflect the habits and manners of

the occupant; the architectural features of a house should, as consistent with its chosen style, body forth the essence of "home" (capacious, welcoming porches; prominent chimneys symbolizing the hearth; bay windows suggesting the love of enjoyment of the scenery, even from within; loggias for relaxed family visiting, etc.)

Finally, we have already seen the importance of the site, not only to set off the architecture, but also to give greatest pleasure to the (ostensibly) refined occupant. But the Dodge houses, contrary to the effect achieved in the Vaux engravings, are actually aligned with other houses, and are close to the sidewalks on both sides. This, obviously, prevented any real sense of the natural setting Downing's houses demanded, and thus vitiated an important consideration. Though their rear yards may indeed have been laid out in appropriate fashion, the houses were treated anomalously, being placed on the property line like an ordinary row house (fig. 192). Ironically, the reporter quoted above notes that the plan by Downing for the Francis Dodge house "was furnished, . . . to be consistent and in symentry [sic] with the size and position of the lot on which it is erected." It seems doubtful if this can be completely correct, as other Downing plans have the houses much less close to the street; perhaps the placement on the slope of the land was all that was actually done. Downing often spoke of the need for privacy from passers-by, but here the bay windows are but a

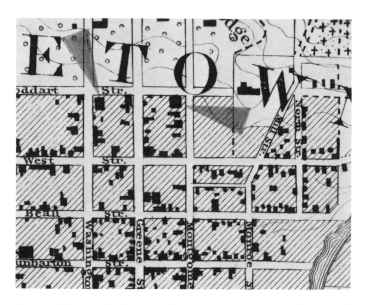

FIGURE 192. Detail, Boschke Map of Georgetown, 1861. Dodge Villas (at arrows) on Washington and Stoddert, and Montgomery Streets.

---

[149] John Clagett Proctor, "Historic Estates once Dotted Boundary Street, now Florida Avenue," *Sunday Star*, Jan. 1, 1939. This home was once on the extreme western part of what later was the Garfield Hospital grounds.

[150] Downing had, of course, used this new openness before, often to achieve cross breezes for all rooms.

few feet from the very sidewalk. The Dodge houses, then, even if surrounded by skillful planting, would not have shown Downing's art to its best effect.

There was, however, a third villa which was also designed, it seems almost certain, by Downing and Vaux; and while the architecture seems less successful (and picturesque) than the Dodge houses, the grounds appear to have been closer to the Downing ideal. This was the Cornelius Barber house, ca. 1851–52 (fig. 193), located on the west slope of Observatory Hill, [151] which was ready for occupancy probably in 1852. It thus would have been designed before Downing's death. The villa itself is apparently more symmetrical, with the tower in the center of a more regular facade; there are, actually, fewer picturesque details such as hood molds.[152]

But it is more the layout of the estate that is important here. From the Boschke map of 1861 (from field inspection of 1857–58), the nature of the grounds is apparent (fig. 194).[153] The villa, located near the center of the farm, faced southeast, and was approached by a number of curving drives at various angles to set its picturesque silhouette to best advantage. While the south (and part of the east) border of the farm was lined with deciduous trees, the central portion of the view, except for one area near the trees which may be meadow (since similar blank spaces to the sides of the villa must surely be lawn), looks out over some sort of planting or crops. The regularity of the symbol may mean orchards.[154] Be that as it may, the villa is clearly well oriented, both for the vista down the Potomac and for the views off

FIGURE 193. Cornelius Barber Villa, Observatory Hill. Photograph taken April 5, 1890.

into the surrounding scenery.[155] The pines, visible in the 1890 photograph, suggest that Downing may well have influenced or planned the grounds, since he was particularly in favor of their use in conjunction with picturesque buildings.

The estate was thus not like the Dodges' "suburban villas," but of the "ferm ornée" type, which combined features of the landscape garden with those of a useable farm, the major concession to beauty being the less efficient, nonrectangular field pattern. One such farm is illustrated in his *Treatise* (fig. 195). Such estates were mainly intended for the gentleman farmer, interested in experimenting with advanced agricultural methods perhaps, and it was specified that "the house and all buildings should be of a simple, though picturesque and accordant character." [156] As Downing advocated in his writing,[157] the nature of the site was to regulate the ar-

[151] In Mary Mitchell, *Divided Town* (Barre, Mass.: Barre Publishers, 1968), the architect of the Barber mansion is given as Calvert Vaux. He is also here credited with the two Dodge Houses. At the author's request, Mrs. Mitchell very kindly searched her own extensive files for the source of this attribution, but could not find the information. Local newspapers, 1851–53 also gave no information. It may be, therefore, that the reference appeared in another context (private letters, etc.) and was not separately identified. Since her source indicated Vaux for all three houses, we can assume that this was, of course, Downing and Vaux. Furthermore, Vaux's houses done after Downing's death are generally more, rather than less, ornate.

[152] After a careful search, the photograph reproduced was the only one of the villa that could be found. I am indebted to Mr. Robert Rhynsburger, Assistant Director, Six Inch Transit Circle Division, U.S. Naval Observatory, Washington, for uncovering this view. The detail is from a construction photograph made Apr. 5, 1890, entitled, "New Naval Observatory, Georgetown Heights, . . . Richard M. Hunt, Architect."

[153] Unfortunately, this map (and his previous one of Washington only) has no key to the symbols used.

[154] Similar dots, though smaller, are found within the limits of Georgetown, suggesting that it may not be tilled land.

[155] An article in the *Washington Star* of Oct. 25, 1890 described the property thus: "It occupies the summit of a ridge of hills, the highest in the vicinity, and commands a superb view for miles around in every direction save the west. Standing on the crest of the hill on which the new [observatory] structure is situated one is delighted with the beauty and extent of the vast picture before him." The views are then described. (Clipping from the files of the Columbia Historical Society library.)

[156] *Treatise*, p. 121. The fields could be bordered with trees, and the circular drives between the fields kept in grass. This would provide very pleasant drives when showing the various agricultural improvements to friends and guests.

[157] See, for example, in *Rural Essays*, pp. 166–171, "How to Arrange Country Places," March 1850.

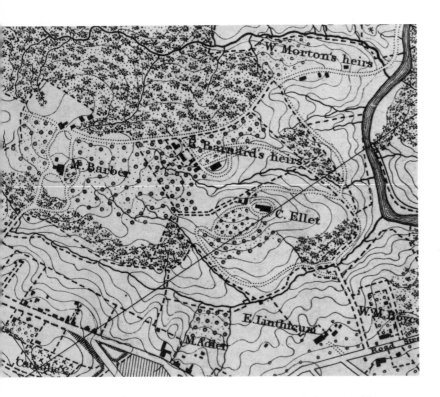

FIGURE 194. Barber Estate in 1861. Detail from Boschke map.

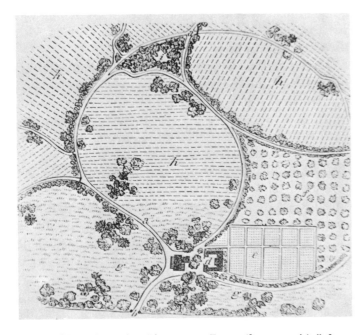

FIGURE 195. "View of a Picturesque Farm (ferme ornée)," from Downing, *Treatise on Landscape Gardening*, p. 120.

rangement. If fine views were available, groups of trees must not shut it out, and when such groves were used, should allow for carefully planned vistas of important features, such as we see here.

But the Barber estate, as the Dodge houses, appar-

ently had little effect. Most other farms around do not show this sort of planting and drives. This may be attributed to a number of factors. Certainly the surrounding country, with many fine views as mentioned above, was already quite picturesque in its natural state. Improving it in the Downing tradition was not worth the cost or effort. Furthermore, Cornelius Barber died within a year of moving into his home; thus the development of the estate as a picturesque farm may have been stunted by his wife's need to spend more of her time on practical matters of running a productive farm.

Finally, the estate existed for only 29 years. The land was purchased in 1881 for use as the new Naval Observatory site, and although the house remained for about 10 more years, the grounds were soon transformed, negating their didactic value.[158] Thus even a landscape design more fully realized than in the Dodge villas appears to have exerted little influence.

If the Dodge houses and the Barber villa did not start a trend toward Italianate homes in Georgetown and Washington, we may well ask what sort of houses were built in the following 10 or 15 years.

We have pointed out before that the houses of the early Nineteenth century tended to favor flat, unmodeled facades, even in rows of adjacent houses, such as 3019–3025 P Street, N.W., of about 1800–30 (fig. 196). Even later buildings, such as at 3001–3039 M Street, N.W., continue this planar quality (fig. 197). We have also seen that, around 1860, these flat facades were sometimes embellished by the addition

[158] *Washington Star*, Oct. 25, 1890; and, Grace Dunlop Peter and Joyce D. Southwick, *Cleveland Park* (Washington, 1958), p. 44.

FIGURE 196. 3019-3025 P Street, N.W.

onto the house facade of wooden bays, such as at 1212–1216 Thirtieth Street, N.W., (fig. 198). This sense of flat surfaces is seen even on large dwellings on corner lots, that might have developed more plasticity, such as the James I. Barrett House (fig. 199) of about 1866.[159] The lack of visible roof enhances this flatness of the exposed sides.

Surprisingly enough, this nonplastic emphasis is seen in the remarkable group of four double villas known as Cooke's Row (fig. 200), built on Q Street in 1868.[160] Only one of them (Villa No. 1, 3027–29 Q Street) has any real plastic sense, with asymmetrical massing, sculptural mansards, prominent bay windows, and a wall surface animated by many projecting hood molds (fig. 201). The other villas, for all their rich detailing, still have rather flat walls with the building obviously compact and square. Villa No. 4 (3007–3009 Q Street, N.W.), in spite of its mansards, still has these qualities. Furthermore, they are lined up neatly along the street, all 25 feet from the public walk, with uniform spaces between them. This flat wall quality can be seen especially in Villa No. 3 (3013–3015 Q Street, N.W.) whose surface detail is too simple to break up the sense of plain walls, and whose recesses are not deep enough to create a truly plastic sense (fig. 202). Interestingly enough, the villa happens to be similar to one published by another architect in 1876 (fig. 203).[161] This may indicate that the flatness was due as much to unimaginative and conservative design as to any local traditions.[162] The plan of Hobbs' villa (fig. 204), for example, is not very different from the older central hall design of 50 or 60 years earlier, showing little adaptation (except in the dining room, H) of the newer spatial concepts. The Georgetown villa's plan (fig. 205), though a double house, is equally conservative.

A similar sense of wall flatness can be seen in a number of Washington villas, visible here and there

FIGURE 197. 3001-3039 M Street, N.W.

FIGURE 198. 1212-1216 Thirtieth Street, N.W.

in overall views of the city. These buildings, ca. 1860–75, are also of the square, boxy, nonplastic form we saw in Cooke's Row (see figs. 124 and 206).

Other houses, which had mansard roofs, also kept

[159] See HABS No. DC-180, published in *Northeast*, pp. 154–166.

[160] The architects were Starkweather and Plowman. See also HABS No. DC-182, published in *Northeast*, pp. 168–183.

[161] Isaac H. Hobbs and Son, *Hobbs's Architecture* (Philadelphia: J. B. Lippincott & Co., 1873); second edition, 1876 with 38 additional plates. The villa is plate 43 in the second edition. The designs in this book had largely been published previously in *Godey's Lady's Book* (p. 13). Thus, this design may date from well before 1872, the date of the first edition's copyright.

[162] It is interesting to note that Hobbs had a "law of architectural proportion" based on the human module. (Contracting or reducing the unit made buildings seem bigger than they were.) This law, he confidently noted, would give his houses "the appearance of being worth twice and three times their cost." p. 13.

FIGURE 199. James I. Barrett House, 1400 Twenty-ninth Street, N.W.

FIGURE 200. Cooke's Row, 3007-3029 Q Street, N.W.

this very severe flat exterior. Often these roofs were added to existing late Greek Revival buildings. Even the frame mansarded house at 1402 Thirty-first, Streets, N.W., built about 1860, is without any bays at all (fig. 207); that on the south side was added in 1952.[163] This flatness continued to be in favor for many years. Holy Trinity Rectory, 3514 O Street, N.W., of 1869 (fig. 208), has its plastic embellishment restricted to brackets, consoles, dormers, and door enframement, set off against the plane surfaces.[164]

The sense of plastic volume did begin to change somewhat after the Civil War. In a few buildings, such as the Grafton Tyler Double House (1868) of 1314 Thirtieth Street, N.W.,[165] the interior spaces begin to open up with sliding doors and openwork screens, and the exterior also becomes considerably more modeled (fig. 209). This is also seen in the double house at 3405–3407 N Street, N.W., (fig. 210), of similar date.

Thus, as this sense of flatness began to slowly change after the war, more plastic treatment in houses could now be found. And with the advent of the Richardsonian Romanesque style beginning in the 1880's, a popular style which was plastic by its very conception and mode of building (with numer-

FIGURE 201. Cooke's Row, Villa No. 1, 3027-29 Q Street, N.W.

ous bays and turrets) carried on this trend with wonderful results. Some were designed by local architects, such as 3099 Q Street, N.W., (fig. 211) of about 1887–90,[166] while others were simply successful essays in the new style by local builders.

[163] See HABS No. DC-253, in *Georgetown Architecture*, pp. 38–53.
[164] Designed by Francis Stanton; see HABS No. DC-201.
[165] See HABS No. DC-178, in *Northeast*, pp. 186–201.

[166] See HABS No. DC-187; published in *Northeast*, pp. 214–227.

FIGURE 202. Cooke's Row, Villa No. 3, 3013-15 Q Street, N.W.

FIGURE 203. Italian Villa, from *Hobbs's Architecture*.

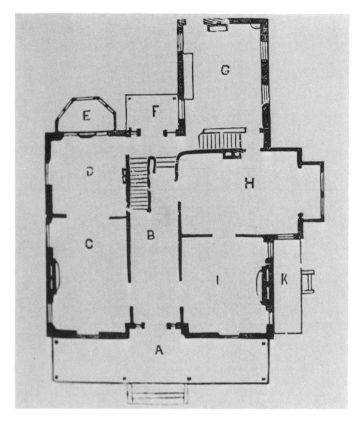

FIGURE 204. Italian Villa, plan, from *Hobbs's Architecture*.

At the same time, however, when very inexpensive workers' rowhouses were desired, such as those at 1021–1037 Thirtieth Street, N.W., of ca. 1890 (fig. 212), the earlier tradition of flat brick walls was again employed.

It is clear, therefore, that the Dodge villas were built well before the sense of the picturesque or volumetric massing and dynamic interior space became accepted locally. They consequently had little influence on the local traditions. But when the local tradition was developing toward more plastic treatment, a style, as the Richardsonian Romansque, which

was basically plastic, would find much ready acceptance.

A similar situation existed in Washington's public architecture, which in part accounts for the lack of influence of Renwick's major structures. The advanced sense of style of his buildings was not compatible with the conservative (and less costly) local solutions which were called upon when large buildings were needed.

There were occasionally, of course, structures of some architectural pretensions. The second Baltimore and Ohio Railroad station of 1851 (fig. 213), erected northwest of the Capitol, was clearly Italianate. It was, however, a rather unique structure (a railroad station) so that superficially it was not readily adaptable to other uses.[167] After the grade changes of the 1870's it was remodeled somewhat and made far less attractive (fig. 214). The Baltimore and Potomac Railroad station (1873), built across the Mall, had a riot of Ruskinian polychromy and was the closest approach to a distinctive, nonvernacular style to have any imitators (fig. 215–216). The Cen-

[167] Washington Topham, "First Railroad into Washington and its Three Depots," *C. H. S. Records*, XXVII (1925), pp. 175–247.

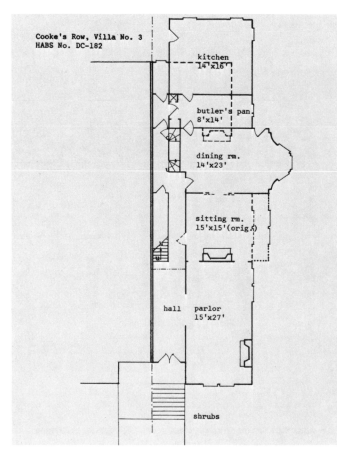

FIGURE 205.   Cooke's Row, Villa No. 3, half-plan.

FIGURE 207.   1402 Thirty-first Street, N.W.

FIGURE 206.   Residence of Mrs. B. B. French (left), from Hutchins and Moore, *The National Capital, Past and Present* (1885), p. 318.

FIGURE 208.   Holy Trinity Rectory, 3514 O Street, N.W.

tral Market, built just to the west of it, carried on its polychromy, but also the station's flat walls, sense of applied details, and the fragmented ornamentation conceived in small patches rather than in an overall program (fig. 217). Only a few Washington houses seem to have followed this style.[168]

The style of building that was generally used for

---

[168] The buildings for Gallaudet College by Withers and Vaux in the 1860's and 1870's also seem to have had few imitators.

FIGURE 209. Grafton Tyler Double House, 1314 Thirtieth Street, N.W.

FIGURE 211. 3099 Q Street, N.W., by T. F. Schneider, 1887-90.

FIGURE 210. 3405-3407 N Street, N.W.

FIGURE 212. Libby Row Houses, 1021-1037 Thirtieth Street, N.W.

was the Winder Building at Seventeenth and F Streets, N.W., (fig. 218) , a fireproof structure erected for Government use.[169] This had the flat wall treatment and local Greek Revival details which we have seen before.

the proliferation of larger buildings was based on the earlier local traditions. In the 1840's one of the few large private structures erected in Washington

[169] Washington Topham, "The Winder Building," C. H. S. *Records,* XXXVII–XXXVIII (1937) , pp. 169–172. The building was erected in 1847–49. The surface was originally stuccoed, as in the view of about 1872. Subsequent changes, with the street lowered; the balcony, stucco, and window caps all removed; and the frieze windows enlarged; alter its appearance considerably for the worse.

FIGURE 213. Baltimore and Ohio Station. Detail of a photograph looking north from the Senate wing, ca. 1856.

FIGURE 215. Baltimore and Potomac Railroad Station (demolished).

FIGURE 214. Baltimore and Ohio Station (demolished).

FIGURE 216. Baltimore and Potomac Railroad Station.

But the mode that was to become most favored was that of brick walls articulated with vertical brick piers, which were used primarily for structural (and economic) reasons, but also tended to give the building a certain sense of architectural style since these piers were analogous to pilasters. We find this mode of building appearing in the 1850's. In Georgetown, two clear examples can be cited. The small Duvall

Foundry at 1050 Thirtieth Street, N.W.,[170] of 1856, makes use of these piers which add considerably to the interest of an otherwise nondescript building (fig. 219). The canal warehouse between Thirty-first Street and Wisconsin Avenue, N.W. built shortly after 1887, is another example of considerably greater size (figs. 220–221); even Mt. Zion United Methodist Church, a modest brick structure begun in 1876, utilized vertical brick ribs on its north and south

170 HABS No. DC-154, published in *Waterfront,* pp. 199–211.

sides.[171] The obvious advantage of this mode was that the windows could be enlarged considerably with the structure still kept sound.[172] With some effort it could be given a passable architectural sense, at "trifling additional cost," such as in the District Armory on the Mall of 1855 (fig. 222), or the Georgetown Market on M Street of 1865 (figs. 223–224).[173] The Eastern Market in Southeast Washington (1871) continues this use successfully (fig. 225) and is embellished with brick machicolation, a feature seen commonly used in the later builder tradition. Inteerstingly enough, the rear and sides of the old Center Market of Washington (fig. 226) mentioned above were not polychromed as was the front, but used this ribbed style.

When adapted to more pretentious use as at the Bureau of Engraving of 1879 (fig. 227) and given a basement story, with the tops of the ribs joined by arches and capped with brick machicolation, a handsome, almost Sullivanesque effect could be achieved. It was this mode, which grew out of a local brick tradition, that was used for local building rather than the more architecturally complex, elaborate, and expensive styles. Even the Franklin School of 1868 (fig. 228) by Adolph Cluss can trace its roots to this style.

There were, as would be expected, other large buildings that are not in this mode; they are even plainer. The old Government Printing Office at H and North Capitol Streets, N.W., (1861) was undecorated, with plain flat walls; the mansarded central pavilion was the only concession to architectural style. The old Washington City Orphan Asylum at 14th and S Streets, N.W., (1866) [174] is ostensibly Italianate, but lacking any of the spatial intricacy or surface richness that the best architects advocated (fig. 229).

It is clear that neither Renwick nor Downing had much architectural influence on Washington for the variety of reasons noted above. Among them, the

FIGURE 217. Center Market, Pennsylvania Avenue and Eighth Street, N.W., (demolished).

FIGURE 218. The Winder Building, Seventeenth and F Streets, N.W. Photograph ca. 1872.

---

[171] HABS No. DC-242, published in *Georgetown Architecture*, pp. 98–116.

[172] This is the form of building used, of course, in New England mills. Those at Manchester, N.H., for example, show a progression of window size that gradually increases from about 1840 to about 1914.

[173] HABS No. DC-123, published in [James Philip Noffsinger and Thomas R. Martinson], *Georgetown Commercial Architecture—M Street* (Washington: Commission of Fine Arts and the Historic American Buildings Survey, 1967), pp. 66–73.

[174] John Clagett Proctor, *Sunday Star*, Jan. 27, 1935. The building was occupied by the State Department from 1866 to 1875.

FIGURE 219. Duvall Foundry, 1050 Thirtieth Street, N.W.

most important were probably the lack of adequate financial resources, or the need for large public buildings; a purely local economy; an uncertain relationship to the Federal Government which, until after the Civil War, was a discouragement to more adventuresome building; and a strong local builder tradition that, until it had far greater contact with architect-designed buildings, would find its own solutions to problems rather than try to imitate more impressive styles. Only in the 1870's, when the economy of the city became more stable, the streets were graded and paved and brought up to decent standards, and the city had greater encouragement from the central government, would the architectural climate also change, to give rise to an astonishingly rich late flowering of architecture in Washington.

FIGURE 220. Canal Warehouse, between Wisconsin Avenue and Thirty-first Street, N.W. Photograph taken 1968; now considerably altered.

FIGURE 221. Canal Warehouse, between Wisconsin Avenue and Thirty-first Street, N.W.

FIGURE 222. District Armory, Mall. Photograph taken August 5, 1896 (demolished).

FIGURE 223. Georgetown Market, 3276 M Street, N.W. Photograph ca. 1937.

FIGURE 224. Georgetown Market, west side. Photograph ca. 1937.

FIGURE 225. Eastern Market, Seventh and C Streets, S.E.

FIGURE 226. South side, Center Market, Eighth Street and Pennsylvania Avenue, N.W.

FIGURE 227. Bureau of Printing and Engraving, Fourteenth and C Streets, S.W., by James G. Hill, 1879.

FIGURE 228. Franklin School, Thirteenth and K Streets, N.W.

FIGURE 229. Washington City Orphan Asylum, Fourteenth and S Streets, N.W., (demolished).

140

CHAPTER V

Epilogue

FOLLOWING the Civil War, two developments combined to start Washington on the way to being a city of wealth and architectural activity. These were the great expansion of the Federal Government, symbolized by the erection of the State, War and Navy Building by Alfred B. Mullett (begun in 1871); and the wide range improvement of the physical city, as seen particularly in the extensive grading and paving of streets, construction of sewers, and planting of avenues of trees, under Alexander Shepherd (1871–73).

The State, War and Navy Building (figs. 230–231) was the symbol for Washington that all efforts to move the Capital (and dissolve the Union) were at an end, and that the government was again willing to spend lavishly on public structures.[1] The building also symbolized, by its very size, the immense growth of the government itself, during and after the Civil War, and indicated that the Federal Government *would* be important, and would increase even more in power over the years. While this might not be looked on with pleasure by states, it was a welcome sign for Washington. Architecturally, the vigorous, plastic building, one of the finest Second Empire edifices in America, drew its vigor not from applied detail or sculpture (of which there was very little), but rather from its massing, a composition of solid and void. It therefore contrasted with, as well as echoed, the neighboring Corcoran Art Gallery (fig. 232) though vastly larger in size. Together with the rapid growth of the Richard-

sonian Romanesque style soon to follow, Washington was here seen visibly moving into a second, more mature phase of later 19th century architecture. Great numbers of fine Romanesque houses, both detached and in speculative rows (figs. 234–237), grew up quickly, and land speculation for peripheral development again became popular. These new rows gave Washington a prosperous look that it had not had before. This period of stylistic evolution lasted until 1902 when the McMillan plan for the development of the central part of Washington was unveiled,[2] and which urged the adoption of a style reminiscent of the Columbian Exposition in Chicago of 1893. This became the accepted mode for major public buildings, and many lesser ones as well.

But equally important as any architectural symbol of a new era was the startling revitalization of the physical layout of the city. Still unimproved during the Civil War, great numbers of people saw—and commented on—the terrible condition of the streets, sewers, and so on. As we have seen, the city's sporadic growth, without any of the original improvements envisioned by L'Enfant, resulted in woefully inadequate street grading, drainage, and sewers. When the District Government was reorganized in 1871, establishing a territorial form of government,[3] a Board of Public Works was also created by the Presi-

---

[1] [Donald J. Lehman], *Executive Office Building* (Washington: U.S. Government Printing Office, 1964).

[2] For a thorough consideration of the origin and development of the McMillan plan, see John W. Reps, *Monumental Washington* (Princeton: Princeton University Press, 1967).

[3] James H. Whyte, "The District of Columbia Territorial Government, 1871–1874," Columbia Historical Society, *Records*, LI–LII (1955), pp. 87–102.

FIGURE 230.   State, War and Navy Building.

dent, with Alexander Shepherd as its head.[4] Under his guidance, a full scale program of city improvement was initiated, perhaps with greater zeal than understanding. A few statistics give an indication of the extent of the work: 180 miles of streets were graded and paved; 208 miles of sidewalks were laid; 127 miles of sewers were constructed; and 6,000 trees were planted.[5]

The necessary grade changes enraged many.[6] Some-

times it would leave houses or public buildings many feet above the new street level (as the Post Office, fig. 238; compare with fig. 28); other times it would bury houses up to the second floor level (fig. 239). But the final effect made it possible for developers to know exactly where they stood when they built. With these improvements and the new climate of government involvement in the affairs of the District,[7] great numbers of people moved into the Capital, and Congressmen more frequently began building houses and bringing their families.[8] Local enthusiasm was considerably improved; as one resident wrote,

> Washington has no equal. Since the war it has so changed that one who knew it then would hardly recognize it now. Its

[4] See Franklin T. Howe, "The Board of Public Works," C.H.S. Records, III (1900), pp. 257–278, and Mrs. Elden E. Billings, "Alexander Robey Shepherd and his Unpublished Diaries and Correspondence," C.H.S. Records, LX–LXII (1963), pp. 150–166. This period is also well treated in Constance McLaughlin Green, Washington, Village and Capital, 1800–1878 (Princeton: Princeton University Press, 1962), pp. 339–362.

[5] Whyte, p. 99.

[6] See, for example, E. E. Barton (ed.), Historical and Commercial Sketches of Washington and Environs (Washington, 1884), pp. 29–33.

[7] In 1878 with the Organic Act, the sharing of local expenses fifty-fifty with the Federal Government was finally implemented.

[8] Henry H. Glassie, "Victorian Homes in Washington," C.H.S. Records, LXIII–LXV (1966), p. 342.

FIGURE 231. State, War and Navy Building, west side.

FIGURE 232. Corcoran Art Gallery, and State, War and Navy Building.

FIGURE 233. Corcoran Art Gallery, and State, War and Navy Building, from McMillan Commission model of 1901.

broad, smooth avenues and streets, its fine dwellings and public buildings, its public libraries and institutions, render it the delight of the educated and people of leisure.[9]

These two major events then, both beginning in 1871, are appropriate symbols for a new era in Washington's development, a period of 30 years that rivaled the rapid growth in any other American city and which saw the widest variety of eclectic styles executed, often in the most lavish manner (figs. 240–241). In such a climate, the utilitarian efforts of Owen and Renwick in the Smithsonian, or the uplifting moral and esthetic effect Downing hoped for in his villas, could inspire little interest.

[9] Barton, p. 37.

143

FIGURE 234. Hay-Adams House, Sixteenth and H Streets, N.W., by H. H. Richardson, 1884-86 (demolished).

FIGURE 235. Richardsonian Romanesque house, 1300 Seventeenth Street, N.W.

FIGURE 236. Row houses, R Street at Seventeenth Street, N.W., ca. 1893.

FIGURE 237. Row houses, 1701-1709 Q Street, N.W

FIGURE 238. Post Office. Photograph taken about 1916.

FIGURE 239. McCleery House, 1068 Thirtieth Street, N.W.

FIGURE 240. Logan Circle, 1970.

FIGURE 241. Connecticut Avenue, 1890.

Bibliography

Public Documents

Adams, John Quincy. *Smithsonian Bequest: Report to the President*, Mar. 4, 1840. H. Rep. 277, 26th Cong., 1st sess., Ser. 370 (155 pp.).

Annual Reports of the Board of Regents of the Smithsonian Institution. From 1846 to present.

Blackford, Charles M. "The Smithsonian Institution," *North American Review*, January 1909. Revised and reprinted as S. Doc. 717, 60th Cong., 2d sess., Ser. 5408 (11 pp.).

Blake, John B. *Report of the Commissioner of Public Buildings*, Oct. 13, 1859. S. Doc. 2, pt. 1, 36th Cong., 1st sess., Ser. 1023, pp. 840–858.

Boutwell, George S. *Expenditures in the District of Columbia. Letter from the Secretary of the Treasury . . . February 19, 1870*. H. Ex. Doc. 156, 41st Cong., 2d sess., Ser. 1418 (11 pp.).

Committee for the District of Columbia. *Street— Capitol to Executive Offices* [Paving of Pennsylvania Avenue]. H. Rep. 184, 21st Cong., 1st sess., Ser. 200 (15 pp.).

Documentary History of the Construction and Development of the United States Capitol Building and Grounds. H. Rept. 646, 58th Cong., 2d sess., Ser. 4585 (1,312 pp.).

Easby, William. *Letter from the Commissioner of Public Buildings, Transmitting his Annual Report*, Feb. 20, 1852. H. Ex. Doc. 79, 32d Cong., 1st sess., Ser. 641 (24 pp.).

French, B. B. *Report of the Commissioner of Public Buildings*, Oct. 5, 1854, in *Report of the Secretary of Interior*. H. Ex. Doc. 1, 33d Cong., 2d sess., Ser. 777, pp. 598–604.

Hughes, George W. *A Report Concerning Obstructions to the Navigation of the Potomac between Washington and Georgtown*, in Levi Woodbury, *Report of the Secretary of the Treasury*. S. Doc. 133, 23d Cong., 2d sess., Ser. 268 (7 pp.).

Memorial of Corporation of City of Washington on the Subject of the Smithsonian Bequest, Feb. 5, 1840. H. Doc. 51, 26th Cong., 1st sess., Ser. 364 (2 pp.).

Michler, Nathaniel. *Communication from Chief of Engineers relative to an Appropriation for Public Buildings and Grounds*, June 10, 1868. H. Ex. Doc. 39, 40th Cong., 2d sess., Ser. 1345.

————. *Report by General Michler on the Examination and Survey of the Potomac River*, in A. A. Humphreys, *Report of the Chief of Engineers*, in E. M. Stanton, *Letter from the Secretary of War*. H. Ex. Doc. 292, 40th Cong., 2d sess., Ser. 1343 (13 pp.).

————. *Report of Brevet Brigadier General N. Michler, Major of Engineers, United States Army, in Charge of Public Buildings, Grounds, Works, &c.*, Oct. 1, 1867, in *Report of the Chief of Engineers*, in *Report of the Secretary of War*. H. Ex. Doc. 1, 40th Cong., 2d sess., Ser. 1325. App. T, pp. 519–531; App. T1 and T2, pp. 532–548.

————. *Report of the Office of Public Buildings, Grounds, and Works*, Sept. 30, 1868, in *Report of the Chief of Engineers*, in *Report of the Secretary of War*. Ex. Doc. 1, pt. 2, 40th Cong., 3d sess., Ser. 1368. App. V, pp. 889–907; App. V2, pp. 911–913.

Moore, Charles (comp.) *Federal and Local Legislation Relating to Canals and Steam Railroads in the District of Columbia, 1802–1903*. S. Doc. 220, 57th Cong., 2d sess., Ser. 4430 (264 pp.).

Mudd, Ignatius. *Annual Report of the Commissioner of Public Buildings for the year 1849*, Jan. 24, 1850. H. Ex. Doc. 30, 31st Cong., 1st sess., Ser. 576 (21 pp.).

————. *Letter from the Commissioner of Public Buildings, transmitting his Annual Report for*

1850. H. Ex. Doc. 47, 31st Cong., 2d sess., Ser. 599 (23 pp.).

Report of the Board of Regents of the Smithsonian Institution . . . January 6, 1848. S. Misc. Doc. 23, 30th Cong., 1st sess., Ser. 511 ¹ (208 pp.).

Smithsonian Institution. Report from the Board of Regents . . . March 3, 1847. S. Doc. 211, 29th Cong., 2d sess., Ser. 495 (37 pp.).

Southard, Samuel L. *Report of the Committee on the District of Columbia,* Feb. 2, 1835. S. Doc. 97, 23d Cong., 2d sess., Ser. 268 (19 pp.).

Spencer, J. C. *Letter from Secretary of the Treasury, transmitting Statements relative to the Smithsonian Fund, &c.,* Feb. 19, 1844. H. Doc. 142, 28th Cong., 1st sess., Ser. 442 (32 pp.).

Thompson, J. *Annual Report of the Secretary of the Interior for the Year 1859* (23 pp.).

Walter, Thomas U. *Report of the Architect for the Extension of the Capitol,* Dec. 23, 1851. H. Ex. Doc. 60, 32d Cong., 1st sess., Ser. 641 (9 pp.).

Articles and Periodicals

Ames, Kenneth. "Robert Mills and the Philadelphia Row House," *Journal of the Society of Architectural Historians,* XXVII, 2 (May 1968), pp. 140–146.

Baker, Geoffrey. "The Smithsonian," *Magazine of Art,* XXXIV, 2 (March 1941), pp. 128–133.

Billings, Mrs. Elden E. "Alexander Robey Shepherd and his Unpublished Diaries and Correspondence," Columbia Historical Society, *Records,* LX–LXII (1963), pp. 150–166.

Brown, Glenn. "The Plan of L'Enfant for the City of Washington and its Effect upon the Future Development of the City," Columbia Historical Society, *Records,* XII (1909), pp. 1–20.

Bryan, Wilhelmus Bogard. "Hotels of Washington Prior to 1814," Columbia Historical Society, *Records,* VII (1904), pp. 71–106.

Campioli, Mario E. "Thomas U. Walter, Edward Clark and the United States Capitol," *Journal of the Society of Architectural Historians,* XXIII, 4 (December 1964), pp. 210–213.

Cantor, Jay E. "The Museum in the Park," *The Metropolitan Museum of Art Bulletin,* XXVI, 8 (April 1968), pp. 332–340.

Caulfield, Philip A. "History of Providence Hospital, 1861–1961," Columbia Historical Society, *Records,* LX–LXII (1963), pp. 231–249.

Clark, Allen C. "Daniel Carroll of Duddington," Columbia Historical Society, *Records,* XXXIX (1938), pp. 1–48.

———. "The Old Mills," Columbia Historical Society, *Records,* XXXI–XXXII (1930), pp. 81–115.

———. "Origin of the Federal City," Columbia Historical Society, *Records,* XXXV–XXXVI (1935), pp. 1–97.

———. "Robert Mills, Architect and Engineer," Columbia Historical Society, *Records,* XL–XLI (1940), pp. 1–32.

Clark, Appleton P., Jr. "Origin of the Building Regulations," Columbia Historical Society, *Records,* IV (1901), pp. 166–172.

Cluss, Adolph. "Architecture and Architects of the Capital of the United States from its Foundation to 1875," *Proceedings of the Tenth Annual Convention of the American Institute of Architects, Philadelphia, October 11 and 12, 1876,* pp. 38–44.

Davis, Henry E. "The Political Development of the District of Columbia," *Proceedings of the Washington Academy of Sciences,* I (1899), pp. 189–220.

Davies, Jane B. "Six Letters by William P. Elliot to Alexander J. Davis, 1834–1838," *Journal of the Society of Architectural Historians,* XXVI, 1 (March 1967), pp. 71–73.

"Death of James Renwick, Recognized as one of the Ablest Architects of this Country," *The New-York Times,* June 25, 1895, p. 9.

"Decatur House," *Historic Preservation,* XIX, 3–4 (July–December 1967). Washington: National Trust for Historic Preservation, 1967.

Donnell, Edna. "A. J. Davis and the Gothic Revival," *Metropolitan Museum Studies,* V (1934–36), pp. 183–233.

"Dreadful Calamity on the Hudson River. Burning of the Steamer Henry Clay. Melancholy Loss of Life . . .," *New-York Daily Times,* July 29, 1852, p. 2.

Elder, William V. III. "Dumbarton House," reprinted from *Winter Antiques Show Catalogue,* (n.d.) (9 pp.).

Evans, George W. "The Birth and Growth of the Patent Office," Columbia Historical Society, *Records,* XXII (1919), pp. 105–124.

Friedlaender, Marc. "Henry Hobson Richardson, Henry Adams, and John Hay," *Journal of the*

Society of Architectural Historians, XXIX, 3 (October 1970), pp. 231–246.

Glassie, Henry H. "Victorian Homes in Washington," Columbia Historical Society, *Records*, LXIII–LXV (1966), pp. 320–365.

Grigg, Milton I. "Thomas Jefferson and the Development of the National Capital," Columbia Historical Society, *Records*, LIII–LVI (1953–56), pp. 81–100.

Hall, Louise. "The Design of the Old Patent Office," *Journal of the Society of Architectural Historians*, XV, 1 (March 1956), pp. 27–30.

Hamlin, Talbot F. "James Renwick," *Dictionary of American Biography*, (New York: Charles Scribner's Sons, 1935), XV, pp. 507–509.

Hamlin, Teunis S. "Historic Houses of Washington," *Scribner's Magazine*, XIV, 4 (October 1983), pp. 475–491.

Heine, Cornelius W. "The Washington City Canal," Columbia Historical Society, *Records*, LIII–LVI (1953–56), pp. 1–27.

"The Henry Clay Disaster. Forty-seven Bodies Recovered . . .," *New-York Daily Times*, July 30, 1852, p. 1.

Hersey, George L. "Godey's Choice," *Journal of the Society of Architectural Historians*, XVIII, 3 (October 1959), pp. 104–111.

Hood, James Franklin. "The Cottage of David Burnes and its Dining-room Mantel," Columbia Historical Society, *Records*, XXIII (1920), pp. 1–9.

Howe, Franklin T. "The Board of Public Works," Columbia Historical Society, *Records*, III (1900), pp. 257–278.

Hunsberger, George S. "The Architectural Career of George Hadfield," Columbia Historical Society, *Records*, LI–LII (1955), pp. 46–65.

Jackson, Cordelia. "People and Places in Old Georgetown," Columbia Historical Society, *Records*, XXXIII–XXXIV (1932), pp. 133–162.

———. "Tudor Place," Columbia Historical Society, *Records*, XXV (1923), pp. 68–86.

Lancaster, Clay. "Builders' Guides and Plan Books and American Architecture, from the Revolution to the Civil War," *Magazine of Art*, XLI, 1 (January 1948), pp. 16–22.

———. "Central Park, 1851–1951," *Magazine of Art*, XLIV, 4 (April 1951), pp. 123–128.

———. "Three Gothic Revival Houses at Lexington," *Journal of the Society of Architectural Historians*, VI, 1–2 (January-June 1947), pp. 13–21.

"Latrobe on Architects' Fees, 1798," *Journal of the Society of Architectural Historians*, XIX, 3 (October 1960), pp. 115–117.

Lee, Ronald F. "Chesapeake and Ohio Canal," Columbia Historical Society, *Records*, XL–XLI (1940), pp. 185–195.

"The L'Enfant Memorials," Columbia Historical Society, *Records*, II (1899), pp. 72–110.

"Local Matters. Modern Building," *Georgetown Advocate*, Dec. 7, 1852, p. 3.

McKenna, R. T. "James Renwick, Jr. and the Second Empire Style in the United States," *Magazine of Art*, XLIV, 3 (1951), pp. 97–101.

Meeks, Carroll L. V. "Creative Eclecticism," *Journal of the Society of Architectural Historians*, XII, 4 (December 1953), pp. 15–18.

———. "Henry Austin and the Italian Villa," *Art Bulletin*, XXX, 2 (June 1948), pp. 145–149.

———. "Picturesque Eclecticism," *Art Bulletin*, XXXII, 3 (September 1950), pp. 226–235.

Metcalf, Frank J. "Octagon Houses of Washington and Elsewhere," Columbia Historical Society, *Records*, XXVI (1924), pp. 91–105.

Milburn, Rev. Page. "How Washington Grew—in Spots," Columbia Historical Society, *Records*, XXVI (1924), pp. 106–120.

Minnigerode, C. Powell. "The Corcoran Gallery of Art," Columbia Historical Society, *Records*, XLVIII–XLIX (1946–47), pp. 227–235.

"Mr. Corcoran Dead," *Washington Evening Star*, Feb. 24, 1888.

Morgan, James Dudley. "Maj. Pierre Charles L'Enfant, the Unhonored and Unrewarded Engineer," Columbia Historical Society, *Records*, II (1899), pp. 116–157.

Neil, J. Meredith. "Latrobe's Professionalism," *Journal of the Society of Architectural Historians*, XXVIII, 3 (October 1969), p. 211.

"Naval Observatory, Its Interesting History and the Results it has Accomplished," unidentified clipping in scrapbook, Columbia Historical Society library, dated Aug. 10, 1884.

Noyes, Theodore W. "Some of Washington's Grievances," *The Evening Star* (Washington), Feb. 18 and 25, Mar. 3 and 10, 1888.

"Oak Hill Cemetery," *National Intelligencer* (Washington), Dec. 23, 1851, p. 3.

Osborne, John Ball. "The Removal of the Government to Washington," Columbia Historical Society, *Records,* III (1900), pp. 136–160.

Pattee, Sarah Lewis. "Andrew Jackson Downing and his Influence on Landscape Architecture in America," *Landscape Architecture,* XIX, 2 (January 1929), pp. 79–83.

Paulin, Charles O. "History of the Site of the Congressional and Folger Libraries," Columbia Historical Society, *Records,* XXXVII-XXXVIII (1937), pp. 173–194.

Peets, Elbert. "The Genealogy of L'Enfant's Washington," American Institute of Architects *Journal,* XV, 4 (April 1927), pp. 115–119; XV, 5 (May 1927), pp. 151–154; XV, 6 (June 1927), pp. 187–191.

Pierson, William H., Jr. "Robert Mills' Treasury Building," *Journal of the Society of Architectural Historians,* XXVIII, 3 (October 1969), pp. 211–212.

Proctor, John Clagett. "Criminals made old Mall a Dangerous Spot [ca. 1880]," *Sunday Star* (Washington), Nov. 24, 1929.

———. "Historic Capital Fires have Caused Irreparable National Loss," *Sunday Star,* Jan. 29, 1928.

———. "Odd Fellows' Hall Noted old Show Place," *Sunday Star* (Washington), Nov. 17, 1929.

———. "The Tragic Death of Andrew Jackson Downing and the Monument to his Memory," Columbia Historical Society, *Records,* XXVII (1925), pp. 248–261.

Rosenberger, Homer T. "Thomas Ustick Walter and the Completion of the United States Capitol," Columbia Historical Society, *Records,* L (1952), pp. 273–322.

Scisco, Louis Dow. "A Site for the 'Federal City': The Original Proprietors and their Negotiations with Washington," Columbia Historical Society, *Records,* LVII–LIX (1957–59), pp. 123–147.

Smith, Norris K. "Frank Lloyd Wright and the Problem of Historical Perspective," *Journal of the Society of Architectural Historians,* XXVI, 4 (December 1967), pp. 234–237.

Spofford, Ainsworth R. "The Coming of the White Man, and the Founding of the National Capital," *Proceedings of the Washington Academy of Sciences,* I (1899), pp. 221–251.

Spratt, Zack. "Rock Creek Bridges," Columbia Historical Society, *Records,* LIII–LVI (1953–56), pp. 101–134.

Sunderland, Byron. "Washington—As I First Knew It, 1852–1855," Columbia Historical Society, *Records,* V (1902), pp. 195–211.

Tindall, William. "A Sketch of Alexander Robey Shepherd," Columbia Historical Society, *Records,* XI (1909), pp. 49–66.

Topham, Washington. "First Railroad into Washington and its Three Depots," Columbia Historical Society, *Records,* XXVII (1925), pp. 175–247.

———. "The Winder Building," Columbia Historical Society, *Records,* XXXVII–XXXVIII (1937), pp. 169–172.

Torres, Louis. "Federal Hall Revisited," *Journal of the Society of Architectural Historians,* XXIX, 4 (December 1970), pp. 327–338.

Washburn, Wilcomb E. "The Influence of the Smithsonian Institution on Intellectual Life in Mid-Nineteenth-Century Washington," Columbia Historical Society, *Records,* LXIII–LXV (1963–65), pp. 96–121.

———. "Vision of Life for the Mall," *AIA Journal,* XLVII, 3 (March 1967), pp. 52–59.

Whyte, James H. "The District of Columbia Territorial Government, 1871–1874," Columbia Historical Society, *Records,* LI–LII (1955), pp. 87–102.

Wilson, J. Ormond. "Eighty Years of the Public Schools of Washington—1805–1885," Columbia Historical Society, *Records,* I (1896), pp. 119–170.

Wright, Carroll D. "The Economic Development of the District of Columbia," *Proceedings of the Washington Academy of Sciences,* I (1899), pp. 161–187.

"The Writings of George Washington Relating to the National Capital," Columbia Historical Society, *Records,* XVII (1914), pp. 3–232.

Books: 19th Century

Barton, Elmer Epenetus (ed.) *Historical and Commercial Sketches of Washington and Environs, Our Capital City, "The Paris of America."* Washington: E. E. Barton, Publisher, 1884.

[Bohn, Casimir]. *Bohn's Handbook of Washington.* Washington: Casimir Bohn, 1861.

Bouligny, M. E. P. *A Tribute to W. W. Corcoran, of Washington City.* Philadelphia: Porter & Coates, 1874.

Ceremonies and Oration at Laying the Cornerstone of the City Hall of the City of Washington, August 22, 1820. Washington: Jacob Gideon Jr., 1820.

Corcoran, W. W. *A Grandfather's Legacy; Containing a Sketch of his Life, and Obituary Notices of some Members of his Family, together with Letters from his Friends.* Washington: Henry Polkinhorn, printer, 1879.

Downing, Andrew Jackson. *The Architecture of Country Houses; including Designs for Cottages, Farm Houses, and Villas, with Remarks on Interiors, Furniture, and the best Modes of Warming and Ventilating.* New York: D. Appleton & Co., 1850.

———. *Cottage Residences; or, A Series of Designs for Rural Cottages and Cottage-Villas, and their Gardens and Grounds. Adapted to North America.* New York: Wiley & Putnam, 1842.

———. *Explanatory Notes to Accompany the Plan for Improving the Public Grounds at Washington.* Mar. 3, 1851 (manuscript).

———. *The Fruits and Fruit Trees of America. . . .* New York: Wiley & Putnam, 1845.

———. *Rural Essays.* Edited, with a memoir of the author, by George William Curtis. New York: George P. Putnam & Co., 1853.

———. *A Treatise on the Theory and Practice of Landscape Gardening, Adapted to North America; with a View to the Improvement of Country Residences.* New York: Wiley & Putnam, 1841.

Force, W. Q. (comp.) *The Builder's Guide: Containing Lists of Prices, and Rules of Measurement, for Carpenters, Bricklayers, Stone Masons, Stone Cutters, Plasterers. . . .* Washington: Peter Force, 1842.

Goode, George Brown (ed.) *The Smithsonian Institution 1846–1896, the History of its First Half Century.* Washington: [Smithsonian Institution], 1897.

Greenough, Horatio. *The Travels, Observations, and Experience of a Yankee Stonecutter.* New York, 1852.

Hobbs, Isaac H. and son. *Hobbs's Architecture: Containing Designs and Ground Plans for Villas, Cottages, and other Edifices, both Suburban and Rural, Adapted to the United States.* Philadelphia: J. B. Lippencott & Co., 1873.

Hutchins, Stilson, and Moore, Joseph W. *The National Capital, Past and Present: The Story of its Settlement, Progress, and Development, with Profuse Illustrations.* Washington: The Post Publishing Co., 1885.

Lamb, Mrs. Martha J. (ed.) *The Homes of America.* New York: D. Appleton & Co., 1879.

Moore, Joseph West. *Picturesque Washington: Pen and Pencil Sketches.* Providence: J. A. & R. A. Reid, 1884.

[Morrison, William M.] *A Picture of Washington.* Washington: Published by William M. Morrison, 1840.

Morrison, William M. *Stranger's Guide to the City of Washington.* Washington: William M. Morrison, 1842.

Owen, Robert Dale. *Hints on Public Architecture, Containing, among other Illustrations, Views and plans of the Smithsonian Institution: together with an Appendix relative to Building Materials.* New York: George P. Putnam, 1849.

Pugin, Augustus Charles. *Examples of Gothic Architecture; selected from Various Antient Edifices in England: consisting of Plans, Elevations, Sections, and Parts at Large.* 3 vols. Vol. I, 2d ed., London: Henry G. Bohn, 1838. Vol. II, by A. C. Pugin and Augustus Welby Pugin, 1839. Vol. III, by A. W. Pugin and T. L. Walker, 1840.

Pugin, Augustus Welby. *An Apology for the Revival of Christian Architecture in England.* London: John Weale, 1843.

———. *Contrasts, or a Parallel between Noble Edifices of the Middle Ages, and Corresponding Buildings of the Present Day, Shewing the Present Decay of Taste.* London: Charles Dolman, 1841.

———. *The Present State of Ecclesiastical Architecture in England.* Republished from the Dublin Review. London: Charles Dolman, 1843.

———. *The True Principles of Pointed or Christian Architecture.* London: John Weale, 1841.

Report of the Investigating Committee Appointed at a Meeting of Lot-Holders of Oak Hill Cemetery on Monday, February 15, 1869. Georgetown: Courier printer, 1869.

Richardson, James Daniel (comp.) *Compilation of the Messages and Papers of the Presidents 1789–1897.* 10 vols. Washington: U.S. Government Printing Office, 1896–99.

Schneider, T. F. *Selections from the Work of T. F. Schneider, Architect.* Washington, 1894.

Thayer, R. H. (comp.) *History, Organization and Function of the Office of the Supervising Architect of the Treasury Department.* (Treasury Department Document No. 817.) Washington: U.S. Government Printing Office, 1886.

Vaux, Calvert. *Villas and Cottages, A Series of Designs prepared for Execution in the United States.* New York: Harper and Bros., 1857.

Watterson, George. *New Guide to Washington.* Washington: Published by Robert Farnum, 1847.

Webb, William B., Woolridge, J., et al. *Centennial History of the City of Washington, D.C.* Dayton, Ohio: H. W. Crew, 1892.

Wightwick, George. *Hints to Young Architects, Calculated to Facilitate their Practical Operations. . . . With Additional Notes, and Hints to Persons about Building in the Country, by A. J. Downing.* New York: Wiley & Putnam, 1847.

Books: 20th Century

Bell, Whitfield J., Jr., et al. *A Cabinet of Curiosities; Five Episodes in the Evolution of American Museums.* Charlottesville: University Press of Virginia, 1967.

Brown, Glenn. *History of the United States Capitol.* 2 vols. (S. Doc. 60, 56th Cong., 1st sess., Ser. 3849 and 3849 ².) Washington: U.S. Government Printing Office, 1900.

Bryan, Wilhelmus Bogart. *A History of the National Capital.* 2 vols. New York: Macmillan Company, 1914–16.

Bunting, Bainbridge. *Houses of Boston's Back Bay: An Architectural History, 1840–1917.* Cambridge: Harvard University Press, 1967.

Caemmerer, H. Paul. *The Life of Pierre Charles L'Enfant, Planner of the City Beautiful, the City of Washington.* Washington: National Republic Publishing Co., 1950.

————. *A Manual on the Origin and Development of Washington.* Washington: U.S. Government Printing Office, 1939.

————. *Washington, the National Capital.* Washington: U.S. Government Printing Office, 1932.

Clark, Kenneth. *The Gothic Revival: an Essay in the History of Taste.* Harmondsworth: Penguin Books, 1964.

Clifford, Derek. *A History of Garden Design.* New York: Frederick A. Praeger, 1963.

Coffin, Lewis A., Jr., and Holden, Arthur. *Brick Architecture of the Colonial Period in Maryland and Virginia.* New York: Architectural Book Publishing Co., 1919.

Coulson, Thomas. *Joseph Henry, His Life and Work.* Princeton: Princeton University Press, 1950.

Cunningham, Harry Francis, Younger, Joseph Arthur, and Smith, J. William. *Measured Drawings of Georgian Architecture in the District of Columbia 1750–1820.* New York: Architectural Book Publishing Co., 1914.

Davis, Deering, Dorsey, Stephen P., and Hall, Ralph Cole. *Alexandria Houses 1750–1830.* New York: Architectural Book Publishing Co., 1946.

————. *Georgetown Houses of the Federal Period: Washington, D.C. 1780–1830.* Cornwall, New York: Architectural Book Publishing Co., Cornwall Press, 1944.

Dupree, A. Hunter. *Science in the Federal Government: A History of Policies and Activities to 1940.* New York: Harper and Row, 1964.

Early, James. *Romanticism and American Architecture.* New York: A. S. Barnes & Co., 1965.

Eberlein, Harold Donaldson, and Hubbard, Cortland Van Dyke. *Historic Houses of GeorgeTown and Washington City.* Richmond: The Dietz Press, 1958.

Embury, Aymar, II (ed.) *Asher Benjamin: A reprint of The Country Builder's Assistant, The American Builder's Companion, The Rudiments of Architecture, The Practical House Carpenter, Practice of Architecture.* New York: Architectural Book Publishing Co., 1917.

Fitch, James Marston. *Architecture and the Esthetics of Plenty.* New York: Columbia University Press, 1961.

Forman, Henry Chandlee. *Tidewater Maryland Architecture and Gardens.* New York: Architectural Book Publishing Co., 1956.

Gallagher, H. M. Pierce. *Robert Mills, Architect of the Washington Monument, 1781–1855.* New York: Columbia University Press, 1935.

Gifford, Don (ed.) *The Literature of Architecture: The Evolution of Architectural Theory and Practice in Nineteenth-Century America.* New York: E. P. Dutton & Co., 1966.

Green, Constance McLaughlin. *Washington: Village and Capital 1800–1878.* Princeton: Princeton University Press, 1962.

Hamlin, Talbot. *Benjamin Henry Latrobe.* New York: Oxford University Press, 1955.

————. *Greek Revival Architecture in America: Being an Account of Important Trends in American Architecture and American Life prior to the War Between the States.* New York: Dover Publications, Inc., 1964.

Heine, Cornelius W. *The Old Stone House*. Washington: U.S. Department of the Interior, 1955.

[Hills, W. H., and Sutherland, J. A.] *A History of Public Buildings under the Control of the Treasury Department*. Washington: U.S. Government Printing Office, 1901.

Hitchcock, Henry-Russell. *Architecture: Nineteenth and Twentieth Centuries*. Baltimore: Penguin Books, 1963.

———. *Rhode Island Architecture*. Providence: Rhode Island Museum Press, 1939.

Howland, Richard H., and Spencer, Eleanor P. *The Architecture of Baltimore, A Pictorial History*. Baltimore: The Johns Hopkins Press, 1953.

Hussey, Christopher. *The Picturesque: Studies in a Point of View*. London: G. P. Putnam's Sons, 1927.

Jacobsen, Hugh Newell, et al. *A Guide to the Architecture of Washington, D.C.* Published for the Washington Metropolitan Chapter, the American Institute of Architects. New York: Frederick A. Praeger, Publishers, 1965.

Kaufmann, Edgar, Jr. (ed.) *The Rise of an American Architecture*. New York: Praeger Publishers, 1970.

Kilham, Walter H. *Boston After Bulfinch: An Account of its Architecture 1800–1900*. Cambridge: Harvard University Press, 1946.

Kimball, Fiske. *Domestic Architecture of the American Colonies and of the Early Republic*. New York: Charles Scribner's Sons, 1922.

Kite, Elizabeth S. *L'Enfant and Washington, 1791–1792*. Baltimore: Johns Hopkins Press, 1929.

[Lehman, Donald J.] *Agriculture—Administration Building*. ("General Services Administration Historical Study," No. 2.) Washington: U.S. Government Printing Office, 1964.

———. *Executive Office Building*. ("General Services Administration Historical Study," No. 3.) Washington: U.S. Government Printing Office, 1964.

[McKee, Harley J., and Fauntleroy, Thomas L.] *Washington, D. C., Architecture—Market Square*. ("Selections from the Historic American Buildings Survey," No. 8.) Washington: Urban Design and Development Corp. and the Historic American Buildings Survey, 1969.

Meeks, Carroll L. V. *The Railroad Station*. New Haven: Yale University Press, 1956.

Morrison, Hugh. *Early American Architecture from the First Colonial Settlements to the National Period*. New York: Oxford University Press, 1952.

Nelligan, Murray Homer. *Custis-Lee Mansion, the Robert E. Lee Memorial, Virginia*. ("U.S. National Park Service Historical Handbook Series," No. 6.) Washington: U.S. Government Printing Office, 1962.

[Noffsinger, James Philip, and Martinson, Thomas R.] *Georgetown Commercial Architecture—M Street*. ("Selections from the Historic American Buildings Survey," No. 2.) Washington: Commission of Fine Arts and the Historic American Buildings Survey, 1967.

———. *Georgetown Commercial Architecture—Wisconsin Avenue*. ("Selections from the Historic American Building Survey," No. 3.) Washington: Commission of Fine Arts and the Historic American Buildings Survey, 1967.

Padover, Saul K. (ed.) *Thomas Jefferson and the National Capital, containing Notes and Correspondence between Jefferson, Washington, L'Enfant, Ellicott, Hallett, Thornton, Latrobe, the Commissioners, and Others*. Washington: U.S. Government Printing Office, 1946.

Peter, Armistead, III. *Tudor Place, Designed by Dr. William Thornton and Built between 1805 and 1816 for Thomas and Martha Peter*. Introduction by Walter M. Whitehill, photographs by Cervin Robinson. Georgetown: [privately printed], 1970.

Peter, Grace Dunlop, and Southwick, Joyce D. *Cleveland Park: An Early Residential Neighborhood of the Nation's Capital*. Washington: The Cleveland Park Community Library Committee, 1958.

Proctor, John Clagett. *Washington and Environs; Written for the Washington Sunday Star 1928–1949*. Washington: [privately printed], 1949.

Public Buildings Commission. *Public Buildings in the District of Columbia*. Washington: U.S. Government Printing Office, 1918.

[Reiff, Daniel D., and Gwin, William R.] *Georgetown Architecture—the Waterfront*. ("Selections from the Historic American Buildings Survey," No. 4.) Washington: Commission of Fine Arts and the Historic American Buildings Survey, 1968.

[Reiff, Daniel D., and Schwartz, Ellen J.] *Georgetown Architecture*. ("Selections from the Historic American Buildings Survey," No. 10.)

Washington: Commission of Fine Arts and the Historic American Buildings Survey, 1970.

Reps, John W. *Monumental Washington: The Planning and Development of the Capital Center*. Princeton: Princeton University Press, 1967.

Roberts, Chalmers M. *Washington, Past and Present: a Pictorial History of the Nation's Capital*. Washington: Public Affairs Press, 1949–50.

[Schwartz, Ellen J., and Thompson, William P.] *Georgetown Residential Architecture—Northeast*. ("Selections from the Historic American Buildings Survey," No. 5.) Washington: Commission of Fine Arts and the Historic American Buildings Survey [1969].

Spreiegen, Paul D. (ed.) *On the Art of Designing Cities: Selected Essays of Elbert Peets*. Cambridge: The M. I. T. Press, 1968.

Stanton, Phoebe B. *The Gothic Revival & American Church Architecture: An Episode in Taste 1840–1856*. Baltimore: The Johns Hopkins Press, 1968.

Tatum, George B. *Penn's Great Town: 250 Years of Philadelphia Architecture*. Philadelphia: University of Pennsylvania Press, 1961.

Tindall, William. *Standard History of the City of Washington, from a Study of the Original Sources*. Knoxville: H. W. Crew & Co., 1914.

U.S. Bureau of the Census, U.S. Department of Commerce. *Historical Statistics of the United States, Colonial Times to 1957*. Washington: U.S. Government Printing Office, 1960.

Waterman, Thomas Tileston. *The Dwellings of Colonial America*. Chapel Hill, N.C.: University of North Carolina Press, 1950.

Weber, Gustavus A. *The Naval Observatory, Its History, Activities, and Organization*. ("Institute for Government Research: Service Monograph of the United States Government," No. 39.) Baltimore: Johns Hopkins Press, 1926.

Young, James Sterling. *The Washington Community, 1800–1828*. New York: Columbia University Press, 1966.

Photographic Credits

J. Alexander
52, 54, 66, 69, 150

J. Alexander, for the Historic American Buildings Survey
41, 47, 74, 75, 76, 88, 146, 180, 207, 208, 209, 211

Jack E. Boucher, for the Commission of Fine Arts
55, 56, 90, 91, 177, 196, 198, 199, 200, 201, 210, 212

Jack E. Boucher, for the Historic American Buildings Survey
144, 145, 151

Brady-Handy Collection, Prints and Photographs Division, Library of Congress
37, 112, 217, 222

James O. Brostrup, for the Historic American Buildings Survey
51, 57, 59, 60, 64, 68, 84, 103

Commission of Fine Arts
1, 3, 4, 5, 6, 7, 16, 22, 23, 26a, 27, 30, 31, 99, 106, 109, 111, 113, 119, 124, 125, 126, 129, 131, 170, 172, 173, 176, 178, 184, 213, 214, 215, 216, 223, 224, 226, 238, 241

George Eisenman, for the Historic American Buildings Survey
46, 72, 73, 239

Fogg Art Museum, Harvard University
12, 163, 164

Arthur Haskill, for the Historic American Buildings Survey
14

Library of Congress, Map Division
174, 192, 194

Library of Congress, Prints and Photographs Division
8, 9, 11, 17, 18, 20, 21, 24, 25, 28, 29, 36, 70, 71, 87, 95, 96, 104, 105, 108, 110, 115, 121, 122, 132, 136, 137, 156, 157, 158, 165, 167, 171, 175, 181, 218, 228, 230

National Archives
19, 85, 169

New York Public Library, I. N. Phelps Stokes Collection
13

Frederick D. Nicholls, for the Historic American Buildings Survey
123

Peabody Collection, Georgetown Public Library
86

John Clagett Proctor Photograph Collection, Columbia Historical Society
65, 127, 130, 141, 168, 179, 191, 206, 229

Daniel D. Reiff
2, 10, 15, 26b, 32, 33, 34, 35, 38, 39, 40, 42, 43, 44, 45, 48, 49, 50, 53, 58, 61, 62, 63, 67, 77, 78, 79, 80, 81, 82, 83, 89, 92, 93, 94, 97, 98, 101, 107, 114, 117, 118, 128, 133, 134, 135, 138, 139, 140, 143, 147, 148, 149, 152, 153, 154, 155, 159, 160, 161, 162, 166, 185, 186, 187, 188, 189, 190, 197, 202, 203, 204, 219, 220, 221, 225, 227, 231, 232, 233, 235, 236, 237, 240

Delos Smith, for the Historic American Buildings Survey
116

William P. Thompson, for the Historic American Buildings Survey
182, 183, 205

U.S. Naval Observatory Library
193

Washingtoniana Collection, D.C. Public Library
100, 142, 234

Index

☆ U.S. GOVERNMENT PRINTING OFFICE: 1972 O—422-441